MULTINATIONAL FIRMS IN CHINA

MULTINATIONAL FIRMS IN CHINA

Entry Strategies, Competition, and Firm Performance

SEA-JIN CHANG

OXFORD

UNIVERSITY PRESS

OXFORD
UNIVERSITY PRESS

Great Clarendon Street, Oxford, OX2 6DP,
United Kingdom

Oxford University Press is a department of the University of Oxford.
It furthers the University's objective of excellence in research, scholarship,
and education by publishing worldwide. Oxford is a registered trade mark of
Oxford University Press in the UK and in certain other countries

© Sea-Jin Chang 2013

The moral rights of the author have been asserted

First Edition published in 2013

Impression: 1

Published in the United States of America by Oxford University Press
198 Madison Avenue, New York, NY 10016, United States of America

British Library Cataloguing in Publication Data
Data available

Library of Congress Control Number: 2013941632

ISBN 978-0-19-968707-7

Printed and bound in Great Britain by
CPI Group (UK) Ltd, Croydon, CR0 4YY

PREFACE

China means different things to different people. Some people equate China with its massive 1.3 billion people. Some call to mind China's vast territory. Others conjure up an image of one of the oldest civilizations, rich in arts and inventions. Others still may think of politics: China is one of the few countries still under Communist rule. Although China technically ascribes to Communism, people traveling to China are often shocked to find it more capitalistic than any other capitalist countries. Government bureaucrats think and behave like businessmen and private incentives motivate hard work. Ironically, China acted as savior of capitalism for a world on the brink of a global financial crisis in 2008. All of these meanings are right; China is so huge and diverse that it can be anything it wants or needs to be.

To me, a non-Chinese academic, China presents a great place to study the competitive dynamics between multinational and local firms. While Korea closely followed the footsteps of Japan in economic development, China's recent economic development dwarfs both Korea and Japan in terms of magnitude and speed. When China adopted the reform and open door policy in 1978, the Chinese economy floundered with tens of thousands of inefficient state-owned enterprises with backward technology and with unmotivated and unskilled workers. Since then, the Chinese government has pursued a gradual opening to multinational firms by initially requiring joint ventures and only gradually allowing wholly owned subsidiaries. This slow transition was precisely orchestrated to buy time to restructure local industries into able competition for these multinational firms. By 2013, press time for this book, many strong local firms had emerged from the restructuring process to challenge well-established multinational firms. China thus provides a great opportunity for business scholars to study how strong local firms emerge and how multinational firms respond to their competitive challenges.

Because of the slow crafting of local powerhouses, China has proven to be a tough territory for unprepared multinationals to navigate. Several early entrants experienced costly failures and retreated from the market. Despite their superior brands and technology, foreign companies could not compete effectively with these strong local firms that suddenly emerged to capture the market share based on low costs, managerial flexibility, extensive distribution networks, and government support. Furthermore, winning competition against these local firms does not necessarily imply winning only in the Chinese market but the international arena as well. As one manager put it: "China is a place like an Olympic game. The best players from all over the world are here and fight to win. Chinese local firms are not only strong in the domestic market but they are also global players. The global competition with them begins in China. We will be stronger as we strive hard to match their prices and costs. If we lose in China, we cannot succeed in the world market." To understand the global marketplace, it is therefore critical to understand competitive dynamics in China.

This book is motivated by this desire to understand global competition in the context of China. More specifically, this book describes how successful multinational firms grew their operations in China, how successful local firms emerged from the restructuring process, and the ensuing competition between and among the two forms. While anecdotal evidence on the fierce competition within China is widespread, there exists no comprehensive research on the topic. Economic research in this vein tends to focus on macroeconomic factors like government policies. Management research, on the other hand, tends to rely on cases or surveys with limited generalizability and cross-validation. This book takes root in my academic research projects over the last 10 years which have sought to address this gap. My earlier work relied on intensive interviews with executives of both key multinational and local firms. I was then fortunate enough to access the annual industrial survey database from the Chinese National Bureau of Statistics, which contains financial information for over 400,000 local and foreign firms in China, almost a population of all industrial firms for each year. Further, the data are available for the years between 1998 and 2009, a critical period when multinational firms substantially expanded operations in China and strong local firms emerged from the restructuring process. Twelve years in China is the equivalent of 30 to 40 years in other countries given the sea changes in the competitive landscape, as reflected by the nation's double-digit growth.

I conducted rigorous statistical analyses, published in academic journals, which I augment here with detailed case studies on five industries: automobiles, consumer products, telecom, beer, and steel. I can therefore confidently describe the entire process of the emergence of both multinational and local firms, the competition between and among them, and the performance implications of this process. Each chapter, except for the introductory one, begins with a detailed case study of one industry, which will be tied to the insights from rigorous empirical studies based on the annual industrial survey database.

While conducting research on this topic, I benefited from scholars and business practitioners who helped me understand the competitive dynamics in China. I would like to thank them for sharing their insights with me. I have several coauthors with whom I have written academic articles in various academic research projects. I acknowledge their intellectual contributions and note special permissions from the journals where academic works were originally published in each relevant place of the book. I would also like to thank the National Research Foundation of Korea, KRF-342-2007-1-B00016 for helping to fund this project. I also appreciate funding from the National University of Singapore, R-313-000-086-133. I also thank Jackie Yan Zheng, Leah Sheng Yan, and Katie Brown for their research and editorial assistance. Lastly, I would like to thank David Musson and Emma Booth, my editors at Oxford University Press, who did a wonderful job turning the manuscript into a book.

Sea-Jin Chang
Singapore
January 2013

CONTENTS

1

Introduction

The global financial crisis of 2008 reversed economic growth around the world. Yet China remained relatively unaffected. Government control continued to be effective, allowing domestic markets to stay vibrant. China ultimately led the global recovery with 7.8% growth in 2012. This fortitude can be traced to China's "reform and open door policy," which brought a massive inflow of foreign investments, amounting to $1048 billion, into China between 1979 and 2010. Today, foreign companies contribute 27.1% of industrial outputs and 54.6% of total exports in China, playing a vital role in the Chinese economy.[1] Now the de facto locomotive of the world economy, China provides an ideal setting to observe fierce competition between and among foreign and local firms.

In his influential book of 2003, *Selling China*, Yasheng Huang explains why foreign direct investment (FDI) inflows into China surged during the 1980s and 1990s. His reasoning counters the conventional belief that China's huge market and growth potential alone attracted foreign multinationals. Instead, Huang argues the surge represented massive privatization of inefficient, insolvent state-owned enterprises (SOEs), as caused by China's inability to pursue privatization without resorting to foreign ownership. Instead of the rapid privatization witnessed in Eastern Europe after the collapse of Communism, the Chinese government pursued gradual reform to turn inefficient SOEs into joint ventures. This allowed foreign multinational firms to maintain operational control while SOE partners became more or less financial investors, mainly interested in dividends. Compared to these government favorites, local private entrepreneurs faced discrimination when securing loans and other resources. Huang thus painted a gloomy picture of China's reform policies: foreign multinational firms did not bring in technology or marketing knowhow but performed a privatization function and enjoyed special privileges (2003, p. xvi).

Changes in China in the decade since Huang's book offer the opportunity to see if his assumptions still hold. First, if FDIs indeed performed a privatization function of formerly inefficient SOEs, how are they performing now? If, on the other hand, foreign multinationals did not bring in technology or knowhow but merely exploited privileges, their performance would suffer as these privileges all but disappeared. Second, several strong local firms emerged during the last decade, e.g. Chery, Geely, and BYD in automobiles, Shanghai Jahwa, Nice, and Longliqi in consumer products, Huawei and ZTE in telecom, Tsingtao and Yanjing in beer, and Baosteel and Shagang in steel. While some of these firms originated from former SOEs, others were newly established by private entrepreneurs. How did emerging local firms like these become stiff competition for previously privileged foreign joint ventures and SOEs? Third, overall competition has intensified. As privileges disappeared, many foreign firms faced cut-throat competition with local firms and other foreign firms. What factors led some foreign multinational firms to survive the competition and prosper and others to exit? Finally, given these changes, what future challenges do both foreign and local firms face in China?

This book is motivated to answer these questions. Specifically, it examines how successful multinational firms grew their operations in China and how strong local firms emerged from the restructuring process. It also considers the subsequent competition between and among these firms. During this transition process, a few large multinational and local firms gained power by acquiring small, weak, and regional players to become truly national players. Some multinational firms were crowded out not only by these strong local competitors but also by other, more successful multinational firms. Further, some emerging local firms that survived competition in China gained global ambitions and so ventured into international markets, challenging foreign multinational firms in the global marketplace. The current introductory chapter reviews relevant Chinese government policies and trends in FDI. In doing so, this chapter identifies key sectoral and regional patterns of FDI and describes key changes in the competitive dynamics between local and foreign firms, laying the groundwork for the future empirical chapters.

Government Policies toward Foreign Multinationals

Reform and open door policy   China experienced periods of confusion and conflict during its recent history. Late to embrace modern technology and industrialize, China was humiliated by the Western imperial forces beginning with the Opium War that led to the concession of Hong Kong to the British. After the Qing Dynasty collapsed in 1911, China suffered civil wars between warlords and invasions by Japan. In 1949, the Communists defeated the Kuomintang and assumed power in China. In the early years of Communist rule, China adopted socialistic planning from the Soviet Union, nationalizing land and industrial firms. Also following in the footsteps of the Soviet Union, China prioritized heavy industries (Lin 2012). The Cultural Revolution, a politically driven campaign by Mao Zedong, further eliminated elements both capitalistic and traditional from Chinese society. As a consequence, SOEs and collective firms dominated China's economy. But these firms had little control over their own operations and, as such, no incentive to improve cost efficiency or product quality, leading to general inefficiency and stagnation (Rawski 1980).

Beginning in 1978, China sought to address these issues with the adoption of a "reform and open-door policy," as promoted by Deng Xiaoping, who took power after Mao's death in 1976. Naughton (2007) divides this liberalization transition from planned economy to market economy into two major phases: the gradual reform phase (1978–1992) and the liberalization phase (1993–present).[2] During the gradual reform phase, China opted to undergo a gradual transition instead of the "big bang" approach, characterized by massive and immediate privatization of SOEs, taken by former Soviet Bloc nations (Redding and Witt 2007). With a gradual approach, the Chinese government sought to increase the efficiency of SOEs by granting increased autonomy and incentives. For example, SOEs were given latitude to make select input and output decisions, as well as the right to retain a percentage of profits for employee benefits (Groves et al. 1994; Li 1996; Schipani and Liu 2002). At the same time, the Chinese government sought to address demands unmet by SOEs by allowing non-SOEs (e.g., private firms, collective firms, and foreign joint ventures) to enter the market. The entry of non-SOEs was facilitated by the introduction of a dual-track pricing system whereby market supply and demand determined the price of inputs and outputs above and beyond predetermined quotas. The capitalist element of this dual-track system offered incentives for SOEs to increase efficiency, while at the same time allowing non-SOEs to gain access to input and output markets. Despite these capitalist elements, however, the first phase of reform primarily sought to enhance the efficiency of SOEs in order to avoid their collapse from competitive market forces (Lau, Qian, and Roland 2000). As such, non-SOEs were treated as a supplement to, rather than a replacement for, SOEs.

China's decentralized economic structure facilitated this gradual transition to economic liberalization. Historically and currently, each region in China acts as a self-contained market in which a variety of industries operate under the control of regional governments. This decentralization aided economic liberalization by promoting the entry and expansion of non-SOEs for two reasons. First, regional governments had incentive to promote non-SOEs as an important source of regional economic growth. Second, the central government could experiment with liberalization by introducing non-SOEs in select regions and, if successful, diffuse the practice across the nation (Qian, Roland, and Xu 1999, 2006).

Although the first phase of reform in China generated encouraging results, two lingering issues prevented further economic growth. First, SOEs experienced limited gains in efficiency, primarily due to vague property rights. Similarly, as noted above, collective firms are owned by all the people in a given community, yet the people do not directly share the profits, nor do they have control over the operations of these collectives. Rather, the community's administration represents the people and exercises control by appointing executives and influencing production decisions (Tian 2000). Thus, given these vague property rights, collective firms parallel SOEs. Some collectives, however, are disguised private firms, known as "red hat" firms, in order to avoid extortion by local government (Boisot and Child 1996; Tian 2000; Walder 1995).[3] Second, the objective of each region was, and continues to be, the maximization of local economic growth, but not necessarily national economic efficiency. Further, the political careers of regional leaders are closely tied to the economic performance of their own regions vis-à-vis other regions (Li and Zhou 2005). This regional competition often leads to regional protectionism, duplicative investments, and misallocation of resources (Young 2000).

In response to these problems, the Chinese government shifted reform policy to enable ownership restructuring and promote market competition during the second phase of reform. This decentralization phase was initiated in 1993, when the National Congress of the Communist Party of China proclaimed the establishment of a "socialist market economy" and a modern corporate system as its primary goals, as reflected in the Corporate Law. After passing the Corporate Law in 1993, many state-owned enterprises were corporatized with the redefinition of government ownership as shareholding. The Chinese government also strengthened the corporate governance practices in the state sector. The central government set up the State-owned Assets Supervision and Administration Commission (SASAC) in 2003, fashioned after sovereign wealth funds. Temasek in Singapore, which was designed to carry out that government's functions as owner of and investor in state assets, served as an important model.[4] The SASAC monitors operation of its portfolio companies and ensures their financial performance. Local governments also created their own SASACs, transforming regional government ownership into shareholding. The Chinese government subsequently issued policies to facilitate the bankruptcy of insolvent SOEs. Private ownership was explicitly legalized with a 1998 constitutional amendment. With these ownership reforms, China came to share important features with other nations characterized by free market economies.

As a consequence of this restructuring, the composition of industry participants changed dramatically between 1998 and 2009, as illustrated by Figure 1.1. The annual industrial survey data comes from the Chinese National Bureau of Statistics, which includes financial information for industrial firms with annual sales of at least RMB 5 million (roughly $732,000 using the 2009 year-end exchange). Appendix 1 provides more information on this database. In 1998, the annual industrial survey included 47,958 SOEs and 54,384 collective firms, together representing 68% of all firms covered by the survey in that year. By 2009, the numbers of SOEs and collective firms decreased to 5118 and 12,917, respectively, together representing just 5% of all firms included in the survey. This sharp decline supports the notion that most SOEs and collectives closed or were privatized during this time period. The number of private firms and incorporated firms, on the other hand, increased from 10,593 to 219,277 and 10,656 to 61,218, respectively, between 1998 and 2009, together representing a rise from 14% to 76%. This dramatic change in market composition in just 12 years is remarkable! In particular, the emergence of private firms run by entrepreneurs in such a short period of time is astonishing, as highlighted by the title of an influential book, *Billions of Entrepreneurs* (Khanna 2008). During the same time period, the proportion of foreign firms, combining HMT firms (from Hong Kong, Macao, and Taiwan) and non-HMT firms (from other countries), remained relatively steady, with a slight increase from 17.6% in 1998 to 18.6% in 2009.

On the other hand, the shares of firms with different ownership types in terms of assets, as illustrated in Figure 1.2, show that foreign firms, incorporated firms, and SOEs are much bigger than private firms and collectives. In 2009, the proportion of foreign firms, as measured by assets, is close to 31%. The asset shares of incorporated firms and SOEs in 2009 are 36.3% and 8.2%, suggesting that they control much larger assets than a simple count of firms would suggest. Considering that the state

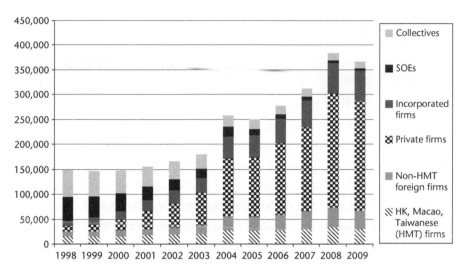

Figure 1.1 Number of firms in annual industrial survey by ownership type

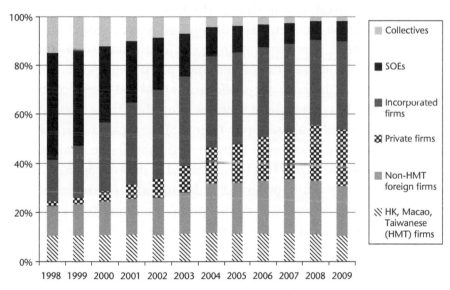

Figure 1.2 Shares of firms with each ownership type in total assets of all industrial firms

owned large shares in incorporated firms via SASACs, the size of state ownership is still fairly large in China. On the other hand, asset share of private firms was just 23% while that of collectives was a mere 1.7% in 2009, suggesting large numbers but minimal assets.

While China has made progress in transitioning to a market-based economy, it still lacks efficient capital, labor, and intermediate goods markets. Governments still play an important role and their policies change frequently, and sometimes, unpredictably. While laws and regulations are clearly written, enforcement remains weak and inconsistent, e.g., intellectual property rights protection. Despite the government's effort to crack down, corruption is prevalent. Personal relationships, known as *quanxi*, still play an important role in conducting business. In other words, China still suffers from "institutional voids," according to Khanna and Palepu (2010). Both foreign and local firms should consider institutional voids in formulating their business strategies.

Regulations governing foreign direct investment   The Chinese-Foreign Contractual Joint Venture Law, introduced in 1979, formally allowed foreign direct investment in China. The Chinese-Foreign Equity Joint Venture Law of 1983 built on this to distinguish between equity joint ventures and contract joint ventures. In equity joint ventures, Chinese and foreign parties contribute capital and share profit in proportion of their equity, while the Chinese party provides only land and takes a contracted share of profit in contract joint ventures.[5] Together, these laws stipulate how joint ventures could set up in China. Since these laws specifically allowed only joint ventures, wholly owned subsidiaries remained de facto prohibited. Realizing that China needed to import capital, technology, and management knowhow in order to industrialize quickly, the Chinese government established four Special Economic Zones (SEZs) to attract FDI in the form of joint ventures. Located in Shenzhen, Zhuhai, Shantou, and Xiamen in 1980, these SEZs were strategically chosen to target maritime neighbors Hong Kong, Macao, nations of Southeast Asia, and Taiwan. Further, the Chinese government provided various subsidies and privileges like cheap land, low tax rates, and exemptions of import tariffs (Naughton 2007). The government subsequently opened and designated 14 other coastal cities in 1984, including Shanghai, to attract more FDI. Due to these various incentives, FDI increased steadily over time.

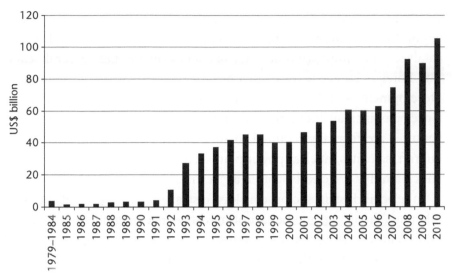

Figure 1.3 Foreign direct investment in China
Note: Actual investment in US$ billion from the National Bureau of Statistics.

However, reform halted momentarily when China experienced a political crisis following the Tiananmen incident in 1989. In 1990, reform resumed with the passage of the Foreign Invested Company Law, which further liberalized the government's FDI regime.[6] The Chinese government also removed a number of sectoral and regional restrictions on FDI. Specifically, it decentralized approval authority from central to local governments, increased market access, and strengthened intellectual property rights protection (Huang 2003). Due to this series of deregulations, FDI regained momentum. Figure 1.3 illustrates the drastic rise of FDI in the 1990s.

Under the 1986 Foreign Invested Company Law, wholly owned subsidiaries were technically possible.[7] In reality, however, they were neither allowed nor encouraged. Wholly owned subsidiaries became popular only when more detailed clauses were added to the Foreign Invested Company Law when China acceded to the World Trade Organization (WTO). In 2001, the law governing joint ventures was again amended to allow FDI without joint ventures, save for in a few strategic industries, while also relaxing the requirement that only Chinese teams could appoint joint venture CEOs. The accession of China to the WTO also catalyzed the elimination of other barriers over the next several years. The Foreign Direct Investment Directory, issued in 1995 by the State Development and Reform Commission and amended several times since, classifies all industries as "encourage," "restrict," or "ban." Joint ventures are formally required in such industries as mining, tobacco, aircraft, satellites, nuclear power plants, telecom service, real estate, and education that are clearly labeled as "restrict."[8]

In select industrial sectors considered strategic, e.g., steel and automobile manufacturing, another set of industry-specific guidelines requires joint ventures, although these industries may be classified as "encourage." For example, Article 48 of the "Automobile Industry Development Policy," adopted in 1994 and amended most recently in 2009, specifies that the Chinese share of a joint venture must exceed 50% in vehicle manufacturing, special vehicles, agricultural vehicles, and motorcycles. While the steel industry likewise requires joint ventures, foreign firms could hold the majority stake prior to 2005. The Iron and Steel Industry Development Policy adopted in 2005, however, specifies that foreign firm share cannot exceed 50%. Foreign firms are allowed to operate wholly owned subsidiaries in other industries such as beer, consumer products, and telecom. Table 1.1 summarizes major laws and regulations geared toward foreign firms in general as well as key, industry-specific guidelines in the five industries selected as case studies for this book.

Foreign firms in China typically receive better treatment than local firms. Until the 1994 Unified Tax Law, foreign firms enjoyed tax breaks and exemptions, including just 15% to 33% taxation, compared to the 55% taxation faced by SOEs (Huang 2003). To be eligible for this tax privilege, foreign firms had to be in SEZs, High-Tech Industrial Zones, and/or Economic and Technical Development zones. Prior to 1994, foreign firms also received additional tax holidays during the first two years of making an operating profit and a 50% exemption for the following three years, an exclusion from the 3% local surcharge tax, and lower taxes on retained earnings (Whalley 2011: 184).[9] The 1994 tax reform abolished the differential treatment of foreign firms and adopted a single unified tax system for both domestic and foreign companies, regardless of wholly foreign-owned or joint venture status. Both foreign and local firms were subject to 30% income tax and a 3% surcharge by local governments. The 1994 tax reform instead provided the same favorable tax treatment to any firm investing in China's priority industries, regardless of foreign or local status. Despite this *de jure* change, however, the government continued to provide a large range of incentives to foreign firms based on industry sector and geographic location.[10] Foreign firms in SEZs and other economic and technological development zones continued to benefit from preferential treatment. Foreign firms could also receive a refund of corporate income tax when they chose to reinvest their profits. In 2008, the Corporate Income Tax Law was further revised to harmonize the income tax rates for foreign invested enterprises and domestic firms, removing many of the remaining incentives for foreign firms. Thus, foreign invested enterprises no longer receive preferential treatment at the national level, though local governments might still offer tax breaks or cheap land to attract FDI.

Trends of Foreign Direct Investment
Overall trends   When the government required foreign firms to form joint ventures with local firms in the early stage of the open door policy, it often designated joint venture partners and dictated the exact terms of the ventures. This joint venture requirement policy is often favored by governments in developing countries in order to facilitate the transfer of technology to local partners so the latter can absorb, innovate, and eventually diffuse it to other firms so that local industries can be developed. For example, Volkswagen entered a joint venture with Shanghai Automobile Industrial Corporation (SAIC) in 1984. Volkswagen committed to transfer technology and increase local content to 26% by 1986 and gradually up to 95% by 1995. In order to achieve this goal, Volkswagen encouraged its parts suppliers in Europe to enter joint ventures with or transfer technology to Chinese firms.

Table 1.1. *Major government policies toward foreign firms*

YEAR	OVERALL ECONOMY-WISE POLICIES	SECTOR-SPECIFIC POLICIES
1979	"Chinese-Foreign Contractual Joint Ventures Law" adopted.	
1980	Four national-level SEZs established at Shenzhen, Zhuhai, Shantou, Xiamen. "Guangdong SEZ regulations" is the first legislation on SEZ. Incentives include tax exemption for FDI for 5 years, 15% corporate tax, further incentives for investment above $5 million, and tariff exempt, etc.	(Telecom) The China Posts and Telecommunication Industry Corporation (PTIC) founded by the Ministry of Posts and Telecommunication (MPT) as a holding company to direct all regional equipment manufacturing corporations.
1982		(Automobile) Government decides to allow joint ventures in automobile industry. (Telecom) MPT prioritizes the modernization of the telecommunication system. MPT acknowledges that China had to import foreign technology and equipment.
1984	The central government opens up 15 ports along the coastal regions including Guangzhou, Fuzhou, Ningbo, Qingdao, Tianjin, Shanghai, Dalian, Qinhuangdao, Yantai, Lianyungang, Nantong, Wenzhou, Fuzhou, Zhanjiang, and Beihai, to attract more FDI.	(Automobile) The central government announces the "Regulations on Individual Farmers Purchasing Motorcyles and Tractors," officially allowing private individuals to own automobiles. From 1984 to 1986, three joint venture projects, such as Beijing Jeep, Shanghai Volkswagen, and Guangzhou Peugeot are approved.
1986	"Foreign Invested Company Law" was enacted. The State Council also published guidelines, which set corporate tax at 15% for export-oriented and high-tech companies and further tax incentives for three years. They also set ceiling for land usage fee at RMB 5–20 per square meter per year. Other incentives include tariff exempt for importing equipments, raw materials, mechanical parts, and preferential rates on foreign exchange and utilities fees.	(Steel) The regulation set in 1984, which allowed steel manufacturing firms to sell 2% of its steel products on its own, priced at no more than 20% above or below the government designated price, removed in 1985.

12

Table 1.1.

YEAR	OVERALL ECONOMY-WISE POLICIES	SECTOR-SPECIFIC POLICIES
1988	Hainan SEZ set up together with the Hainan Province Government, covering the entire province.	
1990	"Foreign Invested Company Law" further liberalizes the government's FDI regime.	
1992	Deng Xiaoping encourages private enterprises and foreign investment. The 14th Conference of the Central Planning Committee states, "We shall widen the field of foreign investment. Foreign investment shall be guided into infrastructure and technology-intensive industry. It should also be invested into finance, commerce, tourism and real estate in a proper way."	
1994		(Automobile) The "Automobile Industry Development Policy" confirms regulation on foreign firms' equity stake to be under 50% for passenger cars. It emphasizes technology transfer as the top priority of joint ventures. New ventures should be minimum RMB 2 billion investment and include R&D organization with minimum RMB 500 million investment.
1995	A broad category of industries labeled for "encourage," "restrict" and "ban" for foreign direct investment announced.	

13

Table 1.1.

YEAR	OVERALL ECONOMY-WISE POLICIES	SECTOR-SPECIFIC POLICIES
1997		(Beer) The China Light Industry Council announces three broad guidelines of industrial policy: modernize production lines; support top 10 local breweries with a goal to increase 10 firm concentration above 40%; support M&A activities of big breweries.
1998	Relaxation of joint venture requirements on banking and financial institutions.	
2000	The central government announces the "Western Development Project," with five major strategic directions: infrastructure improvement; environment protection; industry restructuring; education and technology; and open policy. Government provides incentives for FDI like 15% corporate tax rate and RMB financing for foreign investors.	
2001	China officially joins the WTO.	(Automobile) Deregulations on import with access to WTO: to lower import tariffs in passenger cars to a maximum of 25% by 2006; increase the import quota by 15% each year until it gets eliminated in 2005; foreign firms can acquire a license to import parts and components on a 10% tariff for 3 years; non-bank foreign firms allowed to provide unrestricted auto financing.
2004		(Automobile) A new version of the "Automobile Industry Development Policy" promotes a hybrid car and innovation capability of domestic firms. Foreign firms' ownership stake still limited to 50%.

Table 1.1.

YEAR	OVERALL ECONOMY-WISE POLICIES	SECTOR-SPECIFIC POLICIES
2005		(Steel) The central government announces a restructuring plan in 11 industries including steel to reduce over-capacity. The Iron and Steel Industry Development Policy specifies that top 5 producers' shares should account for 45% of the total output by 2011 and production share of coastal regions should be at least 40% to reduce pollution.
2006	"Regulations on Foreign Acquisitions of Domestic Companies" specify that the Department of Commerce will launch an anti-monopoly investigation if overseas acquirers possess over RMB 3 billion assets and revenue in Chinese market exceeds 1.5 billion, or the market share exceeds 20% or it will exceed 25% with acquisitions.	(Telecom) Government supports national level Information Technology Industrial Park. It encourages foreign investment especially in R&D. It also encourages domestic firms' investment abroad.
2008	New "Corporate Income Tax Law, implemented on Jan 1, 2008, ceases various tax incentives for FDI and JVs to impose a standard tax rate of 25% for both local and foreign companies.	(Automobile) Provides tax incentives for "new energy cars" such as hybrid and electric cars.
2011		(Consumer products) The China Association of Fragrance and Cosmetics Industries launches the 12th five-year plan to lend support to comestic cosmetic industry with a goal to develop 2–3 firms into globally competitive brands, 20 Chinese brands, and 30 famous trademarks.

15

As Huang (2003) points out, the joint venture requirement policy also helped privatize SOEs. According to the political pecking order of Chinese firms, SOEs rank at the top, followed by collectives, and, finally, private firms. The allocation of bank credit and foreign exchanges, business opportunities, political support, and legal protection follows this hierarchy (Huang 2003: 78–29). Due to this political pecking order, the government could not pursue outright privatization of SOEs. It thus promoted joint ventures between inefficient SOEs and foreign multinationals. Due to economic fragmentation, local firms could not move across regions. But foreign multinationals not bound by regional domination could enter any region through such joint ventures. According to Huang (2003: 220), most joint ventures between SOEs and foreign firms were structured in such a way that SOEs transfer all operating assets to joint ventures and then become joint venture partners. In reality, however, they behave more like investment funds interested in dividends. Huang claims the privatization function of FDI was crucial in this early period of reform.

As discussed in the previous section, the Chinese government relaxed joint venture requirements as it prepared to join the WTO, allowing foreign firms to assume full ownership in most non-strategic industries. As a result, foreign multinationals could and did enter China via wholly owned subsidiaries. FDI inflow increased dramatically. Figure 1.4 displays the number of foreign subsidiaries by establishment year. Clearly evident is a sharp increase in FDI beginning in 1993, when the Chinese government removed sectoral and regional restrictions on FDI. Another sharp increase occurs in the early 2000s, when the central government further relaxed joint venture requirements in preparation for ascension to the WTO. The figure also displays a recent increase in wholly owned subsidiary popularity, reflecting a reversal of the initial hesitation of foreign multinationals when the wholly owned subsidiary option was not available due to fear of involuntary technology transfer. Figure 1.4 illustrates that the percentage of joint ventures in total entries declines steadily over the years. While earlier entries came mostly in the form of joint ventures, more than 60% of new entries came as wholly owned subsidiaries in recent years.

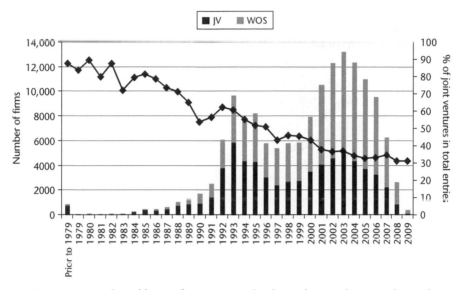

Figure 1.4 Number of foreign firms in annual industrial survey by ownership and establishment year

Figure 1.5 shows FDI by country of origin. The top 10 countries represent 88% of total investments. More specifically, Hong Kong and Macao represent 45% of all accumulated FDI, followed by the British Virgin Islands, Japan, the US, Taiwan, Korea, Singapore, the Cayman Islands, Germany, and, finally, the UK.[11] If we lump together investments from Hong Kong, Macao, and Taiwan, these ethnic Chinese firms represent almost half of all FDI in China. There is an active debate as to whether FDI from Hong Kong and Macao represents genuine FDI. Huang (2003) argues that a substantial portion of FDI from Hong Kong and Macao could be "round-trip FDI," meaning that direct investment capital was originally exported by Chinese firms and then imported back to China. Some Chinese firms might engage in "round trip FDI" in order to exploit various tax benefits and other privileges provided to foreign investors by the Chinese government. For example, Lenovo, one of the most successful local Chinese firms in the personal computer industry, is legally a Hong Kong based foreign firm via "round-trip FDI" (Huang 2008: 3). As there are no official

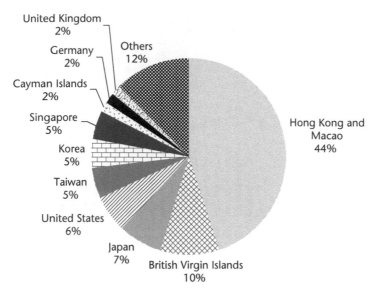

Figure 1.5 Foreign direct investments by country of origin

Note: Accumulated foreign direct investment during 1985–2010 amounting to US$1012 billion.

statistics available regarding the prevalence of "round-trip FDI," we must be cautious in interpreting statistics. On the other hand, the majority of FDI originating from Hong Kong and Macao could be genuine FDI by indigenous Hong Kong and Macao firms, as well as from foreign multinationals' subsidiaries located in these countries.

Sectoral and regional distribution Figure 1.6 and Figure 1.7 illustrate the distribution of foreign firms' combined market shares in 1998 and 2009 according to the 2-digit standard industry classification (SIC) of industries and regions, respectively. On average, foreign firms took 27% in 1998 and 36% combined market shares in all industrial sectors, yet there exists large variation across industries. Several interesting observations emerge from these two figures. Consistent with standard economic theory that emphasizes the monopolistic advantages of foreign firms (Hymer 1976), Figure 1.6 shows that foreign firms hold large shares in high-technology industries like electronics, telecommunication,

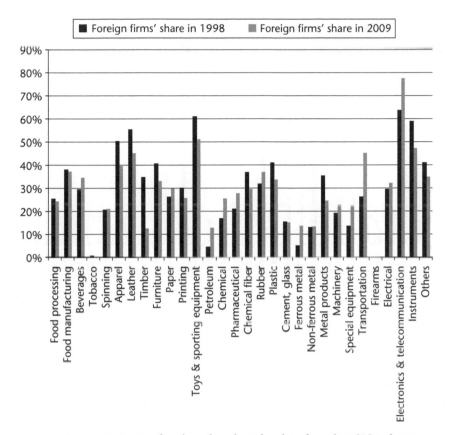

Figure 1.6 Foreign firms' combined market share by 2-digit SIC industry

instruments, and precision machinery. For example, foreign firms had a combined market share of 64% in the electronics and telecommunications industries in 1998. However, to our surprise, foreign firms also maintain large market shares in some labor-intensive industries like apparel, leather, and toys. Foreign firms' combined market share in toys, for example, was as high as 61% in 1998. Huang (2003) argues that this anomaly can be attributed to the government's preferential policy toward SOEs and their foreign partners, to the detriment of private firms. According to Huang, these labor-intensive industries could have been better served by export or contract of local companies, as opposed to FDI. Foreign firms took advantage of various government

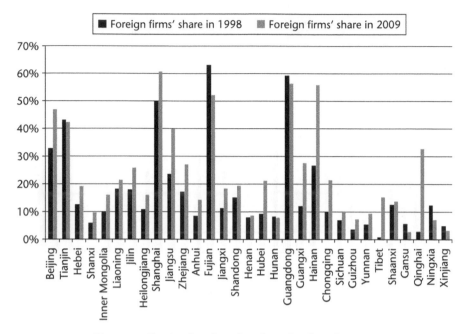

Figure 1.7 Foreign firms' combined market share by region

subsidies and tax breaks in these labor-intensive industries by incurring FDI. Huang supports his conjecture with evidence that the sharp rise in FDI in the 1980s and 1990s was accompanied by a drop in contractual alliances like export processing and assembly in labor intensive and export-oriented industries.

Figure 1.6, however, shows that foreign firms' combined market share in labor-intensive industries declined significantly from 1998 to 2009. For example, foreign firms' combined market shares dropped from 50% in 1998 to 39% in 2009 in the apparel industry, 56% to 45% in leather, 35% to 13% in timber, 41% to 33% in furniture, and 61% to 50% in toys and sporting goods. On the other hand, foreign firms' market shares in more technology- or capital-intensive industries increased substantially during the same time period. Foreign firms' combined market share rose from 17% to 26% in the chemical industry, 21% to 28% in pharmaceuticals, 14% to 22% in special machinery and equipment, 26% to 45% in transportation equipment, and 64% to 78% in electronics and telecommunications. Together, these trends suggest that the driving force of multinational firms' competitive advantages shifted from preferential government treatment, which encouraged FDI in labor-intensive industries in the earlier period of reform, to the possession of intangible resources like technology and brands, which led to a boost of FDI in technology or capital-intensive industries over the last decade. Thus, Huang's claim needs to be re-examined in light of more recent empirical evidence.

In terms of geographic location, foreign firms tend to concentrate in major cities like Beijing, Tianjin, Shanghai, and Chongqing, and coastal regions like Jiangsu, Zhejiang, Fujian, Shandong, Guangdong, and Hainan. Coastal regions in China have attracted the most FDI, as the Chinese government initially opened up various coastal cities to foreign investment, including the creation of the SEZs, as well as other trade and industrial zones. Local governments in coastal regions also competed with each other to attract more FDI to their own regions. As a consequence, these regions developed stronger institutional infrastructures and support systems. Du, Lu, and Tao (2008) demonstrate that foreign firms prefer to invest in regions with greater protection of intellectual property rights, lower degrees of government intervention in business operations, lower levels of government corruption, and better contract enforcement. As such, inland regions with underdeveloped institutional environments failed to attract FDI.

At the same time, as displayed in Figure 1.7, foreign firms' market shares increased substantially in inland areas like Chongqing, Qinghai, Hubei, Gangxi, Jiangxi, and Hebei between 1998 and 2009. Specifically, foreign firms' combined industrial market shares increased from 10% to 21% in Chongqing, 3% to 33% in Qinghai, and 9% to 21% in Hubei. In order to help develop the western inland part of China, such as Chongqing, Qinghai, and Gangxi, the government sought to spur the development of infrastructure and FDI with the Western Development Project. By the end of 2007, the government invested a total of RMB 1.3 trillion in western regions. The government provided various tax incentives and subsidies to multinational firms investing in western regions. Multinational firms followed this government directive to channel investment into this area. High wages, a shortage of workers, and intensifying competition in coastal regions further precipitated this move. As such, FDI in the last decade might be driven by different factors than those observed by Huang, which was based on earlier FDI experience. This book picks up where Huang left off, exploring foreign firms' entry strategies using recent empirical evidence.

Organizing Framework

Changes in competitive landscape in China The preceding discussion of China's reform and open door policy and the trends of foreign firms' combined market shares in China, reveals some important underlying forces changing the competitive landscape in China over the last decade. First, while foreign firms maintained an overall annual combined market share of between 27% and 36% in industrial sectors from 1998 to 2009, as in Figure 1.6, there were substantial shifts within industries. As detailed above, foreign firms gained market shares in technology and capital-intensive industries but lost market shares in more labor-intensive industries. During the same time period, the Chinese government gradually removed special privileges offered to foreign multinationals, essentially leveling the playing field between foreign multinationals and local firms. As a consequence, foreign multinationals relying on government support quickly lost ground and eventually exited the market.

Further, some foreign multinationals perform better than other foreign multinationals, while some local firms perform better than other local firms. When foreign multinationals initially entered China, they tended to zero in on high-end markets via product imports or the local assembly of imported parts. These foreign multinationals competed on the basis of technology and brand. On the other hand, local companies, mostly traditional SOEs and collectives, tended to occupy the low end of the market. Given their positions at opposite ends of the market, multinationals and local firms did not initially compete against each other. However, between 1998 and 2009, our study time

period, the Chinese market changed substantially. As Chinese consumers became more affluent, they demanded better quality products
than conventional local firms supplied. Yet, their incomes were not
high enough to afford imported foreign products. Strong local con-
tenders and multinational firms that developed local competences
in China filled the resulting holes in the market. Among local firms,
private firms and incorporated firms like limited liabilities firms or
joint stock companies were on the rise, replacing the SOEs and collectives that used to control Chinese industries. This new breed of local
competitors emerged from former joint ventures and new startups
by private entrepreneurs. Further, many former SOEs and collectives
transformed into joint stock companies and raised much needed capital by going public. These reformed local firms were able to expand
quickly and capture market shares with their low costs, managerial
flexibility, extensive distribution networks, and government support.
Meanwhile, some multinational firms localized themselves in order to
lower their cost positions and bring in more sophisticated technology
or brands to match the intensified competition from both local and
foreign competitors. As these two new types of firms—"localized multinational firms" and "emerging local firms"—continued their market
expansion, they also began competing head to head with each other in
mid-range markets across China. The intensified competition pushed
out conventional local firms unable to upgrade and conventional multinationals relying on imports. Figure 1.8 illustrates these changes in
China's competitive landscape over the last decade.

Spillover and competition: a theoretical lens   This book is motivated to
examine how localized multinational firms and emerging local firms
grew over the years. China provides an ideal setting to observe fierce
competition between and among foreign and local firms. While FDI has
been an important subject in both economics and management, the conventional FDI theories fall short in explaining this phenomenon because
scholars have mainly approached FDI from the perspective of multinational firms. The literature has paid little attention to local firms, save

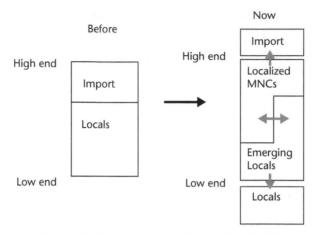

Figure 1.8 Changing nature of competition in China
Note: Adapted from S. Chang and S. Park (2012), "Winning Strategies in China," Long Range Planning 45: 3.

for studies on joint ventures, despite the fact that multinationals must compete with local firms in local markets post-FDI. Similarly, although economists have long considered technology spillover from foreign to local firms (Caves 1974; Blömstrom 1986; Hejazi and Safarian 1999), they have viewed local firms, especially those in emerging and developing economies, as passive recipients of technology spillovers and *not* potential competitors to multinational firms. I argue that, not only do multinationals fiercely compete with local firms in local markets upon making FDI, but that local firms must be considered potential competitors to multinational firms.

The marginalization of local firms in the strategy and economics literature may be attributable to one of FDI theory's underlying assumptions: foreign entrants' monopolistic advantage over local firms is sufficiently large enough to compensate for their liability of foreignness, thereby limiting competition from local firms (Caves 1971; Hymer 1976). This assumption may have been true when multinational firms entered less developed countries in the 1960s and 1970s, but it is no longer valid. Local firms in developing countries are successfully challenging foreign entrants (Dawar and Frost 1999; Zeng and Williamson 2007). In China, in particular, local firms are taking market shares from well established multinationals, creating a great competitive threat.

This book thus examines the evolution of foreign and local firms over time and the competition between and among them with the theoretical lens of "spillover" and "competition." Spillover effects can be defined as the positive influence of one firm group on another firm group's performance. Spillover occurs when the introduction of new technologies and products inspires other firms to develop these entities themselves. The spillover of advanced knowledge and technologies across firms can be facilitated by hiring managers and engineers (Ahn, de la Rica, and Ugidos 1999). In addition, cross-regional greenfield investments and "friendly" mergers and acquisitions of both local and foreign firms may facilitate knowledge spillover across regions. Competition effects, on the other hand, are defined as the negative influences caused by the presence of a group of firms on members of another group, which decrease the latter's performance. Competition is intensifying not only between foreign and local firms, but also among foreign entrants and among local firms, respectively, another possibility overlooked by prior studies. In fact, spillover and competition effects are two sides of the same coin. A firm is simultaneously a source of knowledge spillovers and a source of competition to other firms in the same industry. Thus, what we can observe in reality is the net of positive spillover effects and negative competition effects. When competition is moderate, spillover effects are more likely to dominate; otherwise, competition effects will prevail. Thus, we must examine spillover effects and competition effects simultaneously. Further, we must examine both of these effects from and on both foreign and local firms.

Structure of the book   Chapter 1, presented above, is an introductory chapter that sets the stage for the entire book. It reviews relevant Chinese government policies and trends regarding FDI. In short, as part of its economic reform strategy, the Chinese government initially allowed foreign multinationals to enter the market through joint ventures but gradually shifted to allow wholly owned subsidiaries in non-strategic industries, while removing the privileges they enjoyed in the past. This chapter reviews key sectoral and regional patterns of FDI and describes key changes in the competitive dynamics between foreign and local firms.

Chapter 2 examines multinational firms' strategies in China. For earlier entries, the Chinese government required foreign multinationals to form joint ventures with local partners. Multinational firms do not appreciate forced joint ventures, especially when they must protect intangible resources like technology and brand. Thus, most multinational firms refused to import their sophisticated technology and/or brands when entering China until competitive pressures became too intense. When the joint venture requirement policy relaxed, already entered multinational firms transformed their incumbent joint ventures into wholly owned subsidiaries while other multinationals newly entered the market directly through wholly owned subsidiaries. This enabled foreign firms to bring in more intangible resources and improve firm performance. Chapter 2 also examines the sequential expansion of multinational firms upon entry. Multinational firms tended to expand from affluent and open coastal regions into inland areas in order to capture early mover advantages and avoid competition. More recent investments tend to be larger and favor greenfield investments over acquisitions.

Chapter 3 examines how strong local competitors emerged in China. An important rationale of the Chinese government's gradual opening was to buy time for local firms to restructure and improve operations before entering head to head competition with multinational giants. After the initial effort to increase SOE efficiency by providing them with autonomy and incentives proved unsuccessful, the Chinese government shifted its reform policy to focus on privatizing SOEs. Thousands of SOEs soon transformed into limited liability firms or joint stock companies with SASACs assuming ownership. Many of these former-SOEs were listed on the stock exchanges, allowing them to be run as private firms despite de facto state ownership. At the same time, thousands of other SOEs, usually smaller and less profitable, were closed or sold to private interests. These newly privatized firms were then able to invest more in fixed and intangible assets and, in turn, increase sales and improve productivity and profitability. In addition, tens of thousands firms, typically run by private entrepreneurs with superior technology, newly entered the industry, challenging both incumbent local and foreign competitors.

Chapter 4 examines competition between foreign multinationals and local firms, which were examined independently in the preceding two chapters. Both types of firms gain competences over time and compete fiercely between and among themselves in China. Until the early 1990s, multinational firms entered high-end markets by leveraging their technology and brand, while local companies maintained the low end of the market, with little competition between the two. Between 1998 and 2009, however, competition intensified. Some multinationals expanded Chinese operations by localizing production, sourcing, and management. At the same time, several local firms emerged as serious competitors against multinational competitors. This chapter examines the competitive interactions between firms. We confirm that the greater relative competitive advantage of multinational firms vis-à-vis local firms corresponds to higher technological complexity and marketing knowhow. For instance, foreign firms' market share is the highest when marketing knowhow and technological complexity are important. Weak intellectual property rights protection in China, however, poses a great threat to foreign firms. This chapter details the factors influencing China's changing engagement with intellectual property rights protection. With case studies, we examine major foreign and local firms to understand why and how they emerged as winners.

Chapter 5 considers the performance of foreign multinationals vis-à-vis local firms in terms of survival and profitability. In contrast to earlier concerns that FDI might negatively affect domestic companies' survival (Huang 2003), this chapter suggests that FDI is a double-edged sword, both benefiting and harming Chinese firms. Spillover effects from foreign firms most benefitted local firms in the earlier period of reform when there was less market overlap, and so direct competition with each other was avoided. More recently, however, competition between localized multinational firms and reformed local firms has intensified, forcing weaker firms to exit. As a consequence of tough competition with local firms and fellow foreign multinationals alike, foreign firms are generally less profitable than privately owned local firms and collectives. Yet, there remains the possibility that multinationals may shift income out of China via various internal transfer pricing schemes and thus merely exhibit lower performance.

Chapter 6 discusses important future trends. Chinese industries are becoming increasingly consolidated, with just a few large foreign and local firms emerging as winners from the consolidation process. Furthermore, competition led to uneven growth in industrial activities across regions, creating new regional clusters. Some local firms survived competition in China to act on ambitions to venture into the international market. Foreign multinational firms must now compete with this first generation of multinational firms originating from China not only in China, but in the global marketplace. This chapter contrasts strengths and weaknesses of these emerging Chinese multinationals with those of foreign multinationals to elucidate likely future challenges.

In sum, winning competition against local firms does not necessarily imply winning only in the Chinese market but in the international arena as well. According to one manager:

> China is a place like an Olympic game. The best players from all over the world are here and fight to win. Chinese local firms are not only strong in the domestic market but they are also global players. The global competition with them begins in China. We will be stronger as we strive hard to match their prices and costs. If we lose in China, we cannot succeed in the world market. (Chang and Park 2012)

It is therefore critical to understand competitive dynamics in China. This book seeks to do just that.

Research methodology The evidence presented in each chapter is firmly based on large sample-based statistical analyses and detailed case studies of select industries. The annual industrial survey database from the Chinese National Bureau of Statistics contains financial information for industrial firms with annual sales of at least RMB

5 million, which offers almost population level data, including over 400,000 local and foreign firms operating in China each year. Further, the data exist for the years between 1998 and 2009, a critical period when multinational firms expanded their operations in China and strong local firms emerged from the restructuring process. Twelve years in China during its reform period is equivalent to 30 to 40 years in other countries given the sea changes in the competitive landscape, as reflected in China's double-digit growth. Appendix 1 gives full information on this annual industrial survey database. Using these data, I conducted rigorous statistical analyses, included as technical appendices to each chapter.

I augmented the large sample statistical analyses with detailed case studies. Between 2003 and 2005, I conducted field based work on leading multinationals and local firms in China with a colleague. The results were subsequently published in an academic journal (Chang and Park 2012). We initially selected three to five leading multinationals and one to two local firms in several industries where multinationals and local firms actively competed against each other. We deliberately chose at least one multinational firm from each major economic region, i.e., the United States, Europe, and Asia (specifically, Japan and Korea), to reflect the diverse strategic orientations and different sources of competitive advantages that tend to vary by country of origin. For example, in the consumer products industry, we included Unilever and Henkel from Europe, Johnson and Johnson from the United States, and Kao from Japan. As for local firms, we selected White Cat and Shanghai Jahwa, rapidly emerging local challengers. For each firm included in our fieldwork, we attempted to schedule meetings with the CEO and at least four key managers covering marketing, human resources, and strategy. By conducting interviews with a variety of vital managers, we were able to cross-validate the interviews and cover broad functional areas.

As I prepared this book, I conducted another round of interviews between 2009 and 2012 to update the earlier field research. I selected five narrowly defined industries—automobiles, consumer products,

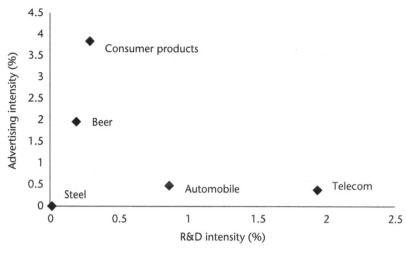

Figure 1.9 Case research design

telecom, beer, steel—and visited the most successful local and foreign multinationals in each. For instance, in the telecom equipment industry, I conducted thorough interviews at Huawei, ZTE, and Cisco. The nature and extent of competitive dynamics between local and multinational competitors differ greatly by industry. Pressure from emerging local players is mounting, while multinational firms engage in strategic moves to hold on to their earlier advantages. Local firms face higher barriers to challenge multinationals when they deal with complex technologies and diverse consumer needs and market structures because local firms may still fall behind well-established multinational firms that possess strong technology and marketing knowhow.

If I measure technological complexity and marketing knowhow with firms' R&D and advertising expenditures to total sales, based on all firms available in the annual industrial survey for each 3-digit industry from 2001 to 2007, when such data are available, these five industries differ greatly from each other, as shown in Figure 1.9. The consumer products industry with such products as shampoo and detergent has the highest advertising intensity, averaging 3.8%. The beer industry boasts the next highest, with 1.9%. Telecom, on the other hand, invests the most in R&D (1.9%), followed by the automobile industry (0.9%). The steel industry

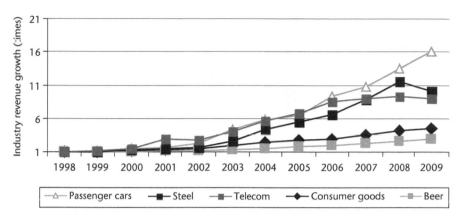

Figure 1.10 Industry revenue growth during 1998–2009

Note: Industry revenue of 1998 is set to one for each industry.

posts both the lowest R&D and advertising intensities. These industries also differ in terms of relative growth (Figure 1.10). The industry revenue almost tripled in the Chinese beer industry between 1998 and 2009, demonstrating the potential for a mature industry in developed countries to be a growth industry in an emerging economy. The consumer products industry, another mature industry, grew five times during the same period. During the same time period, telecom grew nine times, steel ten times, and automobile sixteen times. These phenomenal rates of growth thus pose great opportunities and threats to both foreign and local firms. The fortunes of these firms changed dramatically during this 12 year time period.

I specially chose these five industries to gain insights into how technological complexity and/or marketing knowhow contribute to the competitive dynamics between and within local and foreign firms. I chose one industry for each chapter to illustrate key insights from case studies. Insight from this fieldwork complements and cross-validates the statistical analyses.

Foreign Entry Strategies

When multinational firms formulate strategies to enter China, they consider multiple options. They can enter China via licensing or exporting from home or a third country. Or, they can set up their own subsidiaries through foreign direct investment to ensure the tightest control over operations. Multinational firms also face key decisions when making FDIs: whether to own all or part of the investment, and whether to set up a new operation from scratch or acquire an existing entity. As part of the process, multinational firms also choose location, i.e., which province or city they will enter. These entry decisions are a matter of high strategic importance, as each choice offers specific benefits and risks. This chapter examines the entry mode and location choices faced by multinational firms entering China. These choices are not, however, discrete decisions. Multinational firms make multiple entries in different locations and change their operating modes over time. This chapter further examines these sequential entries and post-entry operational mode choices in order to offer deeper insight into the strategies of multinational firms. The chapter begins with a case study of the Chinese automobile industry, which multinational firms were required to form joint ventures to enter. This in turn posed great management challenges.

The Automobile Industry: A Case Study
The automobile industry in China began with the establishment of the First Automobile Works (FAW) in Changchung, a northern city in the Jilin Province, in 1952. FAW relied on Soviet engineering and equipment

and produced a sedan under its own brand, Red Flag. Red Flag borrowed most of its design from the 1955 Chrysler model and debuted to celebrate the tenth anniversary of the establishment of the People's Republic of China. China set up the Second Automobile Works in 1969 and later renamed it as Dongfeng. Dongfeng was located in Shiyan, Hubei Province, an inland region strategically chosen to geographically diversify industrial bases in case of a possible war with the Soviet Union. Dongfeng started by producing trucks and later introduced passenger cars. In the meantime, numerous automobile manufacturers were set up by all provinces and municipalities. These regional automobile manufacturers included Shanghai Automobile Industrial Corporation (SAIC), Guangzhou Automobile Company (GAC), and Beijing Automotive Work (BAW). Before the beginning of reform in 1979, several hundreds or thousands of automobile manufacturers, all SOEs, had floundered in China. These local automobile manufacturers were small and inefficient, lacked scale economics in production, and were technologically backward and financially broken. Although these issues were not serious concerns during the Communistic planning period, these firms nonetheless failed to thrive.

Only after the economic reform started did the Chinese government realize it would need foreign capital and technology to prop up its automobile industry. From 1984 to 1985, three joint ventures—Shanghai Volkswagen (SVW), Beijing Jeep, and Guangzhou Peugeot—were set up to jumpstart the automobile industry. SVW, for example, was established in 1984 with 50% ownership by Volkswagen, 25% by SAIC, 15% by the Bank of China, and 10% by the China National Automobile Corporation. The joint venture contract mandated a 25-year agreement, very long compared to the three- to five-year Western standard. The Chinese side appointed the managing director and personnel managers, while the German side controlled finance and engineering. SAIC provided an ideal location given its legacy of producing tractors under the guidance of the Shanghai municipal government and thus the built-in base of factories and workers, in addition to established sales and distribution networks. As a large portion of sales went to government fleets or taxis, local partners played a critical role in promoting sales. The Shanghai municipal government helped SVW maneuver through the jungles of bureaucracy, as this venture's success was critical to top government officials' careers. Jiang Zemin, Mayor of Shanghai at that time, was later promoted to Party Secretary and, later, President Zhu Rongji, the next mayor after Jiang, also subsequently enjoyed a successful career.

Volkswagen brought in second-hand machines and equipment from its Brazilian subsidiary to produce its decade-old Santana model, a proven car design that performed well in Brazil's rough road conditions. Initially, the company imported the knock-down kits and assembled them in China. But because the Chinese government considered the automobile industry to be a potential pillar of industry, the ultimate goal in this joint venture was to develop the local automobile industry. Therefore the government pushed Volkswagen to transfer technology and increase local content.[1] Volkswagen in turn encouraged its European suppliers to form joint ventures with local partners in order to build local supply networks. Due to such efforts, SVW reached 31% local content by 1989, 70% by 1991, and over 90% by 1996. SVW's production volume topped more than 200,000 units in 1996, or more than 52% of the market.[2] By any measure, SVW proved to be one of the most successful joint ventures in China. Volkswagen entered another joint venture with FAW in 1990 to produce its Jetta and Audi models and to consolidate dominance in the Chinese market.

The two other early joint ventures, Beijing Jeep established in 1983 and Guangzhou Peugeot established in 1985, proved less successful. Jeep, an American Motors company, later acquired by Chrysler, had a minority stake (31%) in Beijing Jeep. Jeep faced a series of disagreements with its local partner, BAW, including product choice, financing, and import of parts. Similarly, Peugeot had a minority stake (22%) in its joint venture and so was less willing to transfer technology. Instead, Peugeot brought in old models and focused on assembly of knock-down kits and selling parts, making profits in the short term. Its local partner, GAC, owned by the municipal government, also did not lend much support to this venture. Guangzhou Peugeot ultimately dissolved in 1997. In both these cases, foreign multinationals were afraid of leaking technology to local partners and so did not favor rapid localization or introduction of their latest models. Though more successful, Volkswagen had a similar initial trepidation and initially brought in only its decade old Santana model. In fact, Volkswagen did not update its products in China until GM entered the market with its latest model. Yet Volkswagen was more favorable to technology transfer, as it owned 50% of SVW. Further, Volkswagen was newer to the global scene and so had a more urgent need to increase its presence in China. As the Chinese automobile market experienced double-digit growth, SVW became hugely profitable from its near monopoly position.

SVW's near monopoly in the passenger car industry, however, was short lived. The government passed the "Automobile Industry Development Policy" in 1994, which reconfirmed the 50% ceiling of foreign firm ownership. The policy also encouraged foreign firms to transfer technology and improve the capability of local firms. Specifically, it mandated that foreign firms must set up R&D facilities and bring in their latest models. Witnessing SVW's success, other multinational automobile giants that initially hesitated to enter the Chinese market for fear of losing technology could delay no longer. In 1997, GM announced a joint venture with SAIC, an original partner of SVW, to produce Buick models. The deal was worth $1.6 billion, including construction of multiple state-of-the-art research facilities in China. Shanghai GM (SGM) quickly nabbed a large market share with the launch of its Buick brand. This success was largely due to its ability to leverage the mature network built by SAIC and Volkswagen of part-supplying joint ventures already located in Shanghai. While it took SVW 12 years to reach 90% local content, SGM could do the same in just a few years. About 83% of SGM's suppliers also supply SVW (Marukawa 2006). In addition, SGM set up China's first automobile R&D joint venture called the Pan Asia Technical Automotive Center (PATAC) in 1997. With its 1,900 full-time employees, PATAC is now one of the core development centers in the GM global network. SGM, however, decided to build its own dealership network in China, while Volkswagen relied on its joint venture partner SAIC. The dealership network provided SGM tight control over its sales and allowed it to roll out its cars on a national scale. SGM cars sold with the same price tag anywhere in China, where competitors traditionally varied prices by region. In doing so, SGM integrated formerly fragmented regional markets into one consistent national market. More recent joint ventures of other multinational firms followed suit. SGM subsequently expanded into southwest China by setting up Wuling Motors in 2002 to produce minivans and acquired Yantai Body Work to create Shanghai GM Dongyue in Shandong Province in 2002 to make its compact car, Sail. In 2004, SGM acquired the Shandong engine plant of bankrupt Korean automobile producer Daewoo Motors. It also established Shanghai GM Shenyang Norsom in 2004 to manufacture pickup trucks and sport utility vehicles (SUVs).

Japanese automobile producers previously sitting on the fence also jumped in. In 1998, Honda took over the failed joint venture of Guangzhou Peugeot. Unlike Peugeot, Honda demanded 50% ownership in order to bring in its most popular model, Accord. Honda established another joint venture producing engines with Dongfeng in the same year. Nissan set up a joint venture with Dongfeng in 2002. Toyota set up a joint venture with FAW in Tianjin, now called Tianjin FAW Toyota, in 2000 and with GAC, GAC Toyota, in 2004. Hyundai/Kia likewise established joint ventures with BAW and Dongfeng, respectively, in 2002.

Until the early 1990s, the annual production capacity in China hovered around 1 million units. In 2011, it exceeded 16 million units. This dramatic growth is largely attributable to joint ventures. Due to new entries of joint ventures by other multinational firms, SVW's market share continuously dropped down to 36.7% in 1998 and further still to 8.8% in 2009. Together with FAW Volkswagen's market share of 10.5%, Volkswagen's market share in the Chinese passenger car market share remained 19.3% in 2009. SGM's market share went up from 7.4% in 1999, its first year of operation, to 13.8% in 2006. GM's share has since waned as more foreign joint ventures entered China, hitting 10.4% in 2009. The market shares of other multinational competitors like Honda, Toyota, Nissan, and Hyundai/Kia are on the rise. The combined market share of foreign firms remained around 80% during this time period.

The success of foreign firms in the Chinese automobile industry signals a fundamental weakness of local producers. It is hard to find another industry in China that is so reliant on foreign joint ventures. A noticeable trend in the Chinese automobile industry was that most large privileged former-SOEs were turned into joint venture partners with foreign multinationals. FAW partnered with Volkswagen and Toyota, Dongfeng (formerly the Second Automobile Works) partnered with Citroen, Honda, Nissan, and Kia, SAIC partnered with Volkswagen and GM; GAC partnered with Honda and Toyota; BAW partnered with Hyundai; and Changan Motors partnered with Suzuki. These SOEs-turned-joint venture partners benefited greatly from the rapid growth of the Chinese automobile market to become hugely profitable. The Chinese automobile industry grew 16-fold between 1998 and 2009, as in Figure 1.10, while demand consistently exceeded supply. As Huang (2003) points out, these privileged SOE-joint venture partners became financial investors and enjoyed the accompanying dividends.

Yet, importantly, as Huang (2003) further highlights, local joint venture partners failed to fulfill the government mandate to promote local industry. Both structural and technological issues in these local joint venture partners inhibited the development of their own cars and thus they were unable to fulfill the government's directive. While the government hoped Chinese firms would absorb technology from these joint ventures and in turn build a local automotive industry on their own, this transfer did not occur. Rather, incumbent local firms enjoyed profit sharing from joint ventures while their multinational partners prevented technology leakages. These local joint venture partners did not want to upset the profit-making joint ventures, as the development of local brands could sour the relationship with foreign multinationals. Further, technological barriers were much higher than government officials likely expected, as automobiles consist of over 20,000 components while designing a new car requires sophisticated technological and engineering capabilities. For example, Dongfeng continues to face difficulty developing its own passenger car. And, while SAIC acquired Korea's SsangYong Motor Company in 2005 specifically to absorb its technology, it failed miserably due to its poor post-acquisition management.

Earnest challenges of local firms come from new local entrants which do not rely on joint ventures. A rechargeable battery producer in Shenzhen, BYD, entered the automobile industry by acquiring Qinchuan Automobile, a small local firm near Xian, in 2002. BYD Auto gained notoriety in the Western world after Warren Buffet assumed 10% ownership in 2008. As a privately listed company, BYD now sells mass-produced, full hybrid vehicles, and exports to Africa, South America, and the Middle East. Founder Wang Chuanfu is the biggest shareholder, owning 24%. BYD's rise is partly attributable to the 2004 automobile industry policy of promoting local firm innovation and alternative technology such as electric cars. Similarly, Geely was set up by entrepreneur Li Shufu in Hangzhou in 1986. Initially a producer of spare refrigerator parts, Geely acquired a bankrupt SOE and started producing motorcycles in 1994. In 1998, it expanded again to produce a small van. Geely obtained state approval to make automobiles in 2001 and soon began manufacturing cars under such brand names as Emgrand, Englon, and, its namesake, Geely. In 2011, Geely posted revenues of RMB 21 billion and profits of RMB 1.5 billion. Geely is listed on the Hong Kong Stock Exchange. In addition to exporting to several foreign countries, Geely became a truly multinational company with its acquisition of Volvo from Ford in 2010.

Another emerging local firm, Chery, was founded in 1997 as an SOE. Chery soon transformed into a joint stock company with major shareholders tied to the Wuhu municipal government. Led by CEO Yin Tongyao, a former employee at FAW Volkswagen, Chery initially sought a joint venture with foreign firms to no avail, unsurprising given the firm's then novice status. Chery nonetheless started producing cars in 1999 without a production license, instead using a chassis licensed from Volkswagen's SEAT Toledo. The illegal activity continued uninterrupted because the local government that promoted local industry protected Chery from the persecution of the central government. Run by entrepreneurial managers, it took Chery only four years to produce 200,000 cars, starting from scratch. Two years later, Chery manufactured half a million cars, a rapid development rooted in cost efficiency, minimal bureaucracy, and minimal interference from the government, despite its partial ownership. In order to legally introduce its cars to the market, Chery affiliated itself with SAIC by selling 20% ownership to it. In 2003, Chery finally obtained a license with the support of the local government. SAIC dissolved its ownership stake in Chery as the intellectual infringement battle between GM, SAIC's joint venture partner, and Chery over its QQ model intensified in 2004. Chery's rapid growth was attributable to its low price point. Chery could sell its cars at such a cheap price because it copied the designs of competitors and used their parts, at least in its early period, thus saving R&D costs. Despite its poor quality, Chery could sell its vehicles based on the price advantage. As illustrated by Figure 2.1, the market shares of three emerging local companies, e.g., Chery, BYD, and Geely, was miniscule in 1998 but increased to 5.4% in 2009. Important to note is that these local firms' market shares are on the rise.

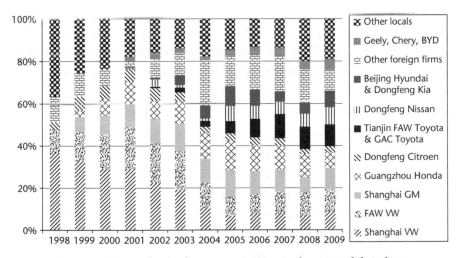

Figure 2.1 Market shares of major competitors in the automobile industry

Entry Mode and Location Choices

Joint ventures vs. wholly owned subsidiaries   The choice between wholly owned subsidiary and joint venture is an important dimension of entry mode choice, as it is a critical issue to multinational firms in maintaining full or partial control over overseas subsidiaries. Another important dimension in entry mode choices is the choice between greenfield investment and acquisition. That is, wholly owned subsidiaries may be achieved either through greenfield investment, i.e., setting up a new plant or other establishment from scratch, or through acquisition, i.e., purchasing a controlling interest in a local firm. Similarly, joint ventures, defined as the pooling of assets of two or more firms in a common or separate organization, may be achieved through either greenfield investment or acquisition. In the case of the automobile industry, foreign firms did not have a choice between joint ventures and wholly owned subsidiaries as they were forced into the former. As local partners converted their old plants into joint ventures, automotive joint ventures were acquisitive ones.

Figure 1.4 in Chapter 1 displays the first choice, i.e., the ownership decisions of all 150,910 foreign subsidiaries included in the industrial survey database by year of establishment.[3] While foreign firms are still required to form joint ventures in several "strategic" industries like automobile and steel, a clear secular trend emerges showing the decline of joint ventures and the rise of wholly owned subsidiaries. Most firms established in the 1980s were set up as joint ventures in response to the Chinese government's mandate that foreign multinational firms enter this way. The joint venture requirement policy is not unique to China. In fact, it is often favored by governments in developing countries to encourage technology transfer from foreign multinational firms to local firms. The most important reason why the Chinese government still imposes joint venture requirements in select industries like automobiles and steel is to encourage the transfer of technology from foreign to local firms and thereby to promote local industry. Another reason specific to China is to facilitate the privatized SOEs by forming partnerships with foreign multinationals, as discussed in Chapter 1 and building on Huang

(2003). The Chinese government often designated local partners and dictated the exact terms for the initial contract to entering multinationals (Puck, Holtbrügge, and Mohr 2009). Foreign multinational firms that wanted to enter China had to agree to these terms. For example, Volkswagen was instructed to form joint ventures with SAIC and FAW, while Peugeot was guided to partner with GAC. Other multinational automobile firms that entered later were likewise married to local firms as designated by the government.

Similarly, all early foreign entries to the telecom industry came in the form of joint ventures. Belgium Bell Company, later acquired by Alcatel, set up Shanghai Bell in 1984 in partnership with the China Posts and Telecommunication Industry Corporation to produce telephone switching and transmission equipment. Similarly, Siemens entered joint ventures with Shanghai Mobile Communications in 1990 and Beijing International Switching Systems Corporation, also in 1990, both of which produced digital telecom devices. However, Motorola successfully negotiated to form a wholly owned subsidiary in Tianjin in 1992, a very exceptional case at the time. To secure this deal, Motorola endured five years of negotiation, ultimately succeeding because of its heightened bargaining position in the post-Tiananmen incident and its commitment to a $100 million investment, the creation of 5000 jobs, and transfer of technology.

The Chinese economy matured just as China sought WTO membership, both of which pushed the Chinese government to slowly relax joint venture requirements. As illustrated in Figure 1.4, less than 40% of foreign subsidiaries established in the 2000s were classified as joint ventures because foreign multinationals could now create wholly owned subsidiaries in most non-strategic industries. For multinational firms, joint ventures are neither all good nor all bad. According to the management literature, multinational firms prefer joint ventures when they need local partners' deep understanding of local markets and access to distribution channels. For example, transaction cost theory specifies that multinational firms form joint ventures with local partners because this enables maximum use of local partners' complementary assets (Hennart

1982; Williamson 1991). Furthermore, when there exists extensive government intervention or regulation, joint venture partners may provide much needed political capital to deal with the government. That is, local partners can manage the relationship with the government, which is important in a transitional economy like China. So sometimes, joint ventures are preferred even when not required.

For example, Ericsson partnered with Nanjing Panda Electronics to produce inexpensive mobile phones under the Panda brand in 1992, the same year that Motorola entered the market with a wholly owned subsidiary. The joint venture entry choice helped Ericsson garner government support; the government even became their customer. Similarly, the Shanghai municipal government not only owned SVW, but was also its customer, purchasing cars for government fleets and taxis. On the other hand, Carlsberg, a brewery, chose to enter Shanghai in 1996 with 95% ownership and struggled. Because the local partner had only a 5% equity share, it lacked incentive to obtain support from the local government. After experiencing huge losses, Carlsberg sold its shares to Tsingtao Beer and exited the market in 2000. Furthermore, joint ventures can also be useful to limit initial risk, while later facilitating expansion or termination of the investment, depending on the joint venture's performance, as well as other strategic considerations. This feature of joint ventures enables a "real option," i.e., the call option to expand or the put option to sell off (Kogut 1991). In fact, many multinational firms in China exercised the call option to buy out local partners when wholly owned subsidiaries were legalized, which will be discussed in more detail later in this chapter.

Yet there are drawbacks to joint ventures. First, they can be very costly. This is especially true when tacit and poorly protected proprietary intangible resources are involved. As intangible assets like technology and trademark are inherently subject to market failure (Arrow 1974), multinational firms that transfer intangible assets find it difficult to prevent joint venture partners from leaking knowledge or free riding on their reputation. In fact, this was, and still is, the gravest concern for multinational automotive firms when forced into joint ventures in

China. It is also hard to price these intangible assets given the difficulty in obtaining price agreement from joint venture partners due to information asymmetry between the two parties. That is, multinationals have more knowledge about the value of these intangible assets than their local partners. For example, multinational firms might assign high value for their technological contribution to the joint venture, which might not necessarily be agreed upon by local partners. Conversely, local firms might attribute high value for their own contribution of local knowledge and political capital, which might not be fully appreciated by multinational partners. In these situations, multinationals have strong incentives to prefer wholly owned subsidiaries. Similarly, multinational firms that possess strong brands tend to prefer wholly owned subsidiaries for fear that joint venture partners may free ride on their reputation and degrade the quality of the products using that trademark.

Second, joint ventures can also be costly when there is a high level of "asset specificity," which refers to durable investments that cannot be easily redeployed to alternative uses or alternative users without a sacrifice in productive value (Williamson 1991). High asset specificity, such as specialized machines, tools, or equipment, may result in self-interested small-number bargaining, which also invites partner opportunism. Wholly owned subsidiaries have better mechanisms for eliminating such hazards.[4] As proprietary intangible resources transferred from the parent are often "transaction-specific" assets, multinational parents may be more willing to transfer them to wholly owned subsidiaries than to joint ventures. Furthermore, most proprietary knowledge is uncodified, making it difficult for foreign parents to transfer it except through close, long-term relationships, which are difficult to set up and maintain in joint ventures (Gatignon and Anderson 1988).

Third, wholly owned subsidiaries can make decisions more quickly than joint ventures, as they need not obtain consent from local partners. That is, many firms also have their own specific management style and culture that may not be compatible with local partners. Wholly owned subsidiaries can increase control by installing their corporate culture and management systems. Industries with a high level of intangible assets frequently face rapid changes in technology and competition. This requires quick decision-making and implementation only possible in the wholly owned option. Consistent with the logic of transaction cost theory, previous studies find that wholly owned subsidiaries are preferred when parent firm R&D and/or advertising intensities, which proxy for tacit and poorly protected intangible assets, are high (Gatignon and Anderson 1988).

To summarize, while joint ventures can lead to higher performance when multinational firms need local knowledge or face government regulations, wholly owned subsidiaries perform better than joint ventures due to higher investment in intangible and tangible resources, greater control, and fast decision-making capabilities. If we apply transaction cost theory to multinational firms operating in China, firms with sophisticated technology or brand should have entered via wholly owned subsidiaries. The automobile industry is certainly characterized by specialized technology and asset-specific investment. If allowed, most multinational firms in the automobile industry would have preferred wholly owned subsidiaries. When forced into joint ventures, these multinational firms often responded by refusing to import their state-of-the-art technology for fear of losing technology to local partners. As detailed above, SVW, formed as a joint venture in 1984, introduced a decade-old Santana model from its Brazilian subsidiary. Volkswagen also brought in another outdated Jetta CL model from Europe to its joint venture with FAW. Then GM, a late entrant in the Chinese market, brought in its most sophisticated model in hopes of penetrating the market. Only at this point did Volkswagen deliver its most recent, technologically advanced models in order to match the new competition.

Similarly, joint ventures were and continue to be required in the steel industry, with the controlling stake maintained by local partners. The government generally intervenes when foreign multinationals try to take a majority share. In 2006, POSCO actively negotiated but failed to acquire 51% of Shagang Steel, a private firm, in a deal ultimately prohibited by the central government. In 2007, Mittal Steel's proposal to acquire Dongfang Group faced similar disapproval.[5] Occasionally, the promise of advanced technologies can circumvent these rules, as in the case of POSCO and ThyssenKrupp, multinationals that hold majority shares in their stainless steel operations. Even the promise of advanced technologies does not always override this rule. When JFE Steel demanded a 51% stake in a joint venture with Guangzhou Steel in order to produce automobile steel sheet, a product that requires extremely advanced technology, a government intervention limited their ownership to 50%. To avoid losing its core technology to its joint venture partner, JFE installed several security measures, including a heavy penalty for employees caught leaking information, storing technical documents in special metal boxes under surveillance, and limiting operators' access to designated segments of the production line to prevent observation of the whole process.[6] Other multinational steel firms similarly hesitate to bring their most advanced technology to their Chinese operations for fear of losing it, which can be a pitfall of the joint venture requirement policy.

While the automobile and steel industries continue to require joint venture entry, the Chinese government relaxed joint venture requirements for non-strategic industries. Unlike automobile assembly, joint venture requirements were relaxed in automobile parts. For example, Delphi utilized joint venture entry in mature parts like air conditioners and batteries, but set up wholly owned subsidiaries for its high tech products like electronic control modules. Moving to consumer products, P&G and Unilever created several joint ventures to enter China in the mid-1980s. They initially used local brands from these joint ventures to develop distribution channels in Guangdong and Shanghai, respectively. P&G and Unilever converted their joint ventures to wholly owned subsidiaries when this option became available, with more recent entries coming in the form of wholly owned subsidiaries.

Figure 2.2 shows the breakdown of entry mode choice by industry sector and major region. Wholly owned subsidiaries are popular in technology-based industries like special machinery, electrical machinery, electronics, and precision instruments. This aligns with multinationals' preference for wholly owned subsidiaries in industries that require transfer technologies, proprietary intangible resources, and/or asset-specific

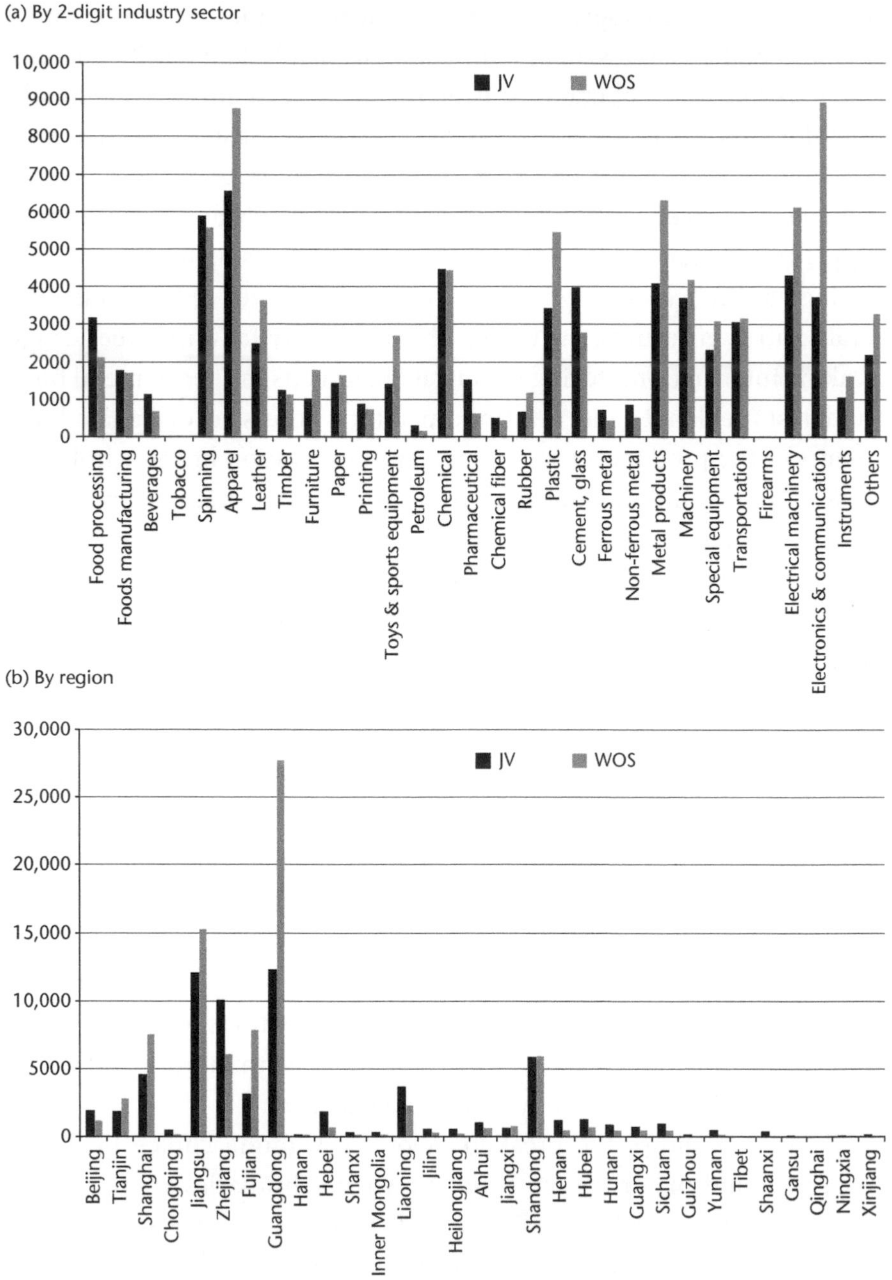

(a) By 2-digit industry sector

(b) By region

Figure 2.2 *Entry mode choices by industry sectors and major region*

investments. Wholly owned subsidiaries also occur frequently in labor-intensive but non-strategic industries like apparel, leather, toys, plastic, and metal products. This does not fit with transaction cost theory but reflects the earlier relaxation of joint venture requirements. In terms of regional distribution, wholly owned subsidiaries are more frequent than joint ventures in coastal regions, where there are fewer restrictions by regional governments.

Appendix 2 details the statistical analysis used to determine which factors motivate the choice between joint venture and wholly owned subsidiary. The analysis uses data from the annual industrial survey between the years 1998 and 2009. Thus, the analysis examines recent entry decisions when joint venture requirements were relaxed except for in a few "strategic" industries. This statistical analysis reconfirms our earlier discussion of industry case studies. Results show that larger investments favor wholly owned subsidiaries over joint ventures, suggesting that multinational firms want to keep full control over their large investments. More recent investments are also more likely to be wholly owned subsidiaries, reflecting the relaxation of joint venture requirements. Wholly owned subsidiaries are preferred in technology-intensive industries, as multinational firms need to protect their intangible assets via full ownership control, a trend consistent with transaction cost theory.

Wholly owned subsidiaries are also preferred in export-oriented industries in which local firms' region-specific knowledge and distribution networks are not needed. Conversely, joint ventures are preferred in domestic market-oriented industries. Joint ventures are also favored in industries dominated by a few large firms and in industries with rapid growth. Perhaps joint ventures help multinational firms penetrate such concentrated or high growth industries inaccessible to wholly owned subsidiaries. Results also suggest that foreign multinationals' entry mode choices are conditioned by the presence of other foreign firms in the same industry, as well as in vertically related industries. Specifically, when there are many multinational firms already in the same industry, multinationals see the wholly owned option as enabling quick responses to competitors' actions. Finally, when there are many foreign buyers and sellers in both upstream and downstream markets, the wholly owned option is preferred, likely because multinational firms do not need the local suppliers or distribution networks offered by joint venture partners.

Greenfield investment vs. acquisitions   The second entry mode option concerns whether multinational firms enter via greenfield investment or acquisition. Acquisition offers the fastest means of building a sizable presence in a foreign market, yet is fraught with the risk of overpayment, an inability to fully assess the value of acquired assets, and post-acquisition challenges like cross-cultural integration. Greenfield investment, on the other hand, offers greater control over local affiliates but requires the longest time to create.

The aforementioned transaction cost theory stresses the extent to which the distinction between exploiting existing resources and acquiring new resources (Hennart 1982) informs a firm's decision between greenfield investment and acquisition. Firms may choose either mode depending on which mode would be more efficient in exploiting or acquiring resources. Yet Madhok (1997) argues that transaction cost theory and its focus on partner opportunism may be limited in its ability to explain choice of entry mode. From his knowledge-based perspective, choice of entry mode is not just a matter of minimizing transaction costs but also reflects the need to devise supporting organizational structures and complementary organizational capabilities that enable the efficient exploration and exploitation of competitive advantages. For instance, when a firm has a strong home-based competitive advantage such as superior organizational and technical expertise, greenfield investment may be the most efficient mode of entry because it allows the firm to structure its operations in such a way that minimizes the loss of knowledge transfer from home country to foreign affiliate. Acquisition, on the other hand, may involve dealing with incompatible organizational routines, different levels of motivation, or low absorptive capacities of the partner or acquired unit, rendering it a less efficient mode of entry. Yet, acquisition may be the preferred mode of entry when a firm enters a foreign country seeking to tap local skills and resources like local sales, distribution channels, and knowledge (Madhok 1997; Barkema and Vermeulen 1998). Data on Japanese direct investment in the US supports the hypothesis that greater R&D intensity increases the likelihood of entry by greenfield investment over acquisition (Hennart and Park 1993).[7]

For example, consumer products firms, e.g., P&G and Unilever, tended to prefer acquisition or acquisitive joint venture, chosen to enable access to sales and distribution channels. Johnson & Johnson similarly acquired the local brand Dabao in order to penetrate the lower end of the market and access distribution channels in lower tier cities and rural areas. Having established distribution networks in China and gained sufficient local recognition, more recent entries by these three firms came in the form of greenfield investment. P&G, Unilever, and Johnson & Johnson built new plants, often in the form of wholly owned subsidiaries, and introduced their own sophisticated brands. As discussed earlier, these sophisticated products need frequent technology transfer from their multinational parents, as well as special machinery or manufacturing processes, which are easier to set up by greenfield investment than acquisition. Multinational beer firms also preferred acquisition, especially when entering new regions, as this enabled them to access already existing distribution channels.

Appendix 2 details the statistical analysis concerning the choice between greenfield investment and acquisition, based on the annual industrial survey between 1998 and 2009. Findings are consistent with our industry case studies. Multinational firms tend to prefer greenfield investment when investment size is large. More recent entries also tend to favor greenfield investment. Multinational firms also prefer greenfield investment in export-intensive industries. Greenfield investment allows multinational firms to transfer technologies from home in the most effective way, which often accompany huge investments. Such big-scale greenfield investment may be a more recent phenomenon, and may also be more relevant in export-oriented industries. Ethnic Chinese foreign firms from Hong Kong, Macao, and Taiwan also tend to prefer

49

acquisition to greenfield investment as compared to non-ethnic Chinese multinational firms. The cultural similarities between these nations and China may make post-acquisition integration easier. Acquisition is similarly preferred in mature industries because greenfield investment can exacerbate the industry overcapacity problem.

Location choices   When multinational firms announce plans to invest in China, they often specify a previously determined location. Most countries consist of many regions that differ greatly from each other in terms of wages, populations, technology bases, and infrastructures. Since multinational firms presumably choose locations that best fit their strategic goals, the location decision *within* a country (e.g., Shanghai vs. Guangzhou) may be more important than the decision at the country level (e.g., deciding to open a factory in China). With its vastly heterogeneous regions, it is especially crucial to examine location decisions at the regional level in China in order to understand multinational firms' overall entry strategies.

Figure 2.2 (b) shows the number of foreign subsidiaries in each province and the breakdown of wholly owned subsidiaries and joint ventures. Specifically, it shows that Guangdong, Fujian, and Shanghai and its neighboring regions Jiangsu and Zhejiang are the three most popular locations for multinational firms since China allowed foreign firm entry. High per capita income and rapid growth make these popular locations attractive to multinational firms, highlighting the importance of market attractiveness in location selection. They are also strategic locations in the sense that they offer access to other neighboring regions. For example, an establishment in Guangdong could cover the southern Chinese market, while one in Shanghai could cover the eastern Chinese market.

Further, governments in these regions are more open and foreign investment-friendly, with many designated as Special Economic Zones (SEZs). For example, Shenzhen, Zhuhai, and Shantou are SEZs located in Guangdong, set up in 1980 to attract foreign investors by providing tax and tariff incentives and cheap land. Due to geographic proximity, Guangdong attracts many investments from Hong Kong and

Macao. Fujian Province opened the Xiamen SEZ, which seeks to attract Taiwanese investors. The Fujian government simplified the procedure for Taiwanese firms to set up operations there, encouraging them to set up R&D centers and providing special incentives to establish headquarters in Fujian. Zhangzhou and Quanzhou were later added to Xiamen to create a "Golden Triangle" in Fujian. Shanghai is another popular location for many Western multinationals. Shanghai was one of the 14 coastal cities to open up for foreign investment. It provided several tax incentives, free land, prioritized loans, and foreign exchanges to multinational firms. Shanghai's Minhang, Hongqiao, Caohejing, and Pudong Districts were chosen to be Economic and Technology Development Zones to provide similar incentives. Stock exchanges were also opened in Shenzhen and Shanghai, further increasing the economic merits of these two regions.

In the consumer products industry, P&G and Unilever chose Guangzhou and Shanghai, respectively, for their initial investments. P&G formed a joint venture at Guangzhou in 1988 with its Hong Kong partner, Hutchison Whampoa. According to P&G's Greater China President, Daniela Riccardi,

> P&G came to Guangzhou in 1988, when Guangzhou was on the frontier of China's reform and open door policy. The policies, ideas, and style of Guangzhou government were very pragmatic. In the past 19 years, our cooperation with the Guangzhou municipal government has been very favorable. The fact that we are settled in Guangzhou was the right decision. Mr. Lafley, Chairman of P&G, mentioned in the meeting with the Guangdong Provincial Party Secretary that locating Greater China headquarters in Guangzhou was one of the most sensible decisions he made during his tenure.[8]

P&G recently expanded operations beyond Guangdong, including construction of its largest global research center in Beijing in 2010. In an interview, Bruce Brown, CTO of P&G, explained this choice as motivated by the desire to recruit the best scientists and engineers from the top Chinese universities, located in this area. The location also provides more opportunities to connect with other global R&D partners.[9]

Similarly, Unilever was attracted to Shanghai for its pro-reform government and affluent customers.

As noted above, government regulation is another important factor to consider in selecting location. Tianjin tried very hard to attract Motorola in 1992, including granting special permission to set up as a wholly owned subsidiary.[10] Similarly, in 1984, regional governments offered such supports as contracts for taxi and government fleets to Volkswagen and Peugeot, leading them to set up in Shanghai and Guangzhou, respectively.

In addition to market attractiveness and government regulation, a multinational firm's location decision can be influenced by the presence of other multinational firms in the same region, a phenomenon known as agglomeration economies or network externalities. Both foreign and local incumbents in the same region can be sources of complementary resources and learning to new entrants. At the same time, these incumbent foreign and local firms can pose a competitive threat to new entrants. Economists have long emphasized the importance of network externalities (Marshall 1920). Porter (1998) summarizes the potential benefits of agglomeration as: (1) improving accessibility to specialized factors and workers; (2) improving access to information about market and technology trends; (3) promoting complementarities among firms and cooperation among firms; (4) improving access to infrastructure and public goods; and (5) increasing competitive pressure among firms.[11]

These network externalities occur when the benefit or surplus that an economic agent derives from a good depends in part on changes in the number of other agents consuming the same kind of good (Katz and Shapiro 1985; Arthur 1990; Liebowitz and Margolis 1995). That is, the more people or firms that use a product or service, the more valuable it becomes. Most agglomeration benefits originate from flows of experience-based knowledge. By hiring specialized workers and purchasing other inputs, a firm can tap the knowledge embedded in such resources. Firms can also share knowledge by detecting market and technological trends and promoting cooperation. Although components of infrastructure like roads, transportation, and housing for expatriates are shared by all firms, it may be easier to share other resources, like specialized suppliers and workers, within industry boundaries. Thus, a large part of network externalities may be industry specific. Several empirical studies find evidence supporting the existence of regional agglomeration patterns among multinational firms.[12] Smith and Florida (1994) and Head, Ries, and Swenson (1995) observe that Japanese firms located manufacturing facilities in states already home to other Japanese firms. These researchers suggest that positive network externalities like technological spillovers, specialized labor, and other inputs might explain this pattern of agglomeration. Chung and Alcacer (2002) similarly find that firms in research-intensive industries are more likely to locate in regions with high R&D intensities.

In the automobile industry, SGM likely benefited more from SVW than it did from any other company in the area.[13] By forming a joint venture with SAIC in 1997, SGM was able to capitalize on the infrastructure of qualified managers, laborers, and suppliers that SVW, SAIC's other joint venture partner, developed beginning in 1984. Multinational firms can also learn from earlier entrants' experiences and avoid making similar mistakes. After Honda's joint venture with Guangzhou started in Guangdong in 1998, other Japanese car companies like Toyota and Nissan set up joint ventures in the same region. Agglomeration of automobile manufacturers also attracted suppliers like POSCO and ThyssenKrupp, both of which supply premium stainless steel to SGM and SVW from their operations in Shanghai. Agglomeration effects are especially substantial for vertically related industries, like automobiles.

For a technology-intensive industry like telecom, the existence of local industry clusters is especially important. Alcatel, Ericsson, and Nokia strategically chose to place their first joint ventures for equipment production near experienced local partners in Shanghai, Nanjing, and Beijing, respectively. These locations also enabled them to recruit China's best college graduates. Because many components need to be imported and a large portion of the products manufactured by joint ventures are exported, preferential local taxation treatment is another important factor. In fact, just such import and export tax breaks, as well as cheap labor and land prices, motivated Nokia to establish plants in Suzhou and, later, Dongguan.

Agglomeration can also have negative externalities. For example, firms can benefit from the spillover of other firms' knowledge and technologies, but their own knowledge and technologies can spill over to other firms. For example, although both SVW and SGM could benefit from spillover from each other, SVW could have lost more than it gained, at least in the early stage of SGM's development. Appold (1995) finds agglomeration to be negatively associated with performance in the US metal working sector. Agglomeration can also lead to intensified competition in both product and factor markets among adjacently located firms. Agglomeration drives up the costs of locally sourced inputs, such as the wages of local managers and engineers, as well as housing expenses for expatriates. For instance, in Shanghai, foreign firms now have to pay top salaries to attract local managers, while housing for expatriates is extremely expensive. Agglomeration can also reduce innovation as it may result in groupthink (Porter 1998). Agglomeration can further push firms in a regional cluster to look only inward for ideas, rejecting innovation from other areas. Detroit's attachment to gas-guzzling automobiles despite the oil shortages of the 1970s is a prime example of such rigidity. In sum, agglomeration decisions are driven by the sum of these negative network externalities.

Agglomeration economies might also be contingent on other factors, such as the identities of the firms targeted as sources of knowledge. It may be easier to transfer knowledge among firms with similar backgrounds since there are higher levels of absorptive capacity among such firms. My earlier empirical work with a research colleague on Korean firms' location choices in China tests whether network externalities are firm specific, nation specific, and/or industry specific (Chang and Park 2005). For example, Samsung Group uses regional organizations to facilitate knowledge sharing among its affiliates. Samsung China coordinates various activities through the subsidiaries of its affiliate firms in China. In turn, these affiliates frequently emulate other affiliates when expanding into new regions. For instance, if Samsung Electronics is located in Tianjin, other affiliates of the Samsung Group like Samsung SDI are more likely to locate in Tianjin because they can learn from Samsung Electronics' experiences in this location. We also show that a firm's country of origin significantly affects the degree of agglomeration economies it can derive from other firms. Since each country has its own culture, national origin may affect the types of experiential knowledge a firm creates (Hofstede 1980). As a consequence, some knowledge or experience may be nation specific, with firms able to learn more from the experience of firms from the same nation than from firms from different nations. For instance, a Japanese firm that transfers labor relationship practices commonly used in Japan may be uniquely qualified to learn from other Japanese firms that previously implemented similar practices in the same foreign location. Similarly, a Korean firm may be more able to recruit a local manager who can speak Korean from a subsidiary of another Korean firm. Further, when there is a large community of firms from the same country, these firms often create country-specific infrastructures, e.g., a Swedish school for Swedish expatriates' children. Thus, agglomeration economies tend to be stronger within firms than across firms, for firms of the same nationality compared to firms of different nationalities, and for firms in the same industry versus those in different industries.

Appendix 3 shows the statistical analysis pertaining to location decisions, again based on the annual industrial survey database from 1998 to 2009. When entering China, multinational firms choose which city or region to enter given the choice of 22 provinces, four major cities, and five autonomous regions. This analysis examines why multinational firms chose a particular location. Results confirm the above discussion centered on case studies. Foreign firms prefer regions with large populations and high per capita income, reflecting market attractiveness. They also prefer regions with higher levels of market development and more reliance on market price mechanisms. Multinationals also tend to enter locations with less government intervention, characterized by fewer government subsidies, smaller government size, and lower levels of SOE share.

The empirical analysis further confirms that agglomeration matters in location choice. It shows that competition effects can offset any spillover effects. For example, the agglomeration of firms in the same industry, whether foreign or local, does not significantly impact location choice. While foreign firms may benefit from the presence of other foreign or local firms in the same region in terms of positive spillover effects, they may also invite more competition. Thus, foreign firms may avoid particular locations, despite initial attraction to the region, with many foreign multinationals or local firms already there in the same industry. After competition effects cancel out spillover effects, agglomeration in the same industry may not have any significant impact. On the other hand, agglomeration of foreign firms, as well as local firms in downstream and upstream sectors, in a given region shows a strong positive impact on a future firm choosing that region. That is, multinational firms tend to locate in areas with well-established suppliers and buyers that can share knowledge with minimal threat of competition.

Post-Entry Strategies
Discussion in the previous sections may seem to suggest that multinational firms make "once and for all" foreign entry decisions, but FDI decisions are not discrete. Rather, they are best understood as part of a series of decisions that determine the volume and direction of resource flows among countries at any given time (Johanson and Vahlne 1977; Davidson 1980; Kogut 1983). Multinational firms that initially enter via joint ventures can convert to wholly owned subsidiaries by acquiring shares from their joint venture partners. Conversely, multinational firms can transform their wholly owned subsidiaries into joint ventures. Similarly, even though multinational firms choose a particular location for their initial entry, they can expand to other provinces or cities by incurring sequential investment.

Joint venture conversion to wholly owned subsidiaries As discussed earlier, China's joint venture requirement policy relaxed with its accession to the WTO. Foreign multinationals could now own wholly owned

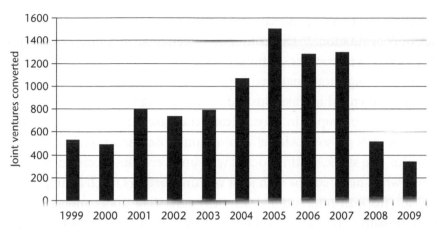

Figure 2.3 Joint ventures converted to wholly owned subsidiaries

subsidiaries, save for in a few "strategic" industries. As a consequence, FDI inflow via wholly owned subsidiaries increased while that from joint ventures dwindled dramatically in recent years, as shown in Figure 1.4. At the same time, many joint ventures converted to wholly owned subsidiaries; Figure 2.3 shows that 9365 of the joint ventures available in the annual industrial survey database converted to wholly owned subsidiaries between 1998 and 2009. This conversion activity gradually increased and peaked between 2005 and 2007, and then tempered down thereafter.

While this joint venture to wholly owned conversion cannot happen in "strategic" industries still restricted by the Chinese government, like automobiles or steel, examples of conversion are easily found in non-strategic industries like consumer products, beer, and telecom. For example, P&G's first Chinese joint venture—shampoo production in Guangzhou, established in 1988—became a wholly owned subsidiary in 2003. P&G's detergent production, established in Beijing in 1993, also transitioned to a wholly owned subsidiary in 2000. Unilever similarly converted its joint ventures in Guangdong, Anhui, and Shanghai into wholly owned subsidiaries between 1999 and 2004, less than a decade after establishment. In an interview, Zeng Xiwen, vice president of Unilever China, said, "According to joint venture agreements, all managerial issues had to be approved by both parties, and each joint venture had its own management, finance, and sales teams, which caused redundancies and lack of coordination."[14] This conversion strengthened Unilever's control over its China operations. At the same time, there exist many other cases in which foreign multinational firms maintain joint ventures, possibly increasing ownership stakes instead of converting to wholly owned subsidiaries. For example, in 2002, Alcatel increased its share of Shanghai Bell from 31% to 50%. Alcatel also optioned one additional stock, i.e., 50% plus one stock, vesting Alcatel with an overriding decision-making power when negotiations with joint venture partners reach an impasse.[15]

Prior work in international business considers the termination (or, more broadly, instability) of joint ventures as an indication of failure. According to this view, joint ventures may be terminated because multinational parents have difficulty coordinating their product portfolio due to shared control (Killing 1983), inability to manage cultural differences (Barkema, Bell, and Pennings 1996), or in order to achieve greater centralization (Franko 1971). Similarly, several researchers argue that "initial conditions," including task definitions, partner routines, and expectations, may create divergent learning and frustration (Doz 1996; Reuer, Zollo, and Singh 2002). The Guangzhou Peugeot joint venture was one such failure likely rooted in uneven ownership structure and misalignment of joint venture partners' interests. Blodgett (1992) demonstrates that uneven ownership structure often causes joint venture instability. However, challenging the notion that joint ventures are inherently fragile, Hennart, Kim, and Zeng (1998) find that international joint venture instability might be comparable to the failure rate of wholly owned subsidiaries, after controlling for firm age and size. More recent studies tend to emphasize that joint venture termination should not be interpreted as a failure but as an optimal adjustment in response to changing environmental or firm-specific conditions. According to this view, foreign firms are likely to enter new markets via joint ventures due to conditions of uncertainty. As uncertainty resolves, foreign firms can either divest joint ventures by exercising a put option or acquire them by exercising a call option (Kogut 1991).

Given the various reasons that motivate firms to terminate joint ventures, it is important to find circumstances in which the transition of joint ventures to wholly owned subsidiaries does in fact improve subsidiary firm performance. Transaction cost theory suggests that wholly owned subsidiaries are preferred to joint ventures in industries characterized by high levels of intangible assets like technology and brand. As noted in the previous section, multinational firms that transfer intangible assets find it difficult to prevent joint venture partners from leaking knowledge or free riding on their reputation. Also, multinational firms do not favor joint ventures when there is a high level of "asset specificity," as this results in self-interested, small-number bargaining and invites opportunism. Furthermore, joint ventures often inhibit quick decision-making, as they need to obtain consent from local partners. To summarize, the conversion to wholly owned subsidiary can improve performance if higher investment in intangible and tangible resources, fast decision-making, and better control are desired.

Following this logic, a large proportion of conversions may occur in an attempt to rectify joint ventures forced by the Chinese government. In these cases, joint ventures may not have been multinationals' optimal mode of operation in the first place. Thus, when allowed, many multinationals converted to wholly owned subsidiaries by buying out their joint venture partners. Yet others remained joint ventures. This provides an interesting setting in which to compare the performance of joint venture conversion decisions. Transaction cost theory suggests that we are more likely to find such cases of suboptimal joint ventures in industries in which intangible assets are important. In this section, we explore whether foreign subsidiaries improve their performance when they convert joint ventures to wholly owned subsidiaries.

Appendix 4 illustrates the two-step statistical analysis procedure used to evaluate the performance implication of the joint venture conversion. In the first step, we examine the conversion decision to see which factors lead joint ventures to switch to wholly owned subsidiaries. Results indicate that smaller, younger, and less profitable joint ventures are more likely to be converted to wholly owned subsidiaries. Perhaps bigger and older joint ventures are so well-established that conversion would prove difficult. Conversion would also be difficult for profitable joint ventures, as the foreign partner would have to pay a higher price to buy out the local partner. Also, if joint ventures are profitable, why would foreign firms bother disrupting them and converting to wholly owned subsidiaries? Results also suggest that export-oriented joint ventures are more likely to be converted to wholly owned subsidiaries, likely because they do not require the local knowledge or distribution channels offered by the local partner. Conversely, joint ventures that focus on domestic markets are less likely to be converted. Joint ventures with a higher level of intangible assets are also more likely to be converted to wholly owned subsidiaries in R&D-intensive industries, in line with transaction cost theory (Hennart 1982). The ratio of fixed assets to total assets has a significantly positive association with the likelihood of conversion, as the large asset base would make it more attractive for multinational partners to take full control. Further, local partners also matter. Results suggest that it is generally difficult to break up joint ventures with state-owned enterprises or collectives, as both are backed by the government. The earlier discussion of P&G and Unilever's experiences support these general empirical findings.

In the second step of the statistical analysis, we match joint ventures converted to wholly owned subsidiaries with the most similar firms that continued as joint ventures, using a technique called propensity score matching. If we do not match them properly, we may end up comparing apples and oranges. Only when we select both converted wholly owned subsidiaries and continuing joint ventures with almost identical characteristics can we single out performance improvement associated with the conversion from joint ventures to wholly owned subsidiaries. Results suggest that converted wholly owned subsidiaries demonstrate a 1.6 percentage point greater increase in return on assets (ROA) compared to firms with similar characteristics that continue as joint ventures (see Figure 2.4). Findings further confirm that the increase in ROA associated with the conversion to wholly owned subsidiary is greater in more technology- and brand-intensive industries. In contrast, there are no significant differences

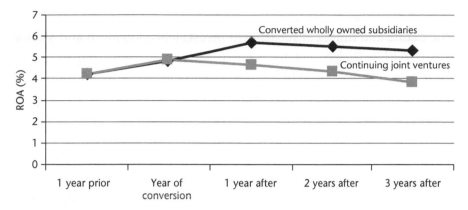

Figure 2.4 Performance improvement with conversion to wholly owned subsidiaries

in ROA in low-technology or low-brand industries. These results are consistent with transaction cost theory in that wholly owned subsidiaries are the preferred mode of entry/operation in technology- or brand-intensive industries in which intangible resources play an important role.

A direct implication of these statistical analyses is that many of the joint ventures that existed in China, especially in technology- or brand-intensive industries, were in a suboptimal position. These multinational firms were forced into joint ventures, and they responded by refusing to bring in their sophisticated technologies and brands for fear of losing them to local partners. The conversion to wholly owned subsidiary meant a correction of this suboptimal condition, in turn enabling them to import advanced technology and brands. Competitive dynamics, as elaborated in Chapter 4, further demonstrate that foreign multinationals eventually gained market shares over local firms, mainly through wholly owned subsidiaries. The Chinese government's move to allow wholly owned subsidiaries proved to be a critical opportunity for multinational firms to reorganize themselves in such a way that facilitated the import of sophisticated technologies and brands to gain competitive advantages over local rivals in China.

Sequential expansion Multinational firms often make multiple entries in a given foreign country. The international business literature describes FDI as a sequential process, whereby initial investments affect the nature and timing of subsequent investments. Johanson and Vahlne (1977) outline the process: firms enter foreign markets through exports, later establish sales subsidiaries, and eventually invest in wholly owned manufacturing subsidiaries. Increasing commitments are made possible by an accumulation of knowledge about the host market. Kogut (1983) observes that multinational firms often use earnings from foreign operations to invest in new projects in the same country, or in other foreign subsidiaries. My earlier work, some with a colleague, similarly finds that Japanese firms sequentially invested in the US by adding more businesses in multiple locations, as prompted by the appreciation of the yen in the late 1980s and early 1990s (Chang 1995; Kogut and Chang 1996). In this sense, sequential expansion makes clear the importance of building local capabilities in foreign subsidiaries, thereby accelerating the evolutionary process and allowing subsidiaries to more quickly benefit from economies of scale and scope within foreign markets (Nelson and Winter 1982).

For example, in the consumer product industry, after first investing in Guangzhou in 1988 to produce shampoo, P&G expanded to Beijing and Chengdu to produce detergent in 1993, and then to Tianjin to produce personal cleaning products in 1993. P&G also expanded its original operations in Guangzhou to produce more products. In 2010, P&G launched its largest global research center in Beijing. P&G invested more than $1.5 billion in China up until 2010, when it announced plans to invest an additional $1 billion over the next five years.[16] Similarly, Unilever set up its initial joint venture in Shanghai to manufacture products like soap, bath gel, shampoo, and skin care in 1986, expanded to Beijing and Guangdong to produce ice cream and tea in 1993, and then moved into Hefei to produce detergent in 1995. Unilever also made several other investments in the Shanghai area to expand production capacity and build a global R&D center in 2009 with a $100 million investment.

Similar patterns emerge in other industries. First, more recent entries tend to be larger investments. For example, Motorola invested $120 million to build a factory in Tianjin in 1992. It later expanded its operations in Tianjin by adding a finance company and mobile technology unit. By 2009, Motorola's accumulated investment in China totaled $4.1 billion, making it one of China's largest foreign investors. Cisco invested $320 million to build an R&D center in Shanghai in 2005. GE announced in 2010 that it would invest $2 billion in the area of energy and railways, including the creation of R&D centers.[17] Anheuser-Busch's 2006 acquisition of Fujian Sedrin for RMB 5.6 billion is the largest acquisition in the history of the Chinese beer industry, while Johnson & Johnson's medical equipment plant, completed in 2008, cost $100 million, making it the largest manufacturing plant in the world.

Second, when allowed, more recent entries tend to take the form of wholly owned subsidiaries over joint ventures. For example, Johnson & Johnson initially entered the pharmaceutical industry through joint ventures. More recent entries in baby care, medical equipment, vision care, and skin care all came in the form of wholly owned subsidiaries. In the beer industry, recent acquisitions are often 100% ownership, including InBev's (then, Anheuser-Busch) acquisition of Fujian Sedrin in 2006 and Daxue Beer in Dalian in 2012. In 2007, Cisco unveiled its plan to invest $16 billion in China, a large portion of which would be used to double its wholly owned manufacturing subsidiaries.

Third, more recent entries tend to be in inland or northern areas, moving away from coastal regions, in line with the Chinese governments' initiative to further invest in inland or northern provinces. In the automobile industry, as previously noted, Volkswagen entered in 1984 with a joint venture with SAIC in Shanghai. Volkswagen's second investment, this time a joint venture with FAW in 1990, moved on to the northeastern city of Changchun. As of 2012, Volkswagen operates 13 plants in various regions. Similarly, after its initial joint venture entry with SAIC at Shanghai in 1997, GM took part in another joint venture in 2002 with SAIC and Wuling Automobile, this time located in Liuzhou, Guangxi, an inland area, to produce minivans. GM invested in assembly plants in Yantai in 2002, Shenyang in 2004, and Wuhan in 2012, expanding its production facilities to northern and western regions. Similarly, after initial difficulties in coastal regions, including its exit from Shanghai in

2000, Carlsberg more recently focused on western markets like Yunnan, Tibet, Gansu, and Qinghai. This pattern shows that, in recent years, multinational firms have tended to move away from congested coastal areas to explore growing markets in inland and northern regions, essentially covering the entire national market.

This chapter examined multinational firms' entry strategies—entry mode and location choices—and their post-entry strategies—operation mode changes and sequential expansions. Although multinational firms were initially forced to enter via joint ventures limited to coastal areas, the government slowly allowed multinationals to incrementally add more investments by creating new wholly owned subsidiaries, converting incumbent joint ventures, and expanding into inland or northern regions. In doing so, some multinational firms developed a strong foothold in China, allowing them to compete effectively with strong emerging local firms, as will be examined in the next chapter.

Emergence of Local Competitors

The gradual nature of China's economic reform deserves attention. As discussed in Chapter 2, the Chinese government gradually relaxed joint venture requirements to allow more foreign firms to enter through wholly owned subsidiaries and gradually opened investment beyond a few SEZs. The gradual nature of this opening was designed to buy time for local firms to restructure themselves and improve performance before being forced to compete head to head with multinational giants. This chapter examines the restructuring process of local firms in order to consider how strong local firms emerge victorious. This chapter begins with a case study of China's consumer products industry, in which several strong local firms that emerged from the restructuring process or were newly created by entrepreneurs compete against giant multinationals.

The Consumer Products Industry: A Case Study

Prior to the reform and open door policy of 1979, the Chinese economy was under strict control by the central government. During this time period, firms produced according to quotas and all output was purchased by a state monopoly distributor. The government allocated tickets to consumers to purchase soap and other daily necessities. The government planned exactly how many bars of soap would be produced and how many would be allocated to each individual. Consumer products did not top the government's list of priorities. Shampoo was considered to be a luxury item and so was unavailable, forcing people to wash their hair with soap, though soap was also in short supply. The Chinese consumer products industry could develop only with the repeal of the ticket system. Soon, the Chinese government allowed its citizens to freely purchase consumer products while local entrepreneurs and foreign firms entered the industry to meet demand.

It was an eye-opening experience for Chinese consumers when multinational firms like P&G, Unilever, and Johnson & Johnson entered China with their well-established multinational brands. In 1988, P&G formed a joint venture in Guangdong with a Hong Kong-based trading company, Hutchison Whampoa. P&G brought in popular brands like Olay, Safeguard, Pantene, Rejoice, Tide, and Pampers. When P&G introduced its Head & Shoulders brand in 1988, it captured a 15% market share in Guangdong within 12 months. P&G clearly positioned its brands in specific market segments and clearly communicated them to Chinese customers. It also trained locally hired employees of their brand management system. P&G expanded its operations to multiple regions and with multiple products. P&G formed P&G Detergent in Guangzhou in 1992 as a joint venture with Hutchison Whampoa to manufacture and market Ariel detergent. It then added several other joint ventures in detergent, including P&G Panda Detergent (Beijing) and P&G Chengdu in 1993, and P&G Lonkey (Guangzhou) in 1994. John Pepper, president of P&G, noted, "One of our globalization strategies calls for expansion into new geographies with strong, established brands in our core categories. These joint ventures in China are right on target with that strategy."[1]

Unilever similarly entered China via a joint venture in Shanghai to manufacture products like soap, bath gel, shampoo, and skin care products in 1986. It also expanded to Beijing and Guangdong to produce ice cream and tea in 1993, and then to Anhui to produce detergent in 1995. These multinational firms initially entered the high-end market because the purchasing power of mass market consumers was limited. They gradually localized their sourcing and production in China and thereby came up with low-priced products for medium and low-end markets. Both P&G and Unilever initially built factories that covered major cities and gradually expanded logistic centers across all major areas of the country. For example, P&G actively developed local contract manufacturers that could supply products at low costs, and a third-party logistics company to handle its distribution. At the same time, distribution channels in China gradually transformed from privately owned local stores to department stores, supermarkets, convenience stores, hypermarkets, and online shopping websites. These new distribution channels helped multinational firms like P&G and Unilever penetrate the Chinese market. Beginning in the mid-1990s, hypermarkets experienced dramatic growth due to their ability to offer lower prices thanks to the high volume of goods and degree of choice. It was at this time that such global giants as Carrefour and Wal-Mart entered China. Several other Hong Kong-based multinational firms like C-bons and MaryKay also expanded their operations in China.

When the ticket system collapsed in the wake of economic reform and the entry of multinational firms via joint ventures, local firms were not ready to meet consumer demand or market competition. Local firms tended to be small, inefficient, technologically laggard, and financially broken. They were isolated to regions due to heterogeneous consumer demand. For example, if a firm were to sell one toothpaste product to the entire national market, the same toothpaste product could melt in the south during the summer and freeze in the north during the winter. Further, customers in coastal areas have larger disposable incomes than those in inland areas. As a consequence, the Chinese consumer products industry used to be extremely fragmented with numerous regional brands and no strong brand reaching the entire nation. While well-known regional brands like White Cat, Panda, and Gaofuli (owned by Lonkey) led certain markets, no national brand existed. Further, many of these old brands could not upgrade themselves. For example, Shanghai White Cat did not have a strong management team, invested little in its own brand and distribution, and so failed to upgrade its marketing skills and products, ultimately leading to a loss in market share.[2] Thomas Tsiang, general manager of Shanghai White Cat, noted, "It had become a sleepy old cat while its competitors were wide awake."[3] In 2006, White Cat was acquired by Hutchison Whampoa. Panda and Lonkey became complacent with their joint ventures with P&G to supply products on the original equipment manufacturer (OEM) supply contract and likewise failed to invest in their own brands. When joint ventures with P&G were terminated, they could not face the stiff competition on their own.

Yet several successful local firms like Nice, Shanghai Jahwa, and Longliqi emerged during this time period. For example, Nice Group is now a leading local firm in detergents.[4] Founded in 1968 as the Lishui 57 Chemical Factory in Zhejiang Province, this SOE transformed into a shareholding company in 1994, with the Zhejiang government owning a large stake. This restructuring became possible with the enactment of the Corporate Law in 1993. When privatized, the Lishui 57 Chemical Factory lacked strong brands and technology but gradually developed brands like Diao and Nice, which eventually became the name of the company. Initially positioned in the low-end market, these brands became associated with respected value products, as embodied by the advertising slogan, "World-class quality but only half the price." Nice invested in advertising even when it lacked financial resources. For example, Nice spent RMB 300 million just on promoting the Diao brand in 2001. Unlike personal care products like soap or shampoo that had direct contact with their skin, Chinese customers proved eager to use a Chinese brand detergent available at a more reasonable price. Nice also improved its technology, enabling it to develop new products like Supra, created in 2003, which uses natural ingredients. As of 2012, Nice holds a 40% market share in washing power products, 67% in soap products, and the largest market share in liquid detergent.[5] Local brands like Nice and Diao also have more power in rural markets than urban markets.

Similarly, Shanghai Jahwa Group is a leading local skin care product firm. Established in 1898 in Hong Kong, this Shanghai plant was nationalized when the Communists took over the country. The Communist regime then merged Shanghai Jahwa with three other plants to form an SOE, Shanghai Mingxing Household Chemical Factory, with such brands as Friendship, Yashuang, Maxam, and Ruby. During the 1980s, it sold moisturizing cream and shampoos under its Maxam and Ruby brands. In 1991, Shanghai Mingxing Household Chemical Factory formed a joint venture with SC Johnson in Shanghai and transferred both the Maxam and Ruby brands to this joint venture. But these two brands were largely neglected and the joint venture floundered. In late 1994, Shanghai Mingxing Household Chemical decided to end this joint venture and reassumed control of Maxam and Ruby.

After its breakup with SC Johnson, Shanghai Mingxing Household Chemicals was restructured into Shanghai Jahwa (Jahwa means household chemical in Chinese), a joint stock company. As with the Nice Group, the restructuring of this SOE into a joint stock company with state ownership became possible with the enactment of the Corporate Law of 1993. As the initial shareholders, the Shanghai municipal government resuscitated Maxam and Ruby in the hopes of developing them into national brands. Shanghai Jahwa's repatriation decision was highly publicized and CEO Ge Wenyao became a national hero. The media coverage of the repatriation helped enhance brand awareness and strongly appealed to the nationalistic sentiment of the general public. The joint venture experience spurred Shanghai Jahwa to strengthen its brand management system. It actively recruited managers and engineers from multinational firms by offering higher salaries and promotions in return for their marketing and management knowhow. Liushen was repositioned to target young women, while Maxam was reconceptualized for mature women. Shanghai Jahwa developed a Herborist brand in 1998, using herbal (medicinal) ingredients rooted in Chinese tradition. In 1999, the Shanghai municipal government proposed Shanghai Jahwa take over Shanghai Daily Chemicals in order to further expand product lines. In 2001, Shanghai Jahwa was also successfully listed on the Shanghai Stock Exchange so that it could raise much needed capital to further invest in brands.

Shanghai Jahwa pursued international expansion with its Herborist brand. In 2005, Shanghai Jahwa entered a joint venture with Sephora, a French cosmetics retailer, in China. Sephora agreed to carry Herborist in its shops in both its Chinese and Western locations, with new packaging by a French designer. The Westernized Herborist products were subsequently imported back to China, adding Western success to its appeal in China. In 2012, the Shanghai municipal government sold its shares of Shanghai Jahwa to a Chinese private investor, Pingan Insurance, for RMB 5.1 billion, completing the privatization process. Ge Wenyao, chairman of Shanghai Jahwa, stated that complete privatization was needed to help Shanghai Jahwa better compete with strong multinational giants like P&G and Unilever.[6] Shanghai Jahwa owns the most extensive distribution network in China, encompassing 40 sales companies in 30 major cities, 350 prefecture level distributors, and more than 400 county level distributors.[7]

Unlike Shanghai Jahwa and Nice, Longliqi is a private firm that was created during the reform period. Jiangsu Longliqi Bioscience, the firm's official title, was founded in 1986 by Xu Zhiwei, an entrepreneur and producer of snake powders and oils. Health-conscious Chinese customers who believed in the power of such natural ingredients supported Xu's development of snake oil facial cleansers and lotions in the late 1990s. Xu later launched products for the mass market, which he differentiated from the high-end products of multinational firms that used chemical compounds. Chinese customers continued to embrace these snake-based skin care products. Longliqi adopted the Six Sigma approach to improve its management and manufacturing process, ultimately reducing product defects and saving costs. Longliqi set up four R&D centers around the world, each focused on different markets: Jiangsu for beauty and health products, Beijing for herbal medicine and biotechnology, New York for skin care, and Kobe, Japan for shampoo. Longliqi also ran extensive advertising campaigns on China Central Television (CCTV) and sponsored various sporting events, making it a well-known brand throughout China.

Figure 3.1 shows the trends of the market shares of major players in the consumer products industry that I define as three 3-digit industries in the annual industrial surveys, i.e., soap and detergent, skin care products including cosmetics, and oral care products such as toothpaste. Despite the success of Nice, Shanghai Jahwa, and Longliqi, multinational brands hold a majority market share in the consumer product industry, hovering around 60% between 1998 and 2009.[8] In 2009, P&G

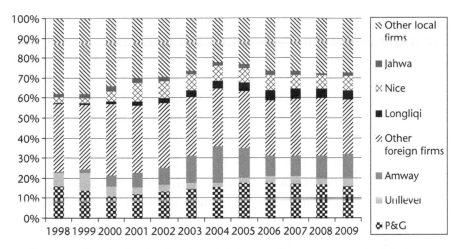

Figure 3.1 Trends of major firms' market shares in the consumer products industry
Note: Market shares are calculated based on firms' revenues in three 3-digit industries, i.e., detergents, soaps, and toothpaste, based on annual industrial surveys.

maintained the highest market share with 16.3%. In cosmetics and skin care products, several well-known local brands like Longliqi, Herborist, and Liushen are profitable. Other local brands are small and remain in the low to middle end of the market. Many of the poorer performing local brands faced bankruptcy and acquisition by multinationals. For example, L'Oréal acquired Mininurse in 2003 and Yuesai in 2004, while Johnson & Johnson acquired Dabao in 2008. These acquisitions enabled multinational companies to further penetrate the market with new access to low-end segments.[9]

In the detergent market, on the other hand, local brands like Diao of Nice Group and Liby of Guangzhou Liby Group led the way. Local firms are now gaining market shares as customer demand for detergent is more homogenous across regions and distribution plays a more important role than brand name in this sector. Local firms therefore maintain advantages over multinational firms in reaching customers in rural areas. Local firms are narrowing the technological gap. For example, Guangzhou Liby partners with Tsinghua University and Zhongsan University in improving its technology. Liby also completely owns five plants, more than 20 OEM partners, and 15 distribution centers, giving it a low-cost advantage in manufacturing and distribution.

Thus, while multinational firms still maintain a general competitive advantage over local competitors, their relative competitiveness also varies by market and product. Further, local firms are quickly catching up by investing in their own brands, as in the skin care industry. Local firms are also consolidating their advantages in distribution channels, as in the detergent market. Multinational firms did, however, overcome their weakness in distribution by tapping into new channels and localizing their products and production, allowing them to reach a national market. As illustrated above, consumer products is one of the most hotly contested markets in China.

The Restructuring Process

As touched upon in Chapter 1, the Chinese government initially tried to increase SOE efficiency by providing autonomy and incentives. The government soon realized this approach to be futile; the earnest restructuring of local firms would require more fundamental reforms to ownership schemes. While technically not allowed under the Communist regime, some firms bypassed the ban on the private ownership of firms and ended up inspiring the government's next step. In southern regions, especially Guangdong, private firms were disguised as collectives. When Deng Xiaoping visited southern China in 1992, he pointed out that the region's superior economic performance was largely attributable to the existence of these then illegal private firms. As such, he called for the privatization of state-owned concerns in other parts of China. In response, the Chinese government shifted its reform policy to enable the privatization of SOEs, a process known as *gaizhi*.

The Chinese government initially tested reform on 55 SOEs, eventually expanding the list to 120, including SAIC and Baosteel, in 1997.[10] In tandem with this experimentation, the government enacted the Corporate Law in 1993. This critical milestone in the privatization process provided a legal framework for converting SOEs into modern corporations. Thousands of SOEs soon transformed into limited liability firms or joint stock companies, with state ownership converted to shares. Initially, the government restricted incorporation to the exchange of shares among SOEs. Soon, though, a private firm could legally take ownership. The first large SOE to be incorporated was Shenyang Jinbei Motor in 1988 (Garnaut et al. 2005). The opening of the Shenzhen and Shanghai stock exchanges in 1990 and 1991, respectively, further enabled firms to issue shares to private investors. Once SOEs incorporated, the state shares could be sold to private interests, creating de facto privatization. Alternatively, the State-owned Assets Supervision and Administration Commission (SASAC), typically set up by local governments, could maintain ownership.[11] The SASAC can continue ownership indefinitely or sell their interests to private investors via stock exchanges, again furthering the privatization process.

For example, Zhongxing Telecom (ZTE), now listed on the Hong Kong and Shenzhen exchanges, began as an SOE originating from a military-affiliated factory. ZTE underwent several rounds of ownership reform. Finally, it settled on existing as a state-owned legal entity with SASAC as a major shareholder, selling its other shares at the stock exchanges. While the Chinese government maintains a large ownership share, it exercises control through state-owned legal entities like SASAC, thereby allowing the firm to run like a private firm with many private shareholders who buy in through the stock exchanges. ZTE was one of the very first to change as a result of China's reform policy, as exemplified by the slogan, "SOE holds control, private company runs the business."[12] In the consumer products industry, both Nice and Shanghai Jahwa, former SOEs, were transformed into joint stock companies around this time. In the case of Shanghai Jahwa, as noted above, the Shanghai municipal government sold its remaining shareholding to a private investor, Pingan Insurance, in 2012 to complete the privatization process.

At the same time, the Chinese government facilitated the bankruptcy of insolvent SOEs. In the early 1990s, many SOEs posted losses and accumulated large debts. In 1995, the Chinese government adopted a policy epitomized by the slogan, "Keep only large firms and let small ones go."[13] "Keeping only large firms" meant that governments would continue owning and controlling strategically important firms like those in resources, utilities, and energy. As of 1997, the 500 largest SOEs—most of which were controlled by the central government—held 37% of the industrial assets, contributed 46% of taxes collected, and earned 63% of profits (Garnaut et al. 2005: 3). In our annual industrial survey data, SOEs appeared to own 43% of assets as of 1998, as illustrated in Figure 1.2. Often monopolies with significant legal and technical entry barriers, these firms proved highly profitable, e.g., China Mobile, a state-owned mobile telecom service, and Sinopec, a state-owned oil giant. As a consequence of reform, these firms became joint stock companies with the government owning large shares. Thus, even though these firms are legally incorporated into joint stock companies, direct government ownership and indirect ownership through SASAC remain common. But despite modern firm ownership structure, these incorporated firms are de facto SOEs. As noted earlier, Shanghai Jahwa became a real private firm only after the government sold its shares to private interests.

Other surviving SOEs grew larger and more profitable, fulfilling the aims of policy reform. As in Figure 1.1 and 1.2, the number of SOEs dropped from 47,958 in 1998 to 5118 in 2009. Those maintaining legal status as an SOE in 2009 represented 8.2% of assets and accounted for roughly 1.3% of all firms in China. In other words, remaining SOEs, although small in number, possess large assets. On the other hand, the number of incorporated firms increased from 10,656 in 1998 to 61,218 in 2009, while their shares in assets increased from 17% to 36%. Overall, despite 30 years passing since the reform and open door policy, the privatization process is still very much in progress.

On the flip side, "letting small ones go" meant that smaller SOEs faced closure or immediate sell-off. Because most were unprofitable, local governments, the owners of the smaller SOEs, had strong incentive to restructure them. According to Garnaut et al. (2005: 47), the years after the initiation of policy-oriented bankruptcy witnessed 3377 cases of bankruptcies, RMB 223.8 billion in write-offs, and 6.2 million layoffs. Restructuring also appeared in such forms as debt equity swap, ownership diversification, and employee shareholding, including management buyout.[14]

For example, Jianlong Steel is a leading private steel firm in China, which would not have been possible without the privatization process. Its predecessor, Zunhua Steel, was an SOE on the edge of bankruptcy in 1998. Steel salesperson Zhang Zhixiang borrowed RMB 50,000 to lease the assets of Zunhua for five years. In 2000, he bought out the firm and changed its name to Jianlong Steel. Over the next nine years, Jianlong acquired and restructured more than ten firms. In 2002, for instance, Jianlong acquired Mingcheng Steel, another SOE on the brink of bankruptcy and in a general state of disarray. Disgruntled workers even picketed the provincial government for unpaid wages. Jianlong acquired the fledgling firm with a promise to settle the unpaid wages. Within two years of acquisition, sales increased 30-fold. Jianlong also applied this turnaround strategy to Ningbo Steel and Heilongjiang Steel. Jianlong's total assets have reached RMB 32 billion, making it one of the largest private steel companies in China.

TCL, a leading local firm in consumer electronics, provides an example of management buyout, also enabled by the government's move toward privatization. A former SOE with majority equity owned by the government of Huizhou City in Guangdong Province, TCL Group signed a five-year contract with the Huizhou government in 1997. According to the contract, all of TCL's assets as of 1996 would be in the name of the Huizhou government. However, a certain percentage of the growth of net assets exceeding 10% would belong to managers in the form of incentive payments. After seven years of rapid growth, government ownership of the TCL Group would dilute to 41% by 2004, with 25% of equity owned by the management team, 18% by other strategic foreign investors, and 16% by other non-management and non-strategic investors.[15] TCL's conversion demonstrates how private incentives can catalyze managerial performance, a nonexistent motivator prior to reform.

Meanwhile, many collectives transformed into private or incorporated firms. Technically, all citizens in a given community jointly owned collectives; in reality, however, local governments controlled them.

Collective firms were efficiently run and profitable, especially in rural areas, where they were known as town and village enterprises (TVEs). However, due to their vague property rights, instability plagued collective ownership and governance structures. For example, Haier, a leading local firm in electronic appliances, was originally established as a collective with employee and other community stakeholders, including local governments. As it grew, Haier needed to raise capital from the stock exchanges. The company transformed itself into Haier Group, a holding company that nonetheless remained a collective firm, while also listing two operating companies, Qingdao Haier and Haier Electronics, on the Shanghai and Hong Kong stock exchanges. On the other hand, many collectives were actually private firms, disguised to avoid expropriation. Known as "red hat" firms, these fake collectives could take off their hats and declare their real identity in 1998 when private firms were fully legalized (Gregory, Tenav, and Wagle 2000).

Included in Chapter 1, Figure 1.1 displays privatization trends from 1998 to 2009. During this time period, the proportion of SOEs and collective firms among all firms in the annual industrial survey decreased from 68% to just 5%. This sharp decline supports the notion that most SOEs and collectives were either closed or privatized. Figure 3.2 shows the number of firms that disappeared from the survey between 1998 and 2009 by ownership type. While some firms may have vanished simply because their sales dipped below the RMB 5 million threshold, most did indeed exit.[16] Figure 3.2 shows that exits of SOEs and collectives were concentrated in the late 1990s and early 2000s, reflecting the restructuring programs of that era. More recent exits, on the other hand, tend to be private, foreign, and incorporated firms that simply failed.

The exit processes of old SOEs and collectives coincide with the privatization of surviving SOEs and collectives, as examined earlier. Figure 3.3 shows that between 1998 and 2009, a total of 44,403 SOEs and collectives privatized or incorporated ownership. At the same time, many new private and incorporated firms entered, as will be examined in more detail later in this chapter. As a consequence of exit and privatization, as well as new entries, the combined proportions of private and incorporated firms

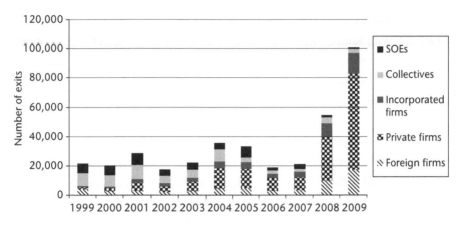

Figure 3.2 Exit activities during 1998–2009

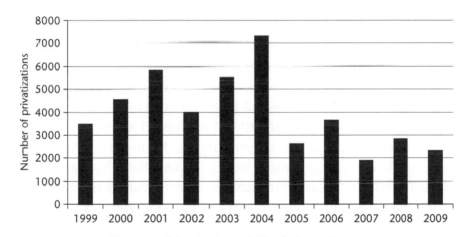

Figure 3.3 Privatization activities during 1998–2009

Note: Privatization is defined as transition from SOEs or collectives to private or incorporated firms.

compared to the total number of firms covered in the annual industrial survey increased from 14% in 1998 to 76% in 2009. This suggests that these two types of local firms—private and incorporated—and foreign firms maintain the majority of the modern Chinese economy. It needs to be emphasized again that privatization and incorporation do not mean firms are then free from government influence, as substantial direct and indirect state shareholdings, e.g., through SASAC, persist. Thus, again, privatization remains in process. In the following two sections, we examine the process of privatization and new entry more closely, evaluating the impact on local firm performance.

Privatization and Firm Performance

Figure 3.3 illustrates the privatization trends from 1998 to 2009, based on the annual industrial survey. I define privatization as the transition of SOEs or collectives into private or incorporated ownership. As shown in Figure 3.3, there are a total of 44,403 cases in which SOEs and collective firms privatized or incorporated during this time period.

The experience of Nice and Shanghai Jahwa in the consumer product industry raises two important questions regarding privatization. First, why did Shanghai Jahwa and Nice privatize while other firms did not? That is, which firms are selected to be privatized and why? Second, does privatization always improve firm performance, as in the case of these two companies? That is, can we generalize from these two case studies? Appendix 5 performs the statistical analysis needed to answer both questions. I again use the two-step method explained in Appendix 4.

In the first step, I examine the privatization decision, i.e., which firms are more likely to be privatized among all potential SOEs and collectives. In order to answer this question, I create data consisting of all SOEs and collectives privatized between 1998 and 2009, as well as all other SOEs and collectives that maintained ownership structure during the same time period. I find that larger firms and younger firms are more likely to be privatized. On the flip side, small-sized SOEs and collectives likely find it difficult to attract attention from buyers and instead exit the market. Older firms have greater inertia, making them more resistant to change and, thus, less attractive to buyers. More productive firms are also more likely to be privatized, as productivity attracts potential buyers for obvious reasons. Financially sound firms, i.e., those with less debt, are more likely to be privatized, as they can be attractive to potential buyers. Similarly, firms with more fixed and intangible assets like technology or brands are more likely to be privatized, as these assets appeal to potential buyers. Firms with lower export ratios, i.e., those focused on domestic markets, are more likely to be privatized, which may attract potential domestic buyers. On the other hand, export-oriented firms may be more likely to be acquired by foreign multinationals rather than privatized. Financial performance, reflected by ROA, does not have any significant relation, as firms with high financial performance likely carry high price tags that offset their attractiveness.

The analysis also considers the role of governments in the privatization decision. As an administrative heritage of the Communist regime, SOEs and collectives reported to various levels of government, depending on their size and relative strategic importance. While large firms and firms in strategic sectors report to central government, i.e., ministries in Beijing, others report to provincial, city, or township-level governments. Results suggest that the lower the level of government that SOEs and collectives report to, the more likely they are to be privatized. In other words, SOEs or collectives that report to central or provincial governments are the least likely to be privatized, followed by those that report to city and township governments, and finally by those that report to all governments below the township level. If we compare SOEs and collectives, collectives are more likely to be privatized than SOEs. This finding may reflect the fact that collectives were more likely to be in non-strategic sectors than SOEs in the first place.

The second question addresses the performance implication of privatization. That is, do privatized firms outperform those that remain as SOEs and collectives? Common sense would suggest they should indeed. Otherwise, there would be no point in privatizing. However, the reality is more complex, as privatizing firms often face resistance. For example, even Jianlong Steel, discussed earlier as an exemplary case that reversed the fate of many poorly managed steel firms, experienced some difficulties. Jianlong acquired 36% of Tonghua Steel, the largest state-owned steel producer in Jilin province in 2005. Jianlong subsequently fired many workers and replaced the management team. The workers felt the welfare they enjoyed under the SOE structure disappeared with

79

the transformation to a private firm structure. In 2009, the provincial government approved the proposal for Jianlong to increase its shares to become the largest shareholder of the firm. This decision led to worker protests that turned violent. A manager from Jianlong was beaten to death and the government had to end the deal by letting Jianlong quit the company completely.[17]

To test this hypothesis, I tracked firm performance up to three years after privatization by utilizing the propensity score matching technique explained in Appendix 5 to calculate the probability of privatization. I matched privatized firms with comparable firms that remained SOEs and collectives based on this probability in order to create comparable groups. The difference-in-difference technique compares these two groups—treatment (privatized) and control (those that were not privatized)—side by side by calculating changes since the privatization event.

As illustrated by Figure 3.4, privatized firms' ROA is 1% higher than the ROA of continuing SOEs and collectives three years after privatization. Privatized firms' productivity demonstrates an average 1.9% point greater increase compared to firms that remained as SOEs and collectives. This result clearly demonstrates that restructuring former SOEs and collectives into private or incorporated firms has a positive impact on firm performance, confirming that ownership reform played an important role in improving the performance of former SOEs and collectives to enable effective competition with foreign multinationals.

I further explore what factors make privatized firms perform better, considering such characteristics as sales, fixed assets, intangible assets, export ratio, and debt to equity ratio. As presented in Appendix 5, privatized firms tend to enjoy higher sales growth, export ratios, fixed asset growth, and intangible asset growth than their SOE and collective counterparts. Privatized firms also possess fewer debts. These results suggest that privatized firms could invest more in fixed assets like factories and machinery, as well as intangible assets like technology and brand. This in turn would increase sales and export and lower their debt to equity ratio, resulting in higher profitability and productivity compared to SOEs and collectives. Thus, this statistical analysis confirms that the success of such

(a) ROA

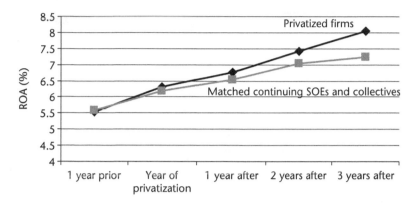

(b) Productivity

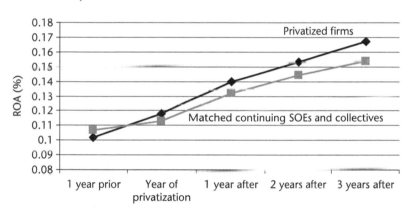

Figure 3.4 Privatization and improvement of firm performance

privatized local firms as Nice and Shanghai Jahwa can be generalized. In short, privatization greatly improves local firm performance.

Productive New Entrants

Figure 3.5 delineates new entry activities by ownership type from 1998 to 2009 using the annual industrial survey. Private firms are the most active new entrant type, followed by incorporated firms, and then foreign firms. New entries by SOEs and collective firms, on the other hand, are small in number and have declined over time. This illustrates the

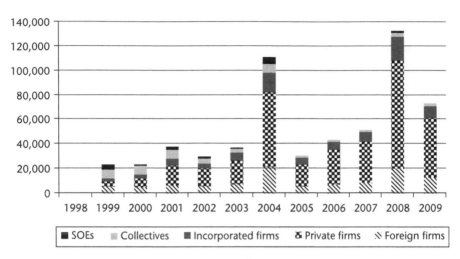

Figure 3.5 New entries from 1998 to 2009

fact that conventional Communistic firms quickly became outdated as China reformed its economy. New entrants challenged and continue to challenge both multinational firms and incumbent local firms, completely changing the competitive landscape in the process.

For example, Longliqi in the consumer product industry is an exemplary case of how new entrants challenge incumbent firms with innovation. Unlike other consumer products that tried to emulate the products of multinational firms, Longliqi tried to differentiate itself by using natural ingredients like snake oils along with traditional formulas. While multinational joint ventures (e.g., Volkswagen, GM, Toyota, Honda) dominated the Chinese automobile industry, new local entrants (e.g., BYD, Chery, Geely) presented a new competitive challenge. As discussed in Chapter 2, BYD was founded by entrepreneur Wang Chuanfu as a rechargeable battery producer in Shenzhen. Now a privately listed company, BYD sells mass-produced, full-hybrid vehicles and exports to Africa, South America, and the Middle East. Similarly, Geely was set up by entrepreneur Li Shufu in Hangzhou in 1986. Initially a producer of spare refrigerator parts, Geely acquired a bankrupt SOE and started producing motorcycles in 1994, expanded to produce a small van in 1998, and to make automobiles in 2001. On the other hand, Chery entered the automobile industry as an SOE in 1997. Chery is an entrepreneurial firm in the sense that it started producing cars in 1999 even without a production license. Run by entrepreneurial managers, despite its partial state ownership. Chery thus exemplified the motto: "SOE holds control, private company runs the business" to demonstrate that SOEs can be entrepreneurial with the right incentives.

Despite the success of the companies detailed above, there exist mixed theoretical arguments and empirical evidence as to whether new entrants are indeed more productive than incumbent firms. Schumpeter (1934) used the term "creative destruction" to describe how more efficient new entrants replace incumbents. Substantial evidence supports the notion that new entrants have higher productivity than incumbents. According to economic theory and much empirical work, newer firms enter the field with state-of-the-art technologies or innovative ideas, which allow them to surpass incumbents and their reliance on obsolete technologies (Caballero and Hammour 1994; Foster, Haltiwanger, and Syverson 2008). Although it is possible to upgrade technology, it is not typically feasible for incumbents given the "adjustment cost" of immediate investments, as incumbent firms may have difficulty handling architectural and disruptive innovations (Henderson and Clark 1990). Christensen (1997) argues that incumbent firms often do not notice the perils of disruptive innovation, which sacrifices performance (e.g., hard disk capacity) but instead offers some new attributes (e.g., small footage) that are not valued by current customers (e.g., minicomputers or desktops). New entrants exploit these new attributes to open up entirely new markets (e.g., notebooks).

The chance that incumbents will fail to upgrade themselves and exhibit lower productivity than new entrants is high in China because incumbent firms are typically not equipped with the organization or incentive to do so. This lack is called "imprinting effects" by organizational theorists (Stinchcombe 1965; Hannan and Freeman 1977). For example, workers for SOEs established under the Communist regime likely lacked incentives to perform while their managers lacked the skills needed to motivate given their acclimation to soft-budget constraints, or the financial safety net provided by governments in case of financial difficulty. Even as SOEs transformed into joint stock companies, the mindset of managers and workers faced greater inertia. Thus, old incumbent firms might face challenges in upgrading their technology and productivity, while new entrants might enter with the most up-to-date technology and strong management teams.

On the other hand, incumbents may exhibit higher productivity than new entrants. After a longer period of operation, inefficient incumbents tend to exit the market (Jovanovic 1982; Hopenhayn 1992), meaning remaining incumbents demonstrate improved efficiency enabled by learning (Baldwin and Rafiquzzaman 1995).[18] Incumbent firms also develop complementary assets like downstream resources (Mitchell 1989; Tripsas 1997), market-specific knowledge (Sosa 2009), complementary technologies (Helfat 1997), and commercialization capabilities (Lee 2009), all of which accumulate with experience. Incumbent firms also have accumulated political connections with the government that can offer competitive advantages in an emerging economy like China. New entrants cannot easily gain access to these complementary assets with internal development due to time compression diseconomies (Dierickx and Cool 1989). Following this logic, incumbent firms may therefore exhibit superior productivity over new entrants.

In order to examine whether new entrants in China exhibit superior or inferior productivity vis-à-vis incumbents, I estimate simple regression models using productivity index as the dependent variable and yearly cohort variables, 3-digit industry, 2-digit region, and year fixed effects as independent variables. Figure 3.6 is based on the estimated coefficients of yearly cohort variables from this regression and illustrates a very clear trend such that newly established firms tend to be more productive than older firms. This is especially true for entry cohorts from 1998 onward, i.e., firms that entered in the post-liberalization period. Yet very recent entrants, i.e., those entering between 2007 and 2009, have yet to fully set up operations and so exhibit lower levels of productivity for the first year or two. These results support the technological change argument that new entrants in China enter the market with state-of-the-art technology or innovative ideas that incumbent firms find it difficult to match, increasing competition in the process.[19]

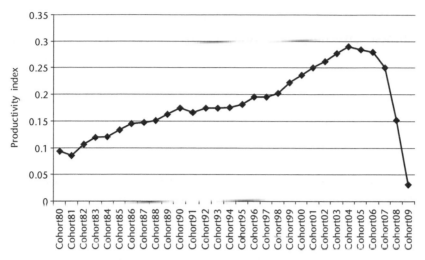

Figure 3.6 *Productivity of firms by entry cohorts*

Spillover from Foreign Multinationals to Local Firms

While privatization and new entries have significantly improved the productivity and profitability of local firms, foreign multinationals in China
have also contributed to this improvement. Figure 1.1 illustrates a 161%
increase in the number of foreign firms in the annual industrial surveys,
from 26,093 in 1998 to 68,223 in 2009. While thousands of new foreign
firms entered each year during this time period, thousands of local firms
were acquired by foreign investors.

As briefly introduced in Chapter 1, foreign direct investment has been
long regarded as a catalyst for economic growth in developing economies. In particular, a popular belief among policy makers holds that FDI
generates positive spillover effects in the form of technology diffused
to local firms. Such optimism regarding possible spillover effects led to
preferential government policies in many countries aimed at attracting
FDI. Among common strategies for promoting inward FDI are exemption from import duties, income tax holidays, and direct subsidies.
China serves as a model case for such preferential treatment to attract
FDI. China set up several economic zones offering special treatment to
foreign firms. Although forced into joint ventures, early entries received

subsidies from the government in the form of cheap land and bank loans. The Chinese government encouraged FDI, especially joint ventures, in the early years of reform to promote technology transfer from foreign multinationals to local firms.

FDI positively affects the productivity of local firms in two main ways. First, FDI spillovers take place through a "demonstration effect," whereby a local firm improves its productivity by simply observing foreign firms and copying their technology (Blomström and Kokko 1998). For example, the introduction of well-established multinational brands like Pantene shampoo, Lux soap, and Colgate toothpaste was sufficient for local firms to emulate their product designs and packaging. Joint ventures maximize demonstration effects, as local partners participate in the operation. Second, technology spillovers from FDI may also occur due to labor turnover, whereby former employees of multinational firms bring the knowhow and technology of foreign firms along with them to their local counterparts (Fosfuri, Motta, and Rønde 2001).[20] A manager from a multinational consumer product firm complained in an interview that the turnover rate of employees in the Shanghai area was as high as 20%. This multinational firm hired college graduates and trained them for several years only to find that they would leave the firm for better pay and promotions. They often ended up in local firms likely to benefit from the management and marketing knowhow acquired by hiring them. Thus, technology transfer from foreign to local firms can be both voluntary and involuntary, as local firms may be able to learn by imitation.

Both voluntary and involuntary technology spillover is evident in the automobile industry. For example, Volkswagen voluntarily transferred its technology to Shanghai Volkswagen, a joint venture with SAIC established in 1984. As discussed in Chapter 2, Volkswagen also encouraged its part suppliers in Europe to license technologies to, or form joint ventures with, parts-supplying local firms. Joint ventures have proven to be a useful way to transfer technology from multinational firms to local firms. Li Xiaowei, chairman of the Hunan Valin Group, mentioned in an interview that its joint venture partner, Mittal, sent its technical director to oversee the joint venture's development of new products like ship plates and silicon steel products. In addition, Valin became a part of Mittal's global procurement system, which helped reduce the cost of raw materials.[21]

There are also many instances of involuntary technology transfer. As mentioned earlier, Chery and BYD's car models closely resemble multinational brands, a common trend. A clear benefit of such copycat design is the learning inherent to the process. That is, in copying, local firms learn how to design a product, conduct market research, and use interchangeable parts and components. However, copycat design can also be infringement on intellectual property, which will be discussed in Chapter 4.

While discussion so far implies that foreign firm presence can be advantageous, this is not always the case. In fact, there is often a "competition effect," whereby local firms face competition from more productive multinationals and so must elevate their own performance in order to compete. Unlike the demonstration effect, which is presumed to be positive, the competition effect can be either positive or negative. While competition with foreign entrants may increase efficiency in the long run, local firms may be forced to cut production in the short run, allowing foreign firms to immediately steal customers. As a consequence, the productivity of local firms may suffer due to decreased demand, forcing them to spread their fixed costs over a smaller production volume. At its extreme, local firms may ultimately be crowded out of the market before any positive competitive effects can be reaped (Aitken and Harrison 1999).

Empirical evidence regarding the relative size of spillover versus competition effects is mixed. Researchers often find rather optimistic evidence, mostly in the context of developed countries, of a narrower technology gap between foreign multinationals and local firms (e.g., Caves 1974; Blömstrom 1986; Keller and Yeaple 2009; Liu et al. 2000; Haskel, Pereira, and Slaughter 2007). On the other hand, scholars often find that the share of foreign firms in a given industry can negatively affect the productivity of domestically owned plants in developing countries, as in Venezuela and Lithuania (Aitken and Harrison 1999; Javorcik 2004). However, Buckley, Clegg, and Wang (2002) find that foreign firms that have invested in China generate spillover benefits for local firms in terms of access to both technology and international markets.

Yet more positive empirical evidence can be found in developed, as opposed to developing, countries, suggesting that host country may matter. Specifically, the magnitude of FDI spillover depends on the absorptive capacity and motivations of host-country firms. Cohen and Levinthal (1990) argue that a firm's absorptive capacity, i.e., the firm's ability to recognize valuable external knowledge, assimilate it, and apply it to commercial ends, is shaped by prior related knowledge. The direct application of this idea to FDI spillover suggests that technologically underdeveloped local firms in China may not be able to acquire new knowledge through mere interaction with foreign multinational firms (Cantwell 1989; Meyer 2004; Buckley, Clegg, and Wang 2007; Blalock and Simon 2009; Liu, Wang, and Weim 2009). Thus, technological absorptive capacity would be required to benefit from the spillover. Recipient motivations or incentives also matter. SOEs enjoy favorable policy treatment and resource concentration, but private firms may have a stronger motivation to improve efficiency and earn profits. In this chapter, we have noted several such cases—ZTE, Nice, Shanghai Jahwa, BYD, Chery, Geely, Jianlong Steel—in which private firms or incorporated firms have strong incentives to excel, which allow them to benefit from FDI spillover and improve their technologies, if only to levels below that of multinational giants.

In this chapter, we examined how strong local firms emerge from the privatization process. We witnessed the inflow of new entrepreneurial firms that challenge incumbent local and foreign firms with their high productivity in China. These local firms benefit greatly from spillover from foreign firms, although they must also compete with them. Chapters 4 and 5 examine spillover effects and competition effects from foreign firms to local firms in more detail. At the same time, spillover and competition effects moving in the opposite direction, i.e., from local firms to foreign firms, will also be explored.

4

Competition Between and Among Foreign and Local Firms

The two preceding chapters examined the process of foreign multinationals entering and expanding their operations in China (Chapter 2) and the process of restructuring local firms and new entries (Chapter 3). Overall, both foreign and local firms gain competences over time and compete fiercely among themselves. This chapter examines the competitive dynamics between and among foreign and local firms. The chapter begins with a case study of China's telecom industry, which demonstrates a drastic contrast between foreign and local firms by sub-industry. That is, foreign firms dominate mobile handsets while local firms dominate telecom equipment. This chapter examines various factors that determine the relative competitive advantages of foreign versus local firms.

The Telecom Industry: A Case Study

The telecom industry is characterized by fast technological changes. Breakthroughs in technology and new services like mobile phones, internet, and mobile internet emerged during the last two decades to spur this rapid change. Incumbent firms often failed to move fast enough to maintain leadership in the next generation of services (Christensen 1997). New entrants could thus exploit the disruptive innovation to unseat incumbent industry leaders.

When China opened up for foreign direct investment, the global telecom industry was dominated by large multinational firms like Alcatel, Lucent, Siemens, and Ericsson. Right after the reform, the Ministry of Posts and Telecom (MPT) founded the China Posts and Telecom Industry Corporation (PTIC) in 1980 as a holding company to consolidate existing regional telecom-related manufacturing plants. But because the telecom infrastructure in China was so underdeveloped, MPT needed to import foreign technology and equipment like modern digital switching and transmission systems. PTIC initially encouraged foreign companies to set up joint ventures. The first joint venture, Shanghai Bell, was formed in 1983 between Alcatel and Belgian Bell, with PTIC taking 60% ownership. Shanghai Bell proved hugely successful as PITC acted as its own customer by purchasing equipment from the joint venture that it owned. Several other joint ventures followed suit. Siemens entered joint ventures with Beijing International Switching Systems Corporation and with Shanghai Mobile Communications, both in 1990. NEC also created a joint venture with Tianjin in 1990, known as Tianjin NEC. Realizing the high cost of production and transportation of imports, long lead time, and huge gap between local demand and foreign supply, multinationals quickly shifted to local procurement and production. For instance, Shanghai Bell created a subsidiary in 1988 to produce integrated circuits for its own use in order to increase local content. The Chinese government encouraged such moves, recognizing the corresponding reductions in imports and increases in technology transfer. These early foreign joint ventures helped modernize the telephone systems in China into digital switching and transmission.

While China's outdated landline telecom system upgraded via foreign joint ventures, mobile telecom services grew at a higher speed than expected beginning in the early 1990s. In many emerging economies, it is common to leapfrog older generations when introducing the latest technology. For example, the Chinese consumer electronics industry skipped video cassette recorders (VCRs) and moved directly to DVDs. Similarly, it was easier and cheaper to build a mobile cellular network than a landline network because it obviated the need to connect individual homes with fixed wires. Motorola, a worldwide leader in cellular services, set up a wholly owned subsidiary in 1992 in Tianjin to manufacture mobile phones, semiconductors, and mobile communication equipment. In 1993, Motorola licensed manufacturing of its cellular phones to Hangzhou-based Eastern Communications Group, a firm owned by PTIC. Although Motorola was late in entering China compared to its European competitors, it quickly grabbed a large market share based on its strengths in analog mobile technology. Witnessing the success of Motorola with its first generation (1G) analog mobile technology, Nokia and Ericsson expanded their operations in China with second generation (2G) digital mobile technology. For example, Ericsson entered a three-way joint venture with Nanjing Panda Electronics and China Putian Information Industry Group in 1992 to produce digital mobile communication systems and switches. In 1995, Ericsson also set up another joint venture, Beijing Ericsson Mobile Communications, with PTIC as a partner, to produce mobile handsets and equipment. In 1995, Nokia set up Beijing Nokia Mobile Telecom, a joint venture with a PTIC-owned firm. As China Telecom adopted Europe's Global System for Mobile (GSM) standard for 2G mobile service, Ericsson and Nokia grew fast and undermined the market share of Motorola during the late 1990s.

While the Chinese government invited several joint ventures with foreign multinationals, it simultaneously tried to promote local firms. Julong, also known as the Great Dragon Group, formed in 1989 out of a military research endeavor. Julong could sell switching equipment at almost half the price of foreign competitors with the help of government subsidies. The Chinese government further consolidated several other SOEs into Julong. By 1995, Julong became the second largest telecom manufacturer in China, after Shanghai Bell. Similarly, Datang was an SOE formed by the China Academy of Telecommunication Technology in 1998. When Datang was formed, the global telecom industry was preparing for the third generation (3G) mobile cellular system, which optimized the wireless transmission of voice and data. The International Telecommunication Union (ITU) adopted Europe's GSM-based Wideband Code Division Multiple Access (W-CDMA) and the US's CDMA2000 as two new global standards. The Chinese government strongly pushed for the TD-SCDMA as the third standard, which was developed by Datang in collaboration with Siemens. Though an unproven technology, TD-SCDMA had the potential to offer superior carrying capacity. Thanks to the support of the Chinese government, TD-SCDMA was adopted as the third standard by ITU. Datang, however, was not able to commercialize TD-SCDMA fast enough to capture the 3G market.

Both Julong and Datang eventually gave way to several private ventures, most notably Huawei and ZTE. Founded in 1988 by former army officer Ren Zhengfei, Huawei has been a private firm ever since. As a solely private firm in the form of a joint stock company with employees owning most shares, Huawei received no government support such as that which Julong or Datang enjoyed. Yet Huawei is now the world's second-largest telecom equipment maker, after Cisco, with sales of $32 billion in 2011. ZTE presents a more complicated case. The state owns one third of the company, parent company Zhongxingxin owns one third, though control for this portion falls to another company privately owned by the founders of ZTE, and the public owns the remaining third through the stock market. Despite de facto state ownership, ZTE is run like a private firm.

In their early days, both Huawei and ZTE backward engineered or imitated foreign firms' technology and products. Lacking sufficient technological advantages to be successful in overseas market, Huawei and ZTE initially focused on the domestic market. Huawei won its first overseas contract from Hong Kong in 1997. In its early days, Huawei sold switching equipment but soon expanded into access markets, optical transmission, and mobile technology. Huawei was also an early investor in 3G technology, ahead of other multinational firms. Such focused investment during this technological shift contributed to its success by allowing it to compete head to head with multinational firms in this 3G space. Huawei used aggressive pricing to penetrate overseas markets, which accounted for 68% of its revenue in 2011. Huawei also invested heavily in R&D, including an army of over 62,000 R&D personnel, representing over 44% of its 140,000 total employees. Huawei's competitive advantages reside in this abundant supply of talented and well-trained engineers working for a low cost, as only China could provide. To tap overseas talents, Huawei also set up R&D centers, like those established in Bangalore in 1999, Stockholm in 2001, and the US in 2001. Huawei also recruited professionals from big companies like IBM to help develop its own technology. As of 2012, Huawei operates 23 R&D centers around the world. Huawei also entered joint ventures in the US: 3Com focused on enterprise data networking, Symantec developed storage and security appliances, and Global Marine provided subsea telecom network solutions. Huawei had filed more than 36,000 patents by 2011. ZTE followed a very similar path as Huawei. ZTE won its first sizable overseas contract in Pakistan in 1998. It set up its R&D center in the US in 1998 and established offices near universities to recruit fresh talent.[1] ZTE's sales reached RMB 86 billion in 2011, 54% of which came from overseas.

The decline of Julong and Datang and the rise of Huawei and ZTE exemplify the shift from SOEs to private firms. As SOEs, Julong and Datang relied on government-sponsored projects and became complacent. As private entities, Huawei and ZTE attracted business through hard work. Furthermore, Julong and Datang were created as the merger of struggling SOEs that could not integrate their operations and management. As such, both lacked stable management teams. Datang focused on TD-SCDMA to the exclusion of other opportunities. Further, where Julong and Datang relied on the domestic market, Huawei and ZTE broadened to the global market.

In telecom, the mobile handset sub-industry is huge, much larger than switching or transmission equipment. Multinational firms initially dominated with mobile handsets, led by Motorola and Nokia, and then Ericsson, Siemens, and Alcatel. Until 1998, local firms did not command any presence in the mobile handset market. As the distribution of mobile handsets was deregulated in 1997, tens of thousands of small, mostly corner stores mushroomed by carrying multiple brands. This resulted in intense price competition. When cheap handsets became available, consumer demand for mobile services exploded and many local firms like Ningbo Bird, TCL, Haier, Lenovo, Kejian, and Konka entered the market. Other local firms without licenses followed suit to produce phones. Others still smuggled in second-hand handsets or counterfeited multinational brands. Although multinational brands had more sophisticated features, local brands were much cheaper and local firms could penetrate rural areas largely inaccessible to multinational firms. By 2003, local brands took more than 17% of the market share in mobile handset revenue, a figure that does not even include illegal local activity. But local firms' market share declined from its peak in 2003 as multinational firms started to fight back by introducing low-end models and expanding distribution networks.

Figure 4.1 shows the market shares of major players in telecom equipment and terminals, which includes mobile handsets, from 1998 to 2009, based on the annual survey. Several clear trends emerge. First, in telecom equipment, local firms' market share grew substantially at the expense of multinational firms' share during this time period. For example, Huawei's market share in telecom equipment grew from a mere 12.9% in 1998 to a whopping 48.9% in 2009. ZTE's market share grew from 3.6% to 16.9% during the same time period. On the other hand, multinational firms that once commanded large market shares lost ground during the same time period. For example, Shanghai Bell, a joint venture with Alcatel, lost its dominant position with market share dropping from 17.3% in 1998 to 5.8% in 2009. In 2009, foreign firms' combined market share shrank to a mere 19.3%. On the other hand, in the mobile handset market, multinational firms like Motorola, Nokia, and Samsung maintained their large market shares. Meanwhile, some local firms like Putian, Ningbo Bird, and TCL captured some of the market thanks to their cheap phones and deep distribution channels but could not maintain their position when multinational firms introduced their own low-end phones. Figure 4.1(b) shows that local firms' market share peaked in 2003 and declined thereafter. On the other hand, foreign multinationals literally dominate this market, with a 91.4% market share in 2009. Unlike telecom equipment, brand names of mobile phones are important to consumers, and are even characterized as fashion goods due to quickly changing trends.

(a) Telecom equipment

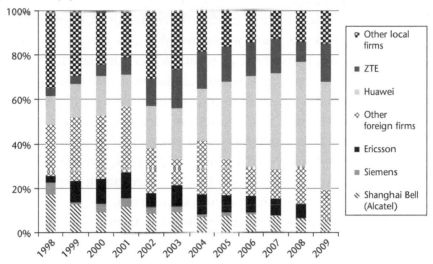

(b) Mobile handsets

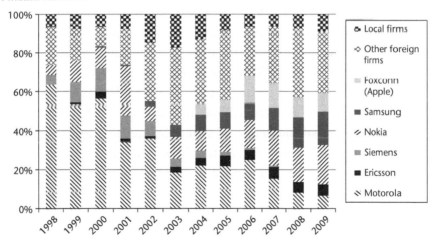

Figure 4.1 Trends of major firms' market shares in telecom equipment and mobile handsets

Multinationals could therefore better protect their market shares in mobile phones than in telecom equipment.

Second, individual firms' market shares within foreign firms and within local firms waxed and waned over this time period. Among local equipment firms, Huawei and ZTE emerged as dominant leaders while Putian, Panda, Datang, and Julong declined over time. Among foreign firms, incumbent leaders in the equipment market like Shanghai Bell, Siemens, and Motorola lost to Ericsson. Incumbent leaders in mobile phones like Nokia and Motorola lost to Samsung. Noteworthy is the case of Cisco. While Cisco entered China early (1994), it relied on subcontractors to manufacture products instead of creating its own manufacturing joint ventures or wholly owned subsidiaries. Thus, Cisco's market share in the annual industrial survey disguised its true business activities in China, as manufacturing of Cisco's products by subcontractors would be reflected in the revenues of those subcontractors. Cisco's own operations in China focused on servicing the high-end market and training, as opposed to manufacturing.

As mentioned earlier, the sudden rise of strong local competitors and the decline of multinational firms in the telecom industry are partially conditioned by rapid technological change. Even multinational firms focused on voice communication quickly lost their competitive advantages. As a consequence, these multinational firms were consolidated in the global market, as in Nokia-Siemens, Alcatel-Lucent, and Ericsson-Marconi. Meanwhile, a new breed of multinational firms like Cisco, Huawei, and ZTE emerged as important players. Both Huawei and ZTE rose quickly because they could exploit the technology shift earlier than multinational competitors since they were privately run, as private ownership allows firms to innovate at a rapid pace. SOEs like Julong and Datang could not match these nimble private firms. Thus, Huawei and ZTE could execute swifter changes, while Datang and Julong could not make timely transitions. In the telecom industry, in particular, missing just one technology generation makes it difficult to catch up in time to innovate for the next generation. The telecom industry shifted rapidly from voice to data and from fixed line to mobile during our study time period. Furthermore, R&D is an increasingly expensive investment.

However, the rise of local firms and the decline of multinational firms in the telecom equipment industry in China cannot be fully explained by the technological changes alone. Weak protection of intellectual property rights in China may also play a role. For instance, in 2003, Cisco sued Huawei for allegedly infringing on its patents and illegally copying source codes, user interfaces, and manuals central in its routers and switches. Cisco demanded a court order to stop Huawei from selling these products. Huawei removed the contested codes, manuals, and command-line interfaces and the case was subsequently dropped.[2] Huawei was also sued by Motorola for alleged theft of trade secrets.[3] ZTE similarly faced setbacks in intellectual property rights, including Ericsson's lawsuit over infringement on its GSM and 3G/UMTS (Universal Mobile Telecommunication System) wireless technology in 2011. ZTE counter-sued Ericsson for patent infringement in China. Both parties settled in a global cross-licensing agreement in 2012 and ZTE agreed to pay royalties to Ericsson.[4] After this series of setbacks, Huawei's proposed acquisition of 3Com in 2008 was blocked for national security reasons, i.e., a possibility of its network gears being used for espionage by the Chinese military.[5,6] In 2012, the Australian government excluded Huawei from tendering for contracts with a government-owned media corporation based on similar security concerns. As both Huawei and ZTE pursue global expansion, they will likely face more intellectual rights infringement litigation as foreign multinationals seek to protect their turf.

Industry Competitive Dynamics

The telecom industry case shows that the entry of foreign firms and the entry/restructuring of local firms dramatically changed the competitive landscape of Chinese and global markets alike. Under the Communist regime, state-owned enterprises remained largely inefficient and continued to produce lower quality goods due to a lack of incentive to innovate. These SOEs were not able to compete effectively with foreign multinationals. Thus, the Chinese government placed various constraints on foreign multinationals even as they opened their markets to them. Initially, multinational firms had to enter as joint ventures, as in Shanghai Bell in the telecom industry. Gradual reform ultimately allowed wholly owned subsidiaries. Motorola was the first foreign firm to enter the telecom industry as such. During the reform, local firms faced the privatization process, with the least efficient forced to shut down. At the same time, many new efficient local firms entered the industry. The weeding out process coupled with new entry developed many strong local firms ready to challenge multinational firms.

When foreign multinationals initially entered China, they entered high-end markets via product imports or the local assembly of imported parts. Foreign multinationals competed on the basis of technology and brand. On the other hand, local companies, mostly traditional SOEs and collectives, like Julong in telecom equipment, occupied the low end of the market. Given their positions at opposite ends of the market, multinationals and local firms did not initially compete against each other. However, between 1998 and 2009, our study time period, competition between foreign and local firms, as well as among local and foreign firms, intensified. In response, some multinationals grew their Chinese operations by localizing production, sourcing, and management. For example, both Shanghai Bell and Motorola initially entered, relying on imported parts. As these companies matured, they moved to locally produced key components like semiconductor chips.

Similarly, multinational firms in the consumer products industry pursued localization in order to stay competitive against emerging local firms and other multinational firms. Up until the mid-1990s, competition between P&G and Unilever was minimal. Geographically, P&G focused on the southern Chinese market with Guangzhou as a base, while Unilever focused on the eastern Chinese market with Shanghai as a base. So, despite similar products with similar price tags, e.g., P&G's Tide and Rejoice vs. Unilever's OMO and Sunsilk, their markets barely overlapped. As local firms like Nice and Shanghai Jahwa began to challenge P&G and Unilever with lower prices, however, Unilever initiated a price war with both local firms and P&G by drastically lowering its prices. For example, OMO detergent for a standard package dropped to RMB 3.5 in 1999. In the meantime, Unilever also launched sales promotions in the southern Chinese market, P&G's turf. In 2001, P&G struck back by lowering the price of Tide from RMB 6.0 to RMB 3.5. In addition to detergent, P&G and Unilever also competed fiercely in other product categories: Sunsilk vs. Eclairol, Lux vs. Pantene, Lux vs. Safeguard, Zhonghua vs. Crest, Ponds vs. Olay, and so on. P&G adopted an aggressive pricing strategy to gain market share, temporarily shifting focus away from profitability. P&G also adopted a "big brand strategy," which gave P&G economies of scale advantages in production, marketing, and advertising, while also allowing entry into many subcategories to further segment the market. For example, under the Pantene brand, there are 10 different product lines tailored to different niche markets. P&G also transformed its pure brand management to category management in order to reduce internal competition, fully leverage internal resources, and allocate resources scientifically, all the while increasing the company's competitive advantage.[7]

In order to respond to P&G more fully, in 2002, Unilever decided to close down all factories in Shanghai and relocate to Hefei's industrial park, located in Anhui Province where wages are lower and the provincial government provides subsidies. Unilever estimated that the relocation could save up to 47% on manufacturing costs. In 2010, Unilever reached an agreement with Hefei to expand its investment with the construction of a second industrial park.[8] Unilever also attempted to localize its products to address the specific needs of Chinese consumers. For example, it licensed the Zhonghua toothpaste brand from Shanghai Toothpaste Company in exchange for 2.5% of net sales. Unilever also launched a new product containing calcium and fluoride with a very affordable price point that became a huge success.

Meanwhile, local firms became strong competitors for these multinationals such as Nice, Shanghai Jahwa and Longliqi in the consumer products industry. This new breed of local competitor emerged from former joint ventures and new startups by private entrepreneurs. Many former SOEs and former collective firms also transformed into joint stock companies and raised much needed capital by going public. In the telecom industry, ZTE and Huawei are examples of successful privatization and new entry respectively. ZTE was a former SOE but transformed into a joint stock company where the government owned one third of shares. Despite its origin and state ownership, ZTE was listed on the stock exchange and behaves like a private firm. Huawei is a strong startup company. These modern local companies accumulated technological skills by benchmarking foreign multinationals and hiring away their engineers and managers. They also moved from low- to high-end markets by expanding their services. Yet not all local firms are mere imitators; rather some develop cutting-edge technologies. As mentioned earlier, Huawei established over 23 global R&D centers and filed more than 36,000 patents globally. In addition to innovation and superior technology, these strong local companies also have greater access to distribution channels. While most foreign multinationals in mobile handsets covered only large cities in coastal areas, local firms like Ningbo Bird and TCL developed dense distribution networks that extended into rural markets. Local firms' deep understanding of local markets and widely penetrating distribution networks also enabled them to better adapt to unpredictable market changes and opportunities.

As these two new types of firms—localized multinationals and emerging locals—continued their market expansion, they began competing head to head with each other in mid-range markets across the country. The intensified competition pushed out conventional multinationals relying on imports and conventional local firms unable to upgrade. Figure 1.8 illustrates such changes.

The extent and nature of these competitive dynamics vary by industry. Specifically, the relative market shares of foreign versus local multinationals differ greatly. While emerging local competitors try hard to catch up with multinational firms by emulating their technology, design, and products, their success depends on the nature of the intangible resources required in a given industry. Kogut and Zander (1993) argue that uncodifiable, unteachable, and complex knowledge is less likely to be imitated by competitors. In other words, if intangible assets such as technology or brand are difficult to explain or put in manuals, and causal relations between intangible assets and other variables are complex, competitors will have a difficult time trying to absorb via imitation.

In earlier field research with a research colleague, I found that two dimensions of intangible assets determine the relative competitive positions of foreign versus local firms: marketing knowhow and technological complexity (Chang and Park 2012). More specifically, when an industry involves complex technologies, it becomes more difficult for local firms to imitate or keep abreast of multinationals' product advantages. According to an executive in an industrial system firm,

> Chinese workers are not particularly strong in complex problem solving, which are essential to be successful in this [industrial system] industry. It takes a high level of abstract thinking and coordination skills to solve a complex problem. Local competitors may be able to copy a product but they cannot copy a system. At the end of the day, we are able to provide solutions to customers but they cannot. (Chang and Park 2012: 5)

For example, the automobile industry requires optimization of more than 20,000 parts. After close to 30 years of joint ventures, local firms are still not able to design and build their own cars.

Likewise, local firms face hardships when trying to catch up with multinationals in industries that require strong marketing knowhow. For example, the consumer products industry requires a high degree of marketing knowhow, as consumer tastes differ by age, income, and region, among other characteristics. Multinational firms like P&G and Unilever have extensive experience analyzing consumer demand and creating brands specific to various customer segments. Often, such knowhow resides in their corporate culture or management system, which may be hard for local firms to imitate. When industries are populated by multinational firms with intangible assets characterized by marketing knowhow and technological complexity, multinational firms may be able to maintain their market share. This is because local firms find it difficult to imitate multinational firms and so face higher barriers in challenging multinationals when working with complex technologies and highly diverse consumer needs and market structures.

Figure 4.2 depicts the trends of the combined market shares of foreign firms in the five broadly defined industries chosen as case studies for this book: automobiles, consumer products, telecom, beer, and steel. These industries differ from each other in terms of marketing know-how and technological complexity, as reflected in advertising and R&D intensities (see Figure 1.9). The consumer products industry has the highest level of advertising expenditures, as brands and distribution are key, followed by the beer industry. Similarly, the telecom industry has the highest level of R&D expenditures, followed by automobiles. If we follow Kogut and Zander (1993), we should expect that the combined market shares of foreign firms over local firms would be greater in the consumer products industry than beer, and greater for telecom than automobiles. The steel industry, low on both the technology and marketing dimensions, should exhibit lowest foreign market share. As illustrated by Figure 4.2, foreign firms gained market shares in each of these

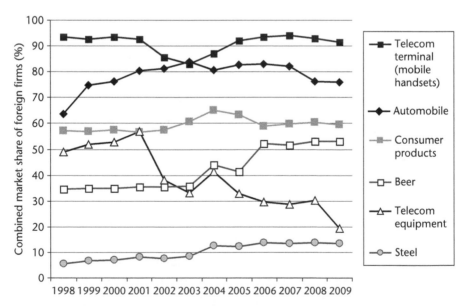

Figure 4.2 Trends of combined market shares of foreign multinationals in five industries

five industries between 1998 and 2009. Yet, the degree of market share differs greatly by industry. Foreign firm dominance seems to increase with technology and marketing knowhow. We also separated telecom equipment and terminals as the competitive dynamics seem to be different from each other and find that overall foreign-firm market share is highest, of all industries under consideration, in the telecom terminals (which includes mobile handsets) industry. Combined market shares of foreign firms in automobiles are also high, reaching 75.9% in 2009, followed by consumer products at about 60%. Foreign firms' market share in the beer industry grew from 30% in 1998 to 50% in 2009. The market share of foreign firms in the steel industry, a commodity product with heavy government regulation, on the other hand, is rather low at 13.6% in 2009.

A noticeable anomaly in Figure 4.2, however, is that foreign firm market share declined substantially in the telecom equipment industry, as Huawei and ZTE are driving out foreign competitors. Unlike mobile handsets, where marketing, brand, and technology play an important role, the main customer of telecom equipment is often large government-controlled telecom service providers like China Telecom or China Unicom. These telecom service providers are SOEs, which exercised their dominant position in procurement to favor local firms. Furthermore, since the product design or the software source code of telecom equipment should be shared with these telecom service providers, it is difficult to protect related intellectual property. The lawsuits between Huawei and Cisco, and ZTE and Ericsson during the 2000s illustrate such difficulties in protecting the intellectual properties in this market.

In order to verify the generalizability of the above observations from case studies, we perform statistical analysis in Appendix 7. To test whether foreign-firm market share is higher when intangible assets, i.e., technology and marketing knowhow, play an important role, we run simple regression models with foreign firms' combined market share as a dependent variable for all 3-digit manufacturing industries. When an industry requires sophisticated technology or marketing knowhow, reflected by high levels of R&D and advertising intensities, local competitors in emerging markets find it hard to catch up with multinational firms by emulating their technology, design, or products. Thus, we expect that the higher the R&D and advertising intensity, the higher foreign firms' combined market shares will be. Conversely, local firms are more likely to capture large market shares in industries low in technology or marketing knowhow.

The statistical analysis shows that, contrary to expectation, the industry R&D intensity is negatively signed and significant in all models. That is, foreign-firm market share tends to be *lower* in technology-intensive industries. On the other hand, industry advertising intensity is positively signed and significant, suggesting that foreign-firm market share is higher in advertising-intensive industries, consistent with our expectation. This result is consistent with the telecom industry case study. The relatively low market share of foreign firms in the technology-intensive industries suggests that weak intellectual property rights protection may be the culprit. In the next section, we will examine intellectual property rights in China.

Intellectual Property Rights in China

Multinational firms face challenges protecting their intellectual property rights in China. The lawsuits between Cisco and Huawei, and Ericsson and ZTE are just a few of many such cases that transcend industry. In the automobile industry, local models closely resemble designs of other well-established multinational firms. For example, the BYD Coupe bears remarkable similarities to the Mercedes CLK model from the front and the Chrysler Sebring convertible from the rear. BYD's F3 model also resembles the Toyota Corolla with Honda Fit design cues.[9] Chery's QQ takes after GM-Daewoo's Matiz compact car, sold in China as the Spark, resulting in a 2004 lawsuit.[10] According to Rob Leggat, vice-president for corporate affairs at GM Daewoo, "The cars are more than similar.... It really approaches being an exact copy...Same cute, snubby nose. Same bug-eyed headlights. Same rounded, high back. And most components in the QQ can easily be interchanged with parts on the Spark."[11,12]

Likewise, in 2005, Honda sued Shuanghuan Automobile for copying its CR-V with Laibao's SRV.

Counterfeit products of multinational brands are also common. Pirated DVDs and knockoff luxury bags ushered in the first era of counterfeiting. In 2000 alone, P&G launched over 670 raids, seizing 790,000 cases of fake products worth a combined RMB 230 million. At the same time, P&G lost a trademark lawsuit against Yaman Cosmetics in Guangzhou for registering Hushibao brand, whose pronunciation is similar to P&G's Whisper brand.[13] Software is even more vulnerable to piracy. About 78% of software sold in China in 2010 was pirated, totaling nearly $9 billion. The legal software market, on the other hand, nets just $2.65 billion.[14] In telecom equipment, as in the case of Cisco vs. Huawei, software accounts for a large portion of the value. Thus, if a firm copies a multinational competitor's software, the former can sell the product for half the price. About 30% of mobile phones in China in 2009 were estimated to be counterfeits,[15] including Hiphone for iPhone, Sumsung for Samsung, and Nckia for Nokia. Other counterfeits even use the original brand names.[16] Most fake mobile phone producers are small outfits, often located in Shenzhen, with 10 or so employees able to produce any kind of fake phone. Since key functionalities of mobile phones are concentrated on a few semiconductor chips and Mediatek, a Taiwanese semiconductor firm, provides a circuit board that easily integrates multiple chips, copying does not require sophisticated skill. These companies avoid the hassle of acquiring production licenses, conducting R&D, and paying taxes. These fake phones are even exported to countries in the Middle East and Africa. Firms making such counterfeits are often called "shanzhai," literally meaning the mountain bandit. Interestingly, this term does not necessarily carry negative connation among the general public in China, which equates this type of bandit with Robin Hood, stealing from the rich to help the poor. The general acceptance of *shanzhai* products reflects the state of intellectual property protection in China.

Although the Chinese government vowed to protect intellectual property rights, actual enforcement is slow to come. China became a member of the World Intellectual Property Organization (WIPO) in 1980; 1982 witnessed the enactment of the trademark law, and 1984 the patent law. Yet, according to a report by the US International Trade Commission, the Chinese government's enforcement proved insufficient due to inadequate resources for enforcement, local protectionism, and a lack of judicial independence (US International Trade Commission 2010: xiii). Raids and seizures result only in temporary slowdown while penalties are not high enough to deter such practices. Although the Chinese government detected massive copyright infringement of Microsoft products by Shenzhen-based local firms in 1992, the penalty was only a slap on the wrist (Gregory 2003). The general public's awareness of intellectual property issues likewise remains low due to inadequate education, with copyright infringement not typically recognized as a crime. When China joined the WTO, it faced increasing demand for intellectual property protection. The Chinese government set up the State Intellectual Property Office in 1998, in addition to specialized courts in major cities and provinces. Multinational firms in China also organized themselves to fight piracy. The Quality Brands Protection Committee (QBPC), under the China Association of Enterprises with Foreign Investment, works with central and regional governments to improve piracy protection. As of 2012, QBPC has 219 members.

Although intellectual property rights protection is in a generally dire state, some positive developments recently emerged. First, as Chinese customers become more affluent, they are beginning to shun counterfeit products. In fact, Chinese customers are now the biggest purchasers of luxury brands. There are many posh shops that sell branded products, while Chinese tourists buy expensive brands en masse. As Chinese consumers grow richer over time, demand for counterfeits or cheap imitations will eventually decline. There have also been several high profile counterfeiting cases that highlight the potential hazards of using fake products. For example, fake mobile phones have exploded and hurt people several times. Increased awareness of potential dangers will likewise dampen demand over time.

Next, local Chinese firms now own their own brands and technologies, which has led to mounting pressure from within for reform. For instance,

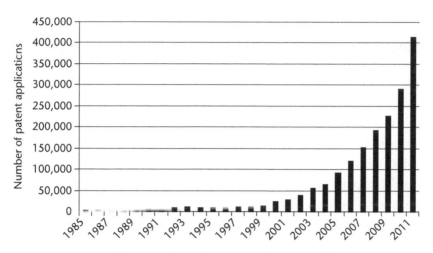

Figure 4.3 Annual patent applications in China

Note: Only inventions, excluding designs and utility models, are considered as patents. Data are from the Chinese patent office.

fake mobile phones hurt multinationals and local firms alike, as local firms invest in R&D and pay taxes to the government. The government provides strong incentives for R&D and patent filing. According to Reuters, China recently became the world's top patent filer, surpassing the US and Japan.[17] Published patent applications from China's patent office neared 300,000 in 2011 and are expected reach 500,000 in 2015. Figure 4.3 depicts this trend. In 2010, ZTE and Huawei ranked second and fourth for number of patents filed; Panasonic and Qualcomm were first and third. The need to protect their brands will push local firms to join the call for stronger protection of intellectual property rights. In addition, civil ligations are on the rise: 2009 witnessed the initiation of more than 30,000 cases, 96% of which were filed by domestic parties. In a document released by the supreme court in 2011, the number of newly filed cases involving intellectual property rights in 2010 hit 42,931, growing 40.18% from the previous year. Intellectual property rights enforcement will improve as the Chinese government realizes that protecting intellectual property rights promotes not only foreign firms but also local firms.

Emerging Winners from the Competition

Emerging local champions   The industry case studies so far suggest that there are some clear winners among local and foreign firms. Successful local firms that challenge multinational firms in these industries share several characteristics. First, they tend to be private firms run by entrepreneurs or incorporated firms run like private firms despite state ownership (e.g., BYD, Chery, and Geely in automobile; Longliqi, Nice, and Shanghai Jahwa in consumer products; Huawei and ZTE in telecom). This enables speed and flexibility (Chang and Park 2012). With minimal organizational heritage, these new companies typically have a down-to-earth, execution-oriented culture that enables quick decision-making. Private entrepreneur owners in particular can make decisions quickly and thus take advantage of new opportunities. Ren Zhengfei could upgrade Huawei's technology fast enough to keep up with the fast moving telecom industry. Wang of BYD and Li of Geely could diversify from battery and refrigerator spare parts businesses, respectively, to develop automobile empires. Longliqi similarly transformed itself from a snake oil business into a skin care business by adapting the concept of traditional medicine to its product line. Thus, these private entrepreneurs enjoyed the speed and flexibility enabled by their ownership structure, unbound by structural or institutional inertia. Some incorporated firms transformed from former SOEs also behave like private firms, as in the Chinese slogan, "SOE holds control, private company runs the business." Chery is one such firm able to move fast, despite its de facto government ownership. On the other hand, SOEs like Julong or Datang could not keep up with the fast development of the telecom industry and eventually dropped out.

Second, successful local firms possess a great capacity for learning. Shanghai Jahwa upgraded its marketing savvy based on knowledge and knowhow obtained from its joint venture with SC Johnson. In particular, Jahwa learned a brand management system that it then used to build its own brands. When Jahwa's state ownership was sold to private investors in 2012, Ge Wenyao, chairman of Shanghai Jahwa, noted, "Just yesterday, Jahwa was still a state owned enterprise, but now it's not. But even when we were an SOE we were different from others."[18] This quote suggests that Jahwa possessed a strong aptitude for learning in order to compete with multinational giants. Similarly, Chery, Geely, and BYD were able to jumpstart China's automobile manufacturing by reverse engineering, though this also won them the label of copycats. More recently, these automobile makers built their own R&D centers and acquired foreign firms in order to upgrade their technologies. In 2010, Geely acquired Volvo for $1.8 billion, seeking its brand and technology. These private firms also actively seek export markets, mostly in developing countries. They further tried to jointly develop products with foreign specialized automotive and engine design companies and trained local engineers through those cooperations. Thus, it would be unfair to call all Chinese firms imitators. As of 2011, Huawei had filed more than 36,000 patents in China, about a third of which were also filed overseas. About 44% of Huawei's 140,000 employees are R&D personnel. In 2010, China produced over 6 million college graduates. Since Huawei could attract China's most talented engineers at a low cost, it could generate low-cost innovation, offering customers high technology for a low price point (Zeng and Williamson 2007). BYD also bet on disruptive innovations like electric cars in order to leapfrog competition. These successful local firms were also able to apply learning to develop products tailored to local customers, as in the case of shampoo based on traditional Chinese herbal formulas. Thus, Chinese firms have come a long way from imitators to become true innovators, following in the footsteps of Japanese, Korean, and Taiwanese firms (Kim 1996).

Third, local firms have low cost advantages and strong distribution channels. While labor costs in China are on the rise, many local firms are located in rural areas characterized by abundant supplies of cheap labor. Further, local firms are not bound by global health and safety standards, which incur substantial costs for multinational firms. Local firms are also free from the expensive overhead costs of multinational firms. Some regional governments also provide subsidies to local firms in the form of cheap land and/or other administrative support. Furthermore, Chinese companies often come up with cost innovations that enable them to offer customers high technology at a low cost (Zeng and Williamson 2007). For example, Haier sold its wine refrigerator for less than a half the price of competitor models, in turn creating a huge market. Local mobile phone producers also came up with cheap phones to attract customers in rural areas, a move which multinational firms could not match. These local firms can also penetrate local distribution channels to reach customers in remote areas. Similarly, local firms in the consumer products industries successfully built many strong local brands. Bawang, a traditional Chinese herbal shampoo designed to prevent hair loss, was a huge success right after its launch.[19] A toothpaste product, Yunnan Baiyao, similarly inspired by traditional Chinese herbal medicine, was also a big success.[20]

Emerging foreign champions   Successful multinational firms share common features, which contrast with successful local counterparts. First, many successful multinational firms tighten control over their Chinese operations. To this end, some multinational firms converted their joint ventures into wholly owned subsidiaries, as discussed in Chapter 2, while recently creating more wholly owned subsidiaries, as in the case of P&G and Unilever. While joint ventures can be helpful in the early stages of investment when multinational firms lack local knowledge, wholly owned subsidiaries provide stronger control over operations, allow faster decision-making, and enable the import of sophisticated technology and brands without the risk of losing them to local partners. Figure 4.4 shows that when wholly owned subsidiaries are allowed, they lead foreign multinational growth in industries like consumer products, telecom, and beer. My field research with a colleague highlights that it is not advisable for multinational firms to emulate the speed and flexibility of local firms. We argue that local firms may be fast, but this speed comes at the expense of precision. Thus, we find that multinational firms that focus more on precision, relying on their well-established procedures, can be more successful (Chang and Park 2012). Strong control over operations in China is likely essential for multinational firms to achieve more

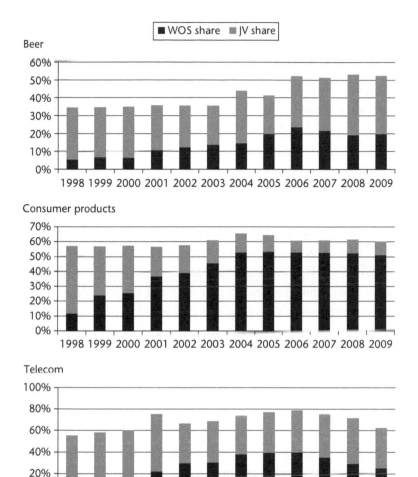

Figure 4.4 Foreign firms' market share by operation mode

precision in decision-making, which in turn enables competition with speedy and flexible local rivals.

Second, like local firms, successful multinational firms also have a great aptitude for learning. This learning manifests itself in the localization of management, production, and sourcing. Successful multinational firms localize production and increase sourcing from China in order to be cost competitive. In 2007, Cisco decided to double its manufacturing in China, a move worth roughly $14 billion. This allowed Cisco to be on a similar cost structure as local competitors Huawei and ZTE. Furthermore, this move granted more authority to local management, facilitating fast decision-making, flexible execution, and quick responses to local market changes. Multinational firms use China as a base for sourcing for their global operations. According to a manager at GE, "With local sourcing, it can act more like a local company. GE cannot compete against the 50,000 local manufacturers of incandescent light bulbs, whose prices are substantially lower, but it can use them as the basis of sourcing, from which it could establish a global level of cost competitiveness" (Chang and Park 2012). These firms also invest in building local distribution channels, especially tapping new outlets like superstores and online shopping. As discussed earlier, in the consumer products industry, P&G gradually expanded its product offering from the high-end market into the low-end market by leveraging local suppliers, OEMs, technological innovations, process optimization, and economies of scale. In order to reduce costs to compete with domestic competitors in medium- to low-end markets, P&G and Unilever chose to use local suppliers and increase local production.

Third, as local firms create low-cost innovations, multinationals similarly tailor products to local customer demand. Johnson & Johnson developed a low-price version of Stay Free, its premium female sanitary napkin, by using low-cost materials without compromising on quality in order to target the mid-level market. Johnson & Johnson sold Stay Free for half the price of its premium product. In doing so, the company could not help cannibalizing its own premium shares. Yet, at the same time, Johnson & Johnson could defend its position against cheaper local brands. Other multinational firms quickly followed suit. Both GE and Siemens developed low-price computed tomography (CT) scanners especially for the Chinese market by keeping only crucial functions and using widely available components.

Common characteristics of successful local firms—speed and flexibility, learning capacity, low cost advantages, and strong distribution—correspond to those of successful multinational firms—control and precision, learning aptitude, and localization. In a sense, each emulates the other in order to respond to each other's advantages in their own ways. These successful multinational and local firms create enormous competitive pressures on other foreign and local firms, eventually crowding out the least successful. Chapter 5 explores key performance indicators of both local and foreign firms such as productivity, profitability, and survival in more detail.

5

Performance of Foreign Firms

Chapter 4 examined competitive dynamics in order to identify common characteristics of successful local and foreign firms. This chapter builds on this to compare the performance of foreign multinational firms and local firms. Competition between localized multinational firms and emerging local firms has intensified in recent years, leading to a decrease in overall profitability and the exit of weak companies. This chapter begins with an examination of the beer industry to help illustrate why and how some firms perform better than others. This sets the stage for a more general evaluation of foreign firm performance in terms of survival and profitability, based on detailed statistical analysis.

The Beer Industry: A Case Study
Of the five industries considered in this book, China's brewing industry provides an ideal setting to look closely at the competition between different types of multinational firms and local firms, as well as the impact of this competition on performance. The beer industry is a historically fragmented market. As of 1998, more than 400, mostly small, brewers served China's regional markets. The fragmentation of the beer industry could be attributed to the following factors. First, regional governments owned local breweries during the economic planning period, and they enacted various trade barriers to protect their own local breweries. For example, a bottle of Yanjing beer sold for 18 cents in its home province of Beijing, could cost as much as a dollar in Sichuan due to provincial

fees and taxes (Gilley 2001). Second, it was prohibitively expensive to move goods between regions in China due to high logistics costs rooted in poor infrastructure. Furthermore, there was a great deal of heterogeneity in consumer demand. The price of beer was higher in coastal and eastern regions, which offered more premium-priced brands, while rural areas had access only to cheap, locally brewed beer. Third, the wholesale distribution sector, dominated by state-owned cigarette and alcohol distribution companies and collective distributors, was also fragmented. Brewers had to deal with more than 20 first-tier wholesalers in each region and second- and third-tier small wholesalers to cover smaller retail outlets (Slocum et al. 2005). As a consequence, both local and foreign breweries could not reap economies of scale and therefore lacked operating efficiency. Lacking scale economies, local beer firms were largely inefficient, selling cheap and low quality beer, often in plastic bags. Although there were some leading brands in each region, no national brand existed. Despite poor supply conditions, demand for beer has grown in recent years as consumer tastes shifted from liquors to low-alcohol content drinks.

The beer industry in China evolved in several phases. The early stage is characterized by aggressive entries of multinational firms. Because the beer industry is not considered "strategic" by the Chinese government, it faces fewer regulations than other industries. Thus, multinational brewers like Anheuser-Busch, Asahi, Kirin, Bass, Carlsberg, Foster's, Heineken, San Miguel, and South African Brewery (SAB) ventured into China in the early 1990s with their well-established, premium brands to primarily focus on first-tier cities. By demonstrating advanced bottling, advertising, and distribution, these foreign multinationals created immense spillover effects for local firms. Many of these multinational firms, however, experienced difficulty tapping the Chinese market. Given the limited income of Chinese consumers, they could not sell enough premium beer to justify marketing and sales expenses. And they soon learned that advertising does not drive the Chinese beer industry. Although many foreign multinational firms introduced international brands in China by spending large sums on advertising in hotels and restaurants in upscale coastal areas, they faced large losses. Rather, price and distribution proved to be the main concerns of the mass market. According to a market analyst,

> Yanjing now has 85% of the Beijing market...It did that by getting control of the guys on tricycles who pedal up and down the hutongs (lanes) peddling beer. By and large, it's not advertising. It's having your products in the right place at the right time. Once you've done that, advertising will help but it isn't the main thing.[1]

Additionally, firms could not utilize national advertising campaigns because they could not supply large volumes of beer outside of their base regions. Yet, foreign multinationals had incentives to push into other regions, which would allow the costs to be spread across a larger sales base. For instance, beer firms could tap into TV advertisements broadcast on a national level, justifiable only if they could reach more markets.

As a consequence, several of these early multinational entrants could not sustain their loss-making Chinese operations. Foster's, one of the earliest multinational firms to enter...and soon exit, sold its two joint ventures to China Resources Snow in 1998 after several years of losing money. A manager at Foster's explains, "It was the corporate Vietnam...when everyone came and looked around and saw no branded products...the trouble was, 80 other companies did the same thing on the same day. And there still isn't a premium market" (Heracleous 2001: 37). Similarly, Carlsberg sold its shares of loss-making Shanghai Brewery to Tsingtao in 2000 after completing construction just four years prior. Carlsberg retreated from markets in coastal areas where competition intensified, turning instead to less crowded western markets like Yunnan.

By the early 2000s, several clear winners emerged from this competition, namely China Resources Snow, Anheuser-Busch, Tsingtao, and Yanjing. During the 2000s, these firms continued to acquire other firms and expand. China Resources Snow Brewery is China's most successful firm in the country's beer market. Hong Kong-based China Resources acquired the Snow Brewery in Shenyang and soon entered the market through a joint venture with SAB in 1994 with a 51.49% equity structure. As a late entrant, SAB originally focused on China's second-tier cities. By combining SAB's technology and China Resources' local knowledge, China Resources Snow substantially increased its market share. According to SAB's managing director for Asia, "Our partners are the China experts. They have experience of doing business there. As a result, they have amazing contacts that can cut the red tape surrounding many issues: they can bring their other commercial operations to bear in a number of areas, they have access to people, they know the market and understand the rate of change required. We have been able to harness our knowledge of the beer industry with their knowledge of China and come up with an awesome team" (Heracleous 2001: 40–1). SAB also had a lot to contribute to this joint venture. SAB had great experience in entering less developed countries in the past, including Eastern Europe and Africa, and so knew how to manage plants with old technology and unskilled labor forces. SAB acquired the US Miller Brewing Company in 2002 and renamed itself SAB-Miller.

Unlike other multinational firms, China Resources Snow did not pursue a premium brand strategy. Like SAB, it aimed for second- and third-tier metropolitan areas. China Resources Snow initially focused in northern provinces and in 1997 expanded to Sichuan, a southwestern province. In 1999, China Resources Snow acquired two failed breweries in Tianjin from Foster's. Further, China Resources Snow did not import any foreign brands. Instead, it created local brands like Snow to deliver good quality at a low price. When China Resources Snow acquired firms, it provided investment, technology, and expertise to the acquired firms to help integrate them into its existing Chinese brands. This approach avoided cannibalization and achieved a clear branding strategy. This strategy also kept prices low with minimal investment in transport and promotion. China Resources Snow is building a strong network in China. In 2010, the company extended its equity stake in several breweries, including a 27% stake in Snow Zhejiang, a 45% stake in Xihu Beer, and a 10% remaining stake in Binzhou to make it wholly owned. It also took over Aoke Beer and opened a new brewery in Henan

Province in 2011. By the end of 2011, the company operated 80 breweries in 21 regions.

While China Resources Snow serves as an exemplary case of a "localized multinational firm," Anheuser-Busch also tried to localize. Anheuser-Busch entered China through Budweiser Wuhan in 1995 with a 97% stake, rendering it a wholly owned subsidiary. In 2002, Anheuser-Busch entered a strategic alliance with Tsingtao Beer, owning its 20% equity, and, in 2004, acquired Harbin Beer. When InBev acquired the global operations of Anheuser-Busch in 2008 for $52 billion, Anheuser-Busch InBev became a major international company. Anheuser-Busch InBev also completed more than ten high-profile acquisitions, including a 24% stake in Zhujiang Brewery in 2002, a 99.6% stake in Harbin Brewery in 2004, and a RMB 5.6 billion 100% acquisition of Fujian's largest brewery, Fujian Sedrin, in 2006. Anheuser-Busch InBev then attempted to position Harbin as a national local brand by increasing production capacity with new breweries and investing in marketing by sponsoring international events like FIFA football matches. Anheuser-Busch InBev also shared distribution systems among its own brands like Budweiser and Harbin in order to fully leverage existing resources so that Harbin could access the rest of China. Anheuser-Busch InBev now includes 33 breweries located in 13 provinces and 25 beer brands, including national favorites like Budweiser, Harbin, and Sedrin, as well as such star regional brands as Zhujiang, Double Deer, and KK. As of 2009, Anheuser-Busch InBev enjoys a 10.7% market share in China.

At the same time, several strong local competitors emerged thanks to their strong distribution channels. Originally founded by an English-German joint venture in 1903, the Chinese government nationalized Tsingtao Brewery in 1949. After the reform and open door policy, it was transformed from an SOE into a joint stock company listed on the Hong Kong Stock Exchange and Shanghai Stock Exchange in 1993. From 1996 to 2001, under the leadership of CEO Peng Zuoyi and his slogan of "Becoming Big, Becoming Strong," as well as the added funds from stock sales, Tsingtao Brewery completed more than 40 acquisitions and expanded its factories into 17 provinces, including acquisition of the Carlsberg's failed operation in Shanghai in 2000 for RMB 150 million. However, the rapid expansion into the low-end market through low-cost acquisitions dramatically increased subsidiary operating expenses and led to financial difficulty. Subsequent CEO Jin Zhiguo reversed the company's strategy to, "Becoming Strong, Becoming Big," signifying his push to integrate operations and save costs. Jin consolidated over 40 brands into four major brands: Tsingtao, Shanshui, Hans, and Laoshan. Tsingtao emerged as the major national brand, with Shanshui, Hans, and Laoshan positioned as secondary brands targeted to regional markets. Tsingtao Brewery now operates more than 55 breweries in 18 provinces and is in the process of internationalizing by exporting beer overseas.

Similarly, Yanjing Beer was established in 1980. Originally known for cheap and low quality "peasant beer," Yanjing Beer imported technology to improve product quality and build a strong sales network in the 1990s. It successfully repositioned itself as a mass market beer. In the late 1990s, Yanjing Beer leveraged its dominance in the Beijing market by acquiring Jiangxi Beer in 1999, Laizhou Beer and Wuming Beer in Shandong Province in 2000, Ganzhou Beer in Jaingxi and Sankong Beer in Shangdong in 2001, Guilin Liquan Beer in Guangxi in 2002, and Huiquan Beer in Fujian in 2003 (Guo 2012).

Both Tsingtao and Yanjing took their local brands into neighboring regions. In a competitive response to Tsingtao's acquisition of Beijing-based Five Star Beer, Yanjing acquired the Shandong-based Wuming Beer and Sankong Beer. Smaller and weaker regional players could not match this play and so were quickly acquired by these emerging locals and successful multinationals or forced to exit the market. As illustrated by Figure 5.1, by 2009, Tsingtao and Yanjing grew to possess 18 and 11.6% market shares, respectively. Yet their profit margins have remained low. To remedy this, successful local firms like Tsingtao and Yanjing recently began moving into the premium market,[2] challenging multinational firms in the medium- to high-end segments and further intensifying competition. Figure 5.1 shows the trend of major firms' market shares between 1998 and 2009.

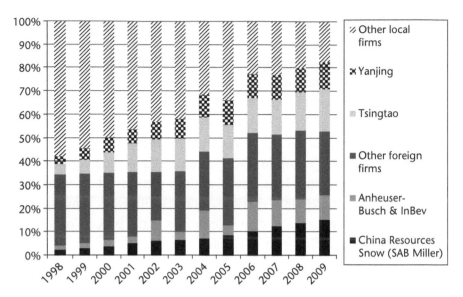

Figure 5.1 Trends of major firms' market shares in the beer industry

As a consequence of the expansion of foreign multinationals and growth of local giants, the Chinese beer industry has become a hotly contested market. The beer industry is characterized by heterogeneous consumer demand, but to a lesser degree than consumer products. As such, we expect multinational firm dominance in the beer industry to be less than in consumer products (Chang and Park 2012). Indeed, as shown in Figure 4.2, foreign firms' combined market share increased from 35% in 1998 to 53% in 2009, lower than in the consumer products industry.

A chronic problem in the beer industry is overcapacity, which affects local and foreign firms alike. Due to cut-throat competition and aggressive acquisition of weak firms in other regions, the beer industry became increasingly integrated into a national market. Competition led both foreign and domestic brewers to undertake aggressive marketing campaigns to increase brand recognition and attract consumers at the point of sale. These campaigns were subject to large scale economies. Organizing efficient distribution networks also became increasingly important. The growth of retail chains required brewers to forge strong ties with these outlets, which helped create deeper market penetration. In many regions, acquisition of local players was required to gain access to established distribution channels. Because only brewers with sufficiently large scale and scope could afford significant investments in technology, marketing, distribution, and acquisitions, financially weak companies were forced to sell off their businesses and exit. The consolidation process of the Chinese beer industry is similar to that of the US beer industry, where technology, marketing, and distribution drive the process.[3] As in the US, technological and marketing-related innovations have been important factors in the consolidation process in China.

Despite these key similarities, there are several differences between the brewing industries in China and the US. First, compared to the US, the consolidation process in China has been heavily conditioned by political factors. Although the US government discouraged competition immediately after the repeal of prohibition, "Government intervention through taxation, regulation, and a period of Prohibition only marginally disrupted the 150-year pattern of development" (McGahan 1991: 282). Only after World War II could large regional brewers engage in national distribution and advertising expansion to unleash the underexploited economies of scale in processing technologies. In China, on the other hand, central and regional governments directly catalyzed the consolidation process, although government intervention is lower compared to other industries. Regional governments owned many local firms, so they decided which products to sell to whom and at what price. They also controlled the regulatory agencies responsible for approving all deals. Local firms were largely dependent on loans from banks controlled by local governments. Thus, governments could implicitly influence incumbent management of a potential target if they supported a given deal. The central government established explicit industrial policies that favored larger brewers. For instance, in 1997, the China National Council on Light Industry granted a package of preferential loans and tax incentives to the 10 biggest domestic breweries. One beneficiary of this policy was Yanjing Brewery, which was majority owned by the Beijing municipal government. It increased sales from RMB 1.3 billion in 1998 to RMB 9.5

billion in 2007, while expanding geographic coverage from one region (Beijing) to 12 regions.

Second, in the US, large breweries could not grow through acquisition because antitrust regulation did not allow it; they therefore had to rely on internal growth (Elzinga 1982).[4] However, the consolidation process in China has been characterized by acquisition. Local Chinese governments favored acquisition in order to protect employment and tax revenue. They also expected acquiring firms to bring in capital and advanced technology without exacerbating the overcapacity problem. There have been over 80 mergers and acquisitions in the beer industry since 2000, including both domestic and foreign players.

Among recent casualties, Kirin sold its share of Daxue Beer to Anheuser-Busch InBev in 2011. In April 2011, Heineken pulled out of its joint venture with Kingway Beer in Shenzhen when its market share dropped from its initial 70% to below 20%. Heineken's Shanghai market share had also declined over the years, forcing the sale of its breweries in both Shanghai and Jiangsu to China Resources Snow in 2011.[5] Figure 5.2 illustrates the more than 237 acquisitions and 439 exits. By 2007, China

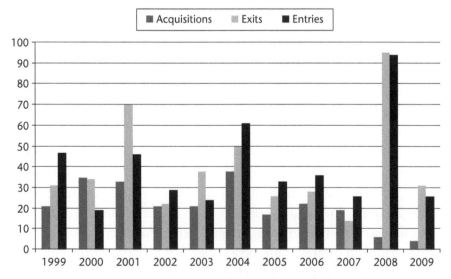

Figure 5.2 New entries, exits, and acquisitions in the beer industry

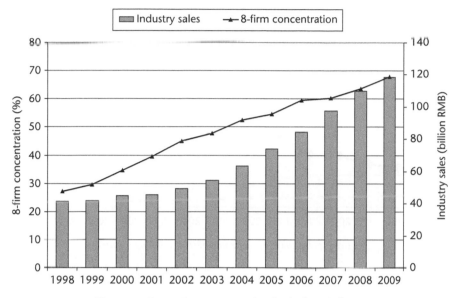

Figure 5.3 Increasing concentration in the beer industry

ranked as the largest beer market in the world, surpassing Germany and the US. Between 1998 and 2009, industry output increased nearly three-fold, from RMB 41.5 billion to RMB 118.4 billion. During the same time period, the industry consolidated through the closing and acquisition of small, weak players by large companies. The eight-firm concentration ratio increased from 27.1% in 1998 to 67.9% in 2009 (see Figure 5.3).

Figure 5.4 displays industry-wide profitability, measured in ROA, defined as the sum of profits of all firms in the beer industry divided by the sum of their assets. We break down the trend of industry profitability by ownership type in Figure 5.5 in order to confirm whether this holds true for both foreign and local firms. Figure 5.4 shows that firm profitability tended to be low in the late 1990s and early 2000s when competition intensified. Foreign firms that originated from outside Hong Kong, Macao, and Taiwan (non-HMT firms) tended to have negative ROAs. As discussed earlier, Foster's and Carlsberg faced difficulty and exited during that time period. Industry profitability began to improve in 2003 when the consolidation process via active acquisitions became mature.

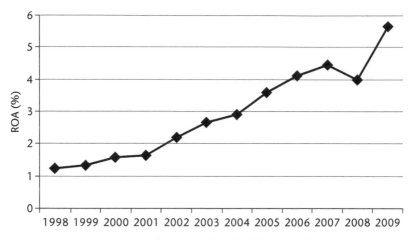

Figure 5.4 Industry-level profitability in the beer industry

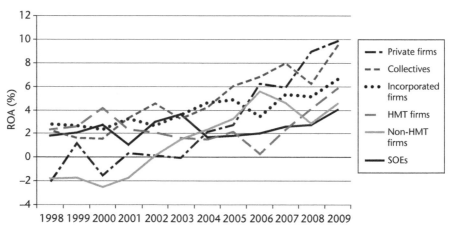

Figure 5.5 Profitability of firms in the beer industry by ownership type

Private firms struggled until the early 2000s, but their profitability has since increased. Collective firms seem to have the most consistent level of profitability during this time period. Both private and collective firms focus on niche markets, often in rural areas where national players like Tsingtao, Yanjing, Snow, and Anheuser-Busch have not yet penetrated, allowing them to enjoy high profitability. For example, Siping Beer from Jilin Province, Tieling Beer and Tianhu Beer from Liaoning

Province, Dezhou Kedaier Beer and Taishan Beer from Shandong Province, Jiujiang Beer and Jingdezhen Beer from Jaingxi Province are small-scale breweries focused on low-end markets in rural areas.[6] Most are unknown outside their home regions, yet these breweries are highly profitable. Other mid-sized private breweries are likewise succeeding. Typically, these mid-sized beer firms focus on a small number of neighboring regions. For example, privately owned Lanbei Group expanded by acquiring former SOEs in the neighboring provinces of Guangdong, Hebei, and Hubei to become highly profitable. As a consequence of consolidation, profitability increased substantially during the late 2000s.

Spillover, Competition, and Firm Survival
This detailed case study of the beer industry exemplifies the existence of both spillover and competition effects. It shows that foreign firm entry and local firm restructuring both offer positive spillover effects, improving individual firm productivity over time. At the same time, foreign firms compete fiercely with local firms and with other foreign firms, while local firms compete fiercely with foreign firms and with other local firms. Over the same time period, many firms, both foreign and local, exited the industry. The industry thus became oligopolistic in nature, dominated by a few large firms. As competition intensified, profitability dipped and will continue to drop until completed consolidation boosts the profitability of surviving firms. Yet, the beer industry's market consolidation in China may be unique as it faces less government intervention than other Chinese industries, enabling market forces like competition and consolidation to play out. This section explores the performance differences between foreign and local firms across all industries in China.

In Chapter 3, we discussed positive spillover effects from foreign multinationals to local firms. Chinese local firms benefitted greatly from foreign multinationals that brought their advanced technology and marketing knowhow. While economists have long considered technology spillover from foreign to local firms (Caves 1974; Blömstrom 1986; Hejazi and Safarian 1999), they have viewed local firms, especially those in emerging and developing economies, as passive recipients of technology spillovers. But multinationals compete with local firms in local markets upon making FDI. We take this one step further to argue that local firms must be considered potential competitors to multinational firms.

There is much evidence that local firms in developing countries are successfully challenging foreign entrants (Dawar and Frost 1999; Zeng and Williamson 2007). As detailed in Chapter 4, local firms like Huawei and ZTE in the Chinese telecom industry are taking market share from well-established multinationals like Alcatel-Lucent, Motorola, and Cisco. Longliqi, Shanghai Jahwa, and Nice in the consumer products industry are similarly challenging P&G and Unilever. For example, Shanghai Jahwa's Liushen body wash brand recently competed head to head with P&G's Zest. P&G ultimately lost the battle and withdrew Zest. While it may be true that local firms historically copied foreign companies' products, in recent years foreign companies have also learned from local firms. The popularity of Bawang shampoo and its herbal concept motivated P&G to launch a similar product with similar packaging.[7]

As touched upon in Chapter 3, we define spillover effects as the positive influence of one firm group on another firm group's performance. Spillover occurs when the introduction of new technologies and products inspires other firms to develop these entities themselves. For example, the introduction of multinational beer brands reinvigorated local firms with advanced packaging and advertisement. The spillover of advanced knowledge and technologies across firms can be facilitated by hiring managers and engineers (Ahn, de la Rica, and Ugidos 1999). In addition, cross-regional greenfield investments and "friendly" mergers and acquisitions of both local and foreign firms may facilitate knowledge spillover across regions.

Competition effects, on the other hand, are defined as the negative influences caused by the presence of a group of firms on members of another group, which decrease the latter's performance. Our analysis in Chapter 4 further suggests that competition is intensifying not only between foreign and local firms, but also among foreign entrants and among local firms, another possibility overlooked by prior studies. In the beer industry, multinational firms like Foster's, Bass, Carlsberg, and Heineken exited because they could not compete with localized multinational firms like China Resources Snow and Anheuser-Busch InBev and emerging local firms like Tsingtao and Yanjing.

In fact, spillover and competition effects are two sides of the same coin. A firm is simultaneously a source of knowledge spillovers and a source of competition to other firms in the same industry. Thus, what we can observe in reality is the net of positive spillover effects and negative competition effects. When competition is moderate, spillover effects are more likely to dominate; otherwise, competition effects will prevail. We must therefore examine spillover effects and competition effects simultaneously. Furthermore, we need to examine these effects both from and on foreign and local firms.

My earlier empirical work with a colleague argues that the relative size of spillover effects vis-à-vis competition effects for a given firm is contingent upon its resource profile (Chang and Xu 2008). Firms differ from each other by strategic resources. Competition tends to be stronger among firms with similar resource profiles (Chen 1996). In analyzing how local companies in emerging markets compete with multinational giants, Dawar and Frost (1999) also note that it is important to consider the type of strategic asset, distinguishing between those that are transferable abroad and those that are customized to a specific home market. Relative to local competitors, multinational firms possess proprietary assets, often in the form of advanced technologies, brand names, and managerial knowhow that they can then transfer to their foreign subsidiaries (Buckley and Casson 1976; Dunning 1988; Hitt et al. 2000). Foreign firms also have abundant capital and experienced expatriate managers who can be assigned to many sites worldwide. In contrast, domestic incumbents typically enjoy locally embedded advantages like marketing and distribution channels, access to information, and network connections. Their managers are usually educated and trained domestically, giving them a thorough understanding of the home market.

Foreign and local firms are not homogenous entities. Further, variations also exist within each group. More localized foreign firms that have acquired country-specific assets will compete more directly with local firms, and so threaten the latter's survival. In particular, ethnic

Chinese firms from Hong Kong, Macao, and Taiwan (HMT firms) may differ substantially from non-ethnic Chinese multinationals (non-HMT foreign firms) while sharing many characteristics with Chinese firms. Because of their common cultural origin, HMT firms enjoy increased access to local knowledge and resources, and so pose a serious threat to local firms. Thus, their entry into local markets is more likely to be seen as an aggressive attack, leading local firms to retaliate. For example, Hong Kong-based China Resources owns 51% and SAB Miller owns 49% of China Resources Snow. China Resources deep knowledge of China proved to be an important factor that led to its success. Similarly, reformed local firms with assets comparable to those of multinationals are more likely to challenge, compete directly with, and crowd out foreign entrants.[8] For example, Tsingtao and Yanjing were transformed into joint stock companies and then listed on the stock exchanges. They have comparable resources with multinational firms.

Although both HMT and non-HMT foreign firms may generate spillover effects for local firms, because HMT firms have resources more similar to local firms than do non-HMT firms, their spillover effects may be offset by the stronger competition effects they exert on local firms. In other words, HMT firms such as China Resources Snow will pose more serious competitive challenges to local firms than non-HMT multinationals. For example, China Resources Snow is a more formidable competitor to Tsingtao and Yanjing as it deliberately pursues a mass-market strategy with good quality beer at a low price, unlike other multinational firms that focus on premium brands. Conversely, reformed local firms such as private or incorporated firms are more likely to effectively respond to entry by multinationals than conventional local firms like SOEs or collectives. This is because the former have done more to imitate the assets, resources, ownership structures, and incentive schemes of multinational entrants (see Appendix 7 for more details regarding the empirical analysis behind these claims). Tsingtao and Yanjing are such reformed local firms that challenge China Resources Snow and Anheuser-Busch InBev.

The relative size of spillover versus competition effects also depends on the degree of market overlap (Chen 1996). Firms in the same region typically share a common geographic market. As discussed earlier, China consists of regional markets with significantly different income levels and customer demands. Thus, firms compete with each other in each of the regional markets they occupy. National markets typically do not exist in most industries due to the absence of such national economic drivers as national distribution systems and national brands. In the case of the beer industry examined earlier, the national market for beer products is just now emerging, thanks to cross-regional acquisitions. As such, the competition effects between foreign entrants and local incumbents were stronger in regional markets than in national markets. In other words, firms compete fiercely with other firms in the same regional market but do not compete with firms in other regional markets.

On the other hand, in a previous article, we argued that spillover effects tend to be a more universal phenomenon in national markets (Chang and Xu 2008). Although the agglomeration literature may suggest that firms can benefit from proximate location to each other within certain geographic boundaries (Krugman 1991; Saxenian 1994; Chang and Park 2005), there are many reasons to believe that such effects extend beyond narrowly defined local boundaries and become more pronounced at the country level (Keller 2002). First, through the demonstration effect, defined in Chapter 3, spillovers can take place across regions within a nation. This effect occurs when the introduction of new foreign technologies and products inspires domestic entrepreneurs and innovators to develop these goods for their home markets. National, not regional, boundaries presumably limit domestic entrepreneurs' access to information about foreign technologies and products. Second, the spillover of advanced knowledge and technologies across regions may be facilitated by the higher mobility of better-educated employees less bound to local job markets (Ahn, de la Rica, and Ugidos 1999). For example, local firms that do not compete directly with foreign firms within their own regional markets can learn from foreign or other local firms by hiring away their managers and engineers. Third, local governments in many regions have encouraged greenfield investments and "friendly" mergers and acquisitions as a way to reach economic growth targets. In China, for instance, an important promotion criterion for local government officials is the amount of investment they attract to their region. Knowledge spillovers are facilitated by cross-regional investments and can easily be used nationwide. Thus, we find that a strong presence of foreign or local firms in a regional market exerts competition effects on both their immediate peers and other firms that compete directly with them in the same regional market.

The presence of those firms in a national market does not, however, pose direct competition to firms in other regions, thus allowing positive spillover effects to dominate nationally. For example, in the beer industry, since many foreign and local firms focused on coastal regions and large metropolitan cities, competition effects outweigh any spillover effects in these regions. Although firms may learn from other firms located in the same coastal regions, they have to compete fiercely with them. On the other hand, spillover effects may outweigh competition effects in inland regions where not many foreign and local firms were located. In other words, firms in inland regions may be able to learn from other firms in other regions without necessarily competing with them. Private and collective beer firms focusing on niche markets in rural areas are such examples.

Our findings, as outlined in Appendix 7, suggest that both spillover and competition effects from various groups of firms affect firms in other groups in China. We measure effects in terms of survival likelihood. We specifically find evidence that competition effects are more likely to outweigh spillover effects among firms of similar resource types than they are among firms with more distinct resource profiles. Further, we find that competition effects are more likely to outweigh spillover effects in regional markets than in national markets. In contrast to prior work that has generally assumed spillovers move only from foreign firms to local firms, we model spillovers as occurring between foreign firms and local firms, among foreign firms, and among local firms. We find that local firms are not passive recipients of technology spillovers or victims of competition. Instead, the presence of reformed local firms, both private and incorporated, has a strong competition effect on all foreign firms in the same market. In contrast, conventional local firms do not exhibit such an effect, likely because they rely on exclusive networks or policy benefits and so do not compete directly with foreign entrants. At the same time, foreign firms and local firms crowd out each other and their peers.

Huang (2003) described a bleak picture of FDI in China that suggests FDI negatively affects domestic companies' survival. Our results, however, depict FDI as a double-edged sword: Chinese firms both benefit and suffer from the presence of foreign firms. This impact can be delineated largely in terms of the resource profiles of both foreign and local firms. The biggest beneficiaries of spillover effects might be local firms located in inland areas, as witnessed in niche market players in rural beer markets, as they can benefit from spillovers from both foreign multinationals and reformed local firms that compete with each other in coastal regions, while avoiding direct competition with either group. Through this process, strong multinational and local firms alike evolve over time.

Profitability of Foreign Firms and Income Shifting

The beer industry case study suggests that industry-wide increased consolidation improves profitability, as illustrated by Figure 5.4. All firms, regardless of ownership type, seem to exhibit higher profitability, beginning in the mid-2000s when consolidation reached a high level, as in Figure 5.5. However, even in the late 2000s, the profitability of private and collective firms seems to be highest (ROA around 10%), followed by incorporated firms and foreign firms, and, finally, SOEs. As discussed earlier, private and collective firms located in rural areas where both multinational firms and large reformed local firms have not yet penetrated enjoy high profitability by targeting niche markets. Foreign firm profitability, whether HMT or non-HMT firms, is between 4 and 6%, substantially lower than private, collective, and incorporated local firms. This poses a puzzle: why is foreign firm profitability lower than that of local firms despite their stronger technology, brand, and capital?

The statistical analysis in Appendix 9 examines the potential for similar profitability patterns in other industries. In this Appendix, I compare the profitability of foreign and local firms based on all firms available in the annual industrial survey database. Consistent with the beer industry, results suggest that private and collective firms are most profitable, followed by incorporated and foreign firms, and, finally, by SOEs. Since SOEs have the lowest profitability, we can measure firm performance while using SOEs as a reference group. For example, private firms, on average, have a 5.8% point higher ROA than SOEs. Collectives, conventional firms, on average, have a 5% point higher ROA than SOEs. The ROA of HMT and non-HMT firms, on average, is 3.6% point higher than SOEs. Thus, ROA of foreign firms is 2.2% point, i.e., the difference between 5.8% point and 3.6% point, lower than that of private firms, after controlling for industry, region, and year fixed effects. Both maintain the same level of profitability as incorporated local firms, much lower than private and collective firms, although their profitability is higher than that of SOEs. *Asia Times* picked up the same point: "About 55% of foreign companies operating reported losses between 2001 and 2004, in 2005, the figure dropped to 42.96%. It seems strange that while Chinese enterprises, including state-owned, joint-stock, and private companies, have been making profit in recent years, nearly half of foreign-invested businesses have been losing money. China witnesses a continual rise in foreign direct investment."[9] Such poor financial performance of foreign firms in China is somewhat puzzling, considering that multinational firms possess the strong technology, brand, and capital available to leverage in China.

Let's consider potential reasons for the poor financial performance of foreign multinationals in China. While the usual suspects are not in fact the culprits, I begin there. First, the international business literature has long pointed out that foreign firms are inherently disadvantaged compared to local firms due to a lack of local knowledge and resources, a.k.a., "liabilities of foreignness." Thus, foreign firms should possess some monopolistic advantages like strong technology or brands to compensate for this inherent disadvantage. Foreign firms may also be able to overcome the liabilities of foreignness as they gain more experience over time. We thus need to consider firm age to control for experience effects. The empirical results presented in Appendix 8, however, suggest that younger foreign firms are in fact more profitable than their older counterparts, suggesting that older multinational firms, which by definition have greater local experience and smaller liabilities of foreignness, may not necessarily perform better. So this possible reason does not pan out and so does not help to solve the puzzle.

Second, one may wonder if ethnic Chinese firms originating from Hong Kong and Macao may be disguised local firms so as to exploit various incentives given to foreign firms by the Chinese government, as discussed in Chapter 1. Huang (2003) labeled such local firms' shifting of funds to Hong Kong and Macao and then back to China as "round-trip FDI." If this is in fact true, some firms that originate from Hong Kong and Macao may not necessarily exhibit high levels of performance, as they are only disguised local firms. Appendix 8, however, shows that these HMT firms are not necessarily performing worse than non-HMT foreign firms. Somehow, they are equally inferior in profitability compared to private firms. So this explanation does not help us solve the puzzle either.

Third, we may also question whether wholly owned firms might exhibit higher performance than joint ventures, as the latter might have difficulties bringing in more sophisticated technology or brands for fear of losing them to local partners, as discussed in more detail in Chapter 2. However, the results in Appendix 8 suggest it is actually the other way around. Somehow, joint ventures exhibit higher profitability than wholly owned companies, contrary to expectation, and so we face another dead end.

Lastly, after exhausting the usual explanations, we are left with one possibility: the poor financial performance of foreign firms may be attributable to income shifting. Multinational firms maximize their

profits around the world by sourcing the best available talents, producing goods in the most cost-competitive locations, and selling these
goods in countries with potential customers. Likewise, multinational
firms actively engage in income shifting among subsidiaries to reduce
their worldwide corporate tax liability and maximize after-tax global
profits. Multinationals' superior ability to maximize profits over each
nation state's welfare is succinctly summarized by the title of an influential book by the late Raymond Vernon: *The Sovereignty at Bay* (1971).[10]

There exists considerable anecdotal evidence regarding tax-motivated
income shifting by multinational firms. By nature, income shifting is
difficult to observe. No multinational firm would openly admit to this
practice, as it is essentially a slap in the face to the host country. Thus,
it would be nearly impossible to directly measure income shifting with
actual transaction-based data. Prior literature has paid attention to two
major means of income shifting: adjustment of transfer prices and the
use of debt contracts. Research in this vein argues that multinational
firms benefit from adjusting internal transfer prices as a way of transferring valuable goods. Specifically, multinational firms can reduce
accounting profits in a high-tax country by overstating the prices of
imports into this country and, conversely, by understating the prices of
exports. Transfer pricing can be particularly important for intangible
assets (e.g., technology, brand), as "arm's length prices," or prices that
unrelated firms would have used in an identical transaction, seldom
exist.[11] This literature further argues that multinational firms use debt
contracts to change the locations of their tax burdens since interest
expenses are tax deductible in most countries and so are more valuable
in countries with high tax rates. Given the constraint of their overall
indebtedness, multinational firms allocate debts across all countries so
that multinational firms as a whole can minimize their worldwide tax
liabilities. Specifically, it makes sense to finance subsidiaries in high-tax
countries with as much debt as possible.[12]

While China removed all formal barriers to profit repatriation with
its accession to the WTO in 2001, multinational firms in China may still
find it difficult to repatriate profit out of China for fear of provoking the

government's protectionist sentiment. As a consequence, multinational subsidiaries in China may have greater incentive to use less transparent means than official profit repatriation to shift profits. Furthermore, the effective corporate tax rate in China was about 33% prior to the 2008 tax reform, one of the highest in the world, though there were substantial tax breaks in various economic zones. According to China's *People's Daily Online* (Yang 2002), Chinese officials from the State Administration of Taxation revealed that China's tax revenue suffers an estimated annual loss of RMB 30 billion due to tax avoidance by multinational corporations. For example, in the automobile industry, foreign companies' income shifting in procurement is an open secret. Foreign joint venture partners insist on purchasing components from parent companies at high prices (sometimes 10 times higher than purchasing from local suppliers), and then selling the vehicles back to the parent companies at a low price. This transfer pricing scheme shifts profits to the multinational parent company at the expense of the joint venture partner.[13] The possibility of income shifting is even higher in wholly owned subsidiaries than in joint ventures, as joint venture partners could serve as monitors to their multinational partners. The finding that wholly owned subsidiaries exhibit lower profitability than joint ventures is consistent with the income shifting hypothesis. According to a research report by the National Bureau of Statistics on foreign companies claiming losses in China, two-thirds have "extraordinary losses," leading officials to believe many are engaging in transfer pricing and other ways to reduce taxable income.[14]

Appendix 10 examines the degree of income shifting among multinational firms in China (Chang, Chung, and Moon 2012). If income shifting regularly occurs among multinational firms in China, foreign subsidiaries with parents from countries where corporate income tax rates are lower have more motivation to shift income to their parent firms in order to minimize global corporate tax liability (e.g., Grubert and Mutti 1991; Hines and Rice 1994). Conversely, foreign subsidiaries with parents from countries with higher corporate income tax rates have more incentive to keep their income in China. Consistent with this income shifting hypothesis, the statistical analysis suggests that the profits from foreign subsidiaries from countries with lower corporate income tax rates are indeed less than the profits from foreign subsidiaries from countries with higher corporate income tax rates. For example, when an industry as a whole expects to earn RMB 1, a foreign subsidiary from a country whose corporate tax rate is 40% will earn RMB 1.348, while another foreign subsidiary from a country whose tax rate is 15% will earn RMB 0.923. Since various economic zones provide preferential tax to firms located there (e.g., Special Economic Zones, Economic and Technological Development Zones), we control for such locations in our model. We find that foreign firms located in these various economic zones with preferential taxes respond more sensitively than those located elsewhere. This finding confirms our conjecture that there are extensive income shifting practices among foreign subsidiaries in China. Thus, the reported low profitability of foreign firms in China does not necessarily mean that they are unprofitable. Rather, they just report less profit to the tax authority in China.

In response, China recently strengthened its anti-tax avoidance laws and implemented stricter transfer pricing regulations, while also becoming more aggressive in investigating transfer pricing (KPMG 2007). Further, the corporate tax reform of 2008 lowered the corporate tax to 25%. The new system also abolished various tax incentives given to foreign firms. After several transitional periods, foreign firms in various economic zones are also subject to the same corporate tax rate as local firms, removing discrimination against local firms. The Chinese government requires local tax authorities to closely monitor cross-border transactions, focusing on multinational companies that seek to transfer overseas operating losses to China or shift profits made in China to overseas tax havens.[15]

This chapter examined the performance of foreign versus local firms. The beer industry case study suggests that profitability increases when poor performing firms exit and the industry consolidates. Such consolidation would benefit surviving firms, both foreign and local. The survival/exit analysis suggests that foreign firms are crowded out by local firms and other foreign firms. Both the beer industry case study and the large sample statistical analysis, however, demonstrate that foreign firms' profitability is substantially lower than that of private or collective firms, hovering close to the level of incorporated firms, though still higher than that of SOEs. This is surprising given the strong technology and brands characteristic of multinational firms and seems largely consistent with income shifting activities, whereby profits are taken out of China by way of an internal pricing scheme. As discussed in Chapter 4, multinational firms complain about weak intellectual property rights protection in China, in particular, about weak enforcement by governments. At the same time, however, this same government may be allowing them to dodge taxes.

6

Competing for the Future

Foreign multinationals in China have faced tough competition from emerging local firms and other multinationals, as detailed in previous chapters. As such, multinationals face several future challenges. As more and more local and foreign firms with stronger technological and managerial capabilities enter the market and as China makes further progress on privatization, competition will continue to intensify, forcing an increasing number of weaker firms to exit. The resulting industry consolidation will also lead to further regional agglomeration, whereby surviving foreign and local firms concentrate in a few regions. Strong local firms are actively seeking globalization so that they challenge multinational firms in international markets beyond China. In tandem, these local firms are upgrading their technology and management knowhow as they call for earnest responses from multinational firms. This chapter begins with the steel industry, by far one of the nation's most regulated markets, which clearly illustrates future challenges.

The Steel Industry: A Case Study

Beginning in 1949, the government built three major steel makers—Anshan Steel, Wuhan Steel, Baotou Steel—with capital and technical assistance from the Soviet Union, the only supporter of the newly born People's Republic of China. Steel output grew rapidly, as aided by such campaigns as the Great Leap Forward. But because this and other programs stalled with China's stagnant economic growth, China ended up with thousands of small-scale, inefficient steel mills. These steel mills produced low quality products so that they could not satisfy the demand when China experienced double-digit growth after the reform. Thus, China was simultaneously one of the largest producers and importers of steel.

Because of the steel industry's classification as strategic, the government limited multinational firm entry into the market, which, in turn, allowed SOEs to remain robust. Right after the reform and open door policy, the Chinese government focused its limited financial resources on building Baosteel, with 100% central government ownership, as a modern, competitive steel maker. The first phase of the project started in 1985, with an annual production capacity of 3 million tons and technology imported from Japan's Nippon Steel. By the second phase, completed in 1992, production capacity expanded to 6 million tons. Baosteel absorbed imported technology and invested in R&D to further develop technology. As a result, while almost 100% of equipment was initially imported, locally sourced equipment surged in the second and third phases to 88% and 95%, respectively. In 1998, Baosteel grew larger still after acquiring Shanghai Metallurgical Holding Groups and Meishan Iron & Steel. Baosteel focused on the high value-added and high-tech steel products like carbon steel, stainless steel, and specially alloyed steel. In 2003, the SASAC converted Baosteel's state ownership into shares and incorporated the company.

During the reform period, several money-losing, small SOEs were privatized. As briefly introduced in Chapter 3, Zunhua Steel was privatized to a steel salesperson, Zhang Zhixaing, who successfully turned around the company now known as Jianlong Steel. Jianlong subsequently acquired more than 10 additional firms on the brink of bankruptcy to further fuel expansion. Additionally, several new private firms entered the market and grew by tapping the rapid growth of the economy and the government's infrastructure investment.

In 2003, the government introduced an aggressive industrial policy to modernize the steel industry by consolidating smaller players. The government tried to restrict output and keep prices stable by ordering steel producers to voluntarily cut down their outputs. The government also tried to force small steel makers to exit, while phasing out low-end products. The government unsuccessfully tried to curb rampant investment by tightening the land approval process and forcing banks to decrease lending to private firms. While large state-owned steel companies followed this industrial policy, smaller private companies did not comply. On the contrary, these private firms increased production capacity, ultimately nabbing the majority market share from SOEs. Private firms controlled the niche market left by large SOEs and enjoyed lower labor costs and less historical baggage than their SOE counterparts. Total volume of crude steel production increased from 180 million tons in 2002 to 500 million tons in 2008. Yet, over this same time period, private steel firms' output grew from 30 million tons to 200 million tons, meaning that private companies came to control two-thirds of the total added capacity.

For example, Rizhao Steel entered the market in 2003, when China started to invest heavily in infrastructure. Despite the Chinese government's effort to promote SOEs in the steel industry, nimble private steel firms like Rizhao seized opportunities much more quickly than their SOE counterparts. Rizhao took only 181 days to build its first plant and launch production. A record in China's steel industry, "Rizhao Speed" became an industry role model. Between 2004 and 2006, Rizhao's assets grew four times to RMB 11.6 billion, all the while recording huge profits. Within just five years of establishment, Rizhao founder and CEO Du Shuanghua ranked No. 2 in China's Hurun Rich List 2008, with personal wealth in excess of RMB 35 billion.[1] Like Rizhao, most steel makers usually start building capacity while applying for approval at the same time. Because it takes a long time to secure approval, these private firms often end up completing capacity before approval, rendering production illegal. To hide this, private firms typically do not report output to the government.[2] This leaves private firms vulnerable to sudden government crackdowns.

The entries of private steel firms like Rizhao aggravated industry fragmentation to the detriment of the 2003 industrial policy in steel. The failure of this policy can be attributed to two main factors. First, the Chinese economy grew faster than expected, increasing demand for steel products. Part of this growth derived from the government itself, with its huge infrastructure investment in highways, high-speed railroads, airports, hydraulic dams, and construction. Because small private firms continued to survive and grow, they could fill and profit from this heightened demand.

Second, and more importantly, the regional government supported private firms that would help maintain employment and increase regional GDP. The central government exercised only limited influence on regional governments, save for a few instances of dissent crackdown. For example, Tieben Steel expanded its plant with generous support from the Changzhou city government in Jiangsu Province in 2004. In fact, the government approved its expansion plan in just one day and even promised to help secure the approval of the central government. But the central government sent in teams to investigate regional investment projects. CEO Dai Guofang landed up in jail, charged with tax evasion, causing the expansion project to cease before completion. When Dai was released, Tieben filed for bankruptcy.[3] Jiangsu government officials were also punished. Around the same time, Ningbo Jianlong Steel, a new plant set up by Jianlong Steel Group and run by entrepreneur Zhang Zhixiang, also flaunted several government investment requirements. Ningbo Jianlong was forced into an acquisition by Hangzhou Steel, an SOE.[4]

In 2005, the government issued a stricter industrial policy. The Iron and Steel Industry Development Policy encouraged mergers and acquisitions and dictated that the combined output of the top 10 producers should account for 50% of the nation's output by 2010 and 70% by 2020. It also announced plans to create two giant steel mills with 30 million ton capacities and several additional firms with 10 million ton capacities. The policy also set the stage for SOEs to acquire other SOEs and private firms. In 2005, the SASAC of Hubei Province transferred 51% ownership of Echeng Steel to Wuhan Steel for free. In 2005, the SASAC of Guizhou Province transferred 85% of Shuicheng Steel to Shougang for free. Baosteel acquired Bayi Steel in Xinjiang in 2007, Guangzhou

Steel and Shaoguan Steel, both in Guangdong, in 2008, and Ningbo Steel in Zhejiang in 2009, all with support from both central and regional governments. Hebei Steel, created by a merger between Handan Steel and Tangshan Steel in 2008, is now the largest steel producer in China. In 2010, Shandong Steel, an SOE, acquired Rizhao Steel, noted above as one of the most successful private steel firms.[5] In 2009, the government reconfirmed its policy to consolidate the steel industry around large players like Baosteel, Anben, and Wuhan and so added another initiative to expand steel mills in coastal areas in order to curb the transportation costs associated with imported raw materials while also easing inland pollution.

Yet regional governments continue to hinder the central government's consolidation efforts in the steel industry, as the former are concerned with losing tax revenue, employment, and control. When Baosteel approached Maanshan Steel in Anhui regarding a merger, the Anhui provincial government launched its own industry development guidelines that nullified the possibility. Similarly, when Wuhan Steel acquired 51% of Liuzhou Steel in Guangxi province, it faced tough resistance from Liuzhou in the post-merger integration process. As Liuzhou Steel contributes one-third of the total tax revenue in Guangxi Province, the regional government did not favor transferring control of this revenue-generating entity to a central SOE. The slow integration between Anshan Steel and Benxi Steel after the merger was also largely due to different levels of government control between the two companies, as Anshan Steel was owned by the central government and Benxi Steel was owned by the regional government.

Regional governments also intervened in the consolidation process by initiating pre-emptive mergers to avoid cross-regional acquisitions. The establishment of Hebei Steel, now one of the largest players, blocked Baosteel from expanding into Hebei Province. In anticipation of acquisition, Baosteel had already formed a joint venture with Handan Steel. However, when Handan Steel was subsequently acquired by Hebei Steel, Baosteel had to withdraw its capital from the joint venture. Hebei Steel's affiliation with Tangshan Steel likewise thwarted

Shougang's attempt to merge with Tangshan. Hebei Province thus kept all regional steel firms under its own control while strengthening the scale and competitiveness of the regional steel industry against the central government's consolidation plan. Similarly, the Shandong provincial government actively pushed the deal between Jinan Steel and Laiwu Steel to form Shandong Steel, which later acquired Rizhao Steel by force. To help push the merger, the provincial government replaced top executives from either company who resisted the consolidation initiative. This merger killed the negotiations between Jinan Steel and Baosteel regarding acquisition.

The steel industry remains one of the most restricted industries in China. Opportunities for foreign investors are limited, as foreign multinationals are required to form joint ventures. Contrary to other industries in which the government relaxed various restrictions, foreign steel firms have faced tighter regulation in recent years. Prior to the 2005 industrial policy, multinational firms could acquire large shares in joint ventures. For example, POSCO, a Korean steel producer, secured majority ownership in its earlier investments, e.g., 55% of Dalian POSCO in 1995, 82% of Zhangjiagang POSCO in 1997, 90% of Shunde POSCO in 1997, and 80% of Qingdao POSCO in 2002. Being an early mover allowed POSCO to benefit from relaxed government policies. The 2005 industrial policy, however, clearly specifies that a foreign partner's share in a joint venture may not exceed 50%. POSCO lobbied hard but ultimately failed to acquire 51% ownership of Shagang Group in 2005, the largest private steel firm. POSCO holds a large market share in stainless steel, a premium segment. Other multinational firms also focused on high-value added products such as steel sheets for the automobile industry. ThyssenKrupp entered a joint venture producing stainless steel with Baosteel in 1999. Similarly, Nippon Steel formed a joint venture with Baosteel in Shanghai in 2004 to produce steel sheets for the automobile industry.

As a consequence, unlike the automobile industry in which foreign ventures dominate despite the joint venture requirement, the combined market share of foreign firms in steel was just 13.6% as of 2009

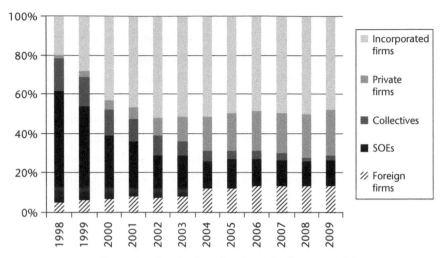

*Figure 6.1 Trends of market shares by firm ownership
in the steel industry from 1998 to 2009*

(see Figure 6.1). Meanwhile, the market share of private firms steadily increased from 2% in 1998 to 23.2% in 2009. The share of conventional SOEs declined from 56.2% in 1998 to 13.5% in 2009. On the other hand, the share of incorporated firms under state ownership by SASAC increased from 19.6% in 1998 to 47.9% in 2009. In addition to their growing stake in the steel industry, private firms are more profitable. According to estimates by the Vice General Secretary of the China Steel Association, while 60% of steel companies lost money in 2009, private firms continued to profit thanks to their flexibility and efficiency.[6] China's steel industry is still largely fragmented, as market shares of large firms like Wuhan, Baosteel, Anben, and Hebei are between 4 and 5%, as of 2009.

Reducing State Control and Further Privatization

For the last three decades, the reform and open door policy has pushed for privatization and foreign direct investment. As a consequence of reform, SOEs and collectives, legacies of the Communist regime, were transformed into incorporated and private firms. Foreign multinationals formed joint ventures and, when allowed, wholly owned subsidiaries, bringing advanced technology and marketing knowhow to China. Yet recent incidents in the steel industry show a clear reversal of this trend. The central government cracked down on several private steel firms and then forced them to be acquired by SOEs, as in Tieben Steel, Ningbo Jianlong Steel, and Rizhao Steel. These more efficient, profitable private firms were being acquired by inefficient and money-losing SOEs backed by the government. If market forces worked, the outcome would have been the other way around. Scholars call this phenomenon, "the state advances, the private retreats" (Naughton 2009).

In fact, some may even argue that state control never gave way to private firms despite the 30-year reform process. When the Chinese government adopted a policy of "keep the large and let the small go," it clearly stated that the government would maintain control of large firms and only small firms would be let go. While the proportion of industrial SOEs' assets relative to total industrial firm assets shrunk from 43.6 to 8.2%, as shown in Figure 1.2, the remaining SOEs remain in near-monopoly positions, like China Telecom and Sinopec. For many incorporated firms, the SASACs hold shares on behalf of the state, rendering the firms de facto SOEs. As of 2009, the share of assets controlled by incorporated firms was as high as 36.3% of all industrial firms' assets. Thus, state-controlled firms have remained very important in China. In a practical sense, the state never retreated.

The global financial crisis of 2008 might have facilitated "the state advances, the private retreats" phenomenon. In 2008, the Chinese government announced a RMB 4 trillion stimulus package to boost the domestic economy. The government pumped money through state-owned banks, which in turn extended credit to SOEs. SOEs could use this fund to acquire private firms. Since private firms were not on priority lists for official bank loans, they barely survived during the crisis and did not have much leverage against acquisition proposals. Only private firms successful enough to be qualified as "national champions" could receive overt and covert support from the government. For example, Geely, Chery, and BYD in automobiles, Huawei and ZTE in telecom,

Shanghai Jahwa and Nice in consumer products, and Tsingtao and Yanjing in beer are considered such "national champions," and so could enjoy state support in terms of acquiring land, permits, and bank loans. Private entrepreneurs, especially those who start their own business, still face high barriers of entry.

It remains to be seen whether "the state advances, the private retreats" may be a phenomenon specific to some sectors, like the steel industry, in the wake of the global financial crisis or will be pervasive in other sectors in the future. At one extreme, *The Economist* magazine featured an article in 2012 claiming that state capitalism may be reviving around the world, especially in emerging markets.[7] With developed countries in the middle of a financial crisis, developing countries consider SOEs to be viable alternatives to private firms. Singapore, where many firms are owned by the sovereign wealth fund, e.g., Temasek and GIC, and perform well, provides an exemplar model for more efficiently run SOEs. There exists much evidence that the Chinese Communist Party holds Singapore as a model case. Temasek is often visited by both central and regional SASACs that are interested in learning how to make their portfolio companies run more efficiently. SOEs might thus have gained confidence over time. Premier Wen Jiabao once mentioned: "The socialist system's advantages enable us to make decisions efficiently, organize effectively and concentrate resources to accomplish large undertakings."[8]

Yet, the applicability of the Singaporean model, based on the city state, to China remains to be seen. The Singaporean model is based on meritocracy and a lack of corruption. China, on the other hand, is an economy of a much bigger scale. There is a much larger scale pervasive corruption, and the legacy of Communism. Although SASACs may want to become smart institutional investors like Temasek, they must follow policy directives from different levels of government and hire ex-government officials as managers. The close relationship between top management and government officials, known as *quanxi*, will likely compromise professional management. Thus, "the state advances, the private retreats" poses some practical concerns. Privatization experiences during the last three decades has enabled the emergence of several strong local firms that can compete against well-established multinational firms. Investing financial resources in inefficient SOEs for the acquisition of private firms that are in fact more efficient is clearly a waste of resources. "The state advances, and the private retreats" will likely undermine future economic growth. Thus, earnest privatization is incomplete. Rather, it remains in progress.

Competition and Further Consolidation

Industry consolidation The consolidation process of China's steel industry is in marked contrast to the consolidation of its beer industry. The beer industry, discussed in Chapter 5, is an exemplary case of industry consolidation that emerged out of intense competition between foreign and local firms. The beer industry transformed itself from a fragmented industry with small brewers serving regional markets into an oligopolistic structure dominated by a few large national players. This emergence of strong national firms closely resembles what happened in the US and Europe at the turn of the 20th century, as documented by Chandler (1962, 1977, 1990). A business historian, Chandler argued that then modern transportation and communications systems like railroads and telegraphy knit previously fragmented regional markets into integrated national markets. This in turn led to the consolidation of industries into an oligopolistic structure. Railroads forced many small, regional firms to compete in the national market. The telegraph and, later, the telephone helped these firms maintain control over geographically dispersed operating units. As regionally focused firms were exposed to nationwide competition, many industries faced the critical problem of overcapacity. Firms responded to this challenge by collusion or merger. For example, Standard Oil was created as a trust that engaged in extensive price fixing practices, which ended up being broken into several pieces by the US Supreme Court for violating the Sherman Antitrust Act in 1911. Several small automobile firms, including Pontiac, Chevrolet, Buick, and Cadillac merged to create General Motors. By the 1950s, these

multidivisional firms with the ability to exploit scale and scope economies became the standard form of modern business enterprises in
major sectors of advanced economies.

Chandler emphasizes the role of scale and scope economies as
the fundamental drivers of the emergence of large, nationwide, and
multinational firms, as embodied in the title of his influential book,
Scale and Scope. Economies of scale occur, "when the increase of
the size of a single operating unit producing or distributing a single product reduces the unit cost of production or distribution"
(Chandler 1990: 17). A large fixed-cost investment, like specialized machinery or investment in distribution facilities or networks,
is often viewed as a source of scale economies (Scherer and Ross
1990). Firms can achieve scale economies in production and distribution by concentrating production facilities in select geographic
locations and serving adjacent regional markets. On the other
hand, scope economies arise from "the use of processes within a
single operating unit to produce or distribute more than one product" (Chandler 1990: 17). Scope economies are generated when
common inputs can be leveraged in multiple markets. Technology
and brands are known to generate substantial scope economies.
Common distribution channels can also contribute to scope economies. For example, a firm can lower the unit distribution cost and
coordinate procurement and inventory by handling multiple products and multiple regions simultaneously. Scherer et al. (1975) iden-
tified the economies of multi-plant operations as a root cause of
industry consolidation.

Scale and scope economies also exist in advertising and R&D.
Large advertising purchases can lead to media discounts, while the
fixed costs of advertising can be spread over a larger sales base.
According to Chandler (1977: 208, 298), advertising became a major
competitive weapon for industries like canned food, cereals, and cig-
arettes because the relatively low unit price per package created ine-
lastic demand. As such, a firm with large scale and scope can afford a
broader mix of media coverage at any point in time while sustaining

advertising over a longer period of time. Since brand equity has a quasi-public good nature, it can benefit all products and plants without incurring additional costs. More recent economic models have shown that competitive escalation in both R&D and advertising investments among firms can drive industries to oligopoly (Sutton 1991, 1997).

Although the process of consolidation of fragmented regional industries in the US and Europe and the emergence of these regions as international players is now decades old, it is currently taking place in China. Chinese industries remained in a competitive vacuum during the Communist economic planning period until recent liberalization. Liberalization policies primarily drive consolidation in transitional economies like China as they remove institutional barriers that have prohibited economic forces from functioning. As Chinese liberalization policies removed high entry and trade barriers, inefficient firms were exposed to competition and subsequently forced to exit.

As detailed in the previous chapter, China's beer industry likely observed the most pronounced consolidation for two reasons: less government intervention and industry maturity. First, when the government intervenes to protect firms according to policy directives, as in the steel industry, consolidation may slow. Conversely, when there is less government intervention, as in the beer industry, market selection forces can better function by driving weak companies out of business. The example of the steel industry suggests that China's decentralized government system seems to hinder industry consolidation. The Chinese economic system classifies firms according to their level of administrative supervision. While some large firms with strategic importance report to central government, others report to regional governments. This system also determines who collects taxes and so cultivates a sense of local protectionism. Thus, local governments protect their local firms through various measures that obstruct firms from other regions. This in turn inhibited cross-region acquisition and integration in the steel industry. Even central SOEs supported by the central government faced

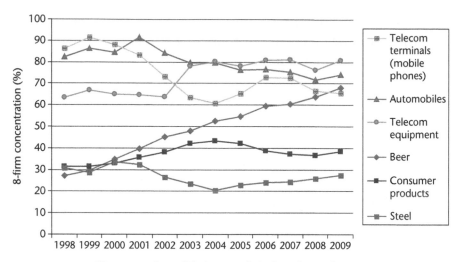

Figure 6.2 Consolidation trends in five select industries

difficulties acquiring firms in some regions due to objections by regional governments.

Second, industry consolidation becomes more likely as an industry matures. As an industry becomes mature, competition becomes a zero-sum game and fierce, forcing weaker firms to drop out. On the other hand, if an industry grows at a faster speed, there will be more room for new firms to enter or small firms to grow, and so the industry becomes less consolidated. Figure 1.10 shows that, between 1998 and 2009, the steel, telecom, and automobile industries literally exploded, recording 1000% or higher growth over a 12-year time period.

Industry consolidation has been a slower process in China's automobile and steel industries, likely due to strong government interventions and sharp increases in demand. Local governments prohibit cross-border acquisitions and encourage consolidation only within their regions. Small private firms have exploited rapid demand growth to expand their operations. As a consequence, the eight-firm concentration in the steel industry declined from its peak at 33.5% in 2000 to 20.4% in 2004, reflecting the growth of smaller, private firms during this time period (see Figure 6.2). Eight-firm concentration started to increase again in 2005 when the central government took a tougher stance against regional governments and established a clearer industrial policy for consolidation. However, increasing consolidation since 2005 is not a consequence of competition but merely reflects government-staged acquisitions of more efficient private firms by less efficient SOEs. Further, mergers of small, regional players to create regional champions do not necessarily increase efficiency unless there is tight post-merger integration and exploitation of scale and scope economies. Thus, it remains to be seen whether government-staged consolidation in the steel industry will in fact result in higher efficiency.

The automobile industry, characterized by joint venture requirements and government production licensing, is moving toward a more competitive structure (i.e., less consolidation) via relaxed regulations. In 1998, the top eight firms accounted for 82.3% of market shares in the automobile industry. This high level of concentration, however, was not a competitive outcome, but an outcome of regulation. Since the Chinese government initially protected the monopoly of Volkswagen for its technology transfer to local industries, other multinational firms were not allowed to enter. When the government allowed other multinational firms like GM, Honda, Toyota, and Hyundai to enter in the late 1990s, they took market share away from Volkswagen. As a result, the eight-firm concentration dropped from its peak in 2001 at 91.3% to 74.2%% in 2009. In addition to relaxed regulation, the automobile industry grew 16 times between 1998 and 2009. Because it takes time to build capacity, incumbent firms could not meet this rate of demand growth, enabling new entrants to meet unmet demand.

As discussed in each industry analysis, intense competition resulted in consolidation in the beer, consumer products, and telecom industries. Between 1998 and 2009, eight-firm concentration increased from 27.1 to 67.9% in the beer industry and from 31.3 to 38.5% in the consumer products industry. In telecom equipment, the eight-firm concentration increased from 63.5 to 80.8% while decreasing in tele-com terminal (including mobile phones) from 86.3% in 1998 to 60.8% in 2004, when local mobile phone producers mushroomed. When multinational firms introduced low priced phones and expanded aggressively into rural areas, they took back market shares and the eight-firm concentration ratio increased again, to 65.7% in 2009. Thus, consolidation is most evident in the telecom equipment seg-ment because it is a more mature market than telephone terminals. In the same time period, the market size for telecom equipment grew only 5.5 times while the market for telecom terminals grew a whop-ping 32 times.

As discussed in Chapter 5, firm profitability improves when an indus-try becomes more consolidated, as weak firms exit making it more difficult for new firms to enter. Large multinational and local firms in consolidated industries are thus the survivors of competition. Since market structure depends on scale economies and entry barriers, the degree of future consolidation remains to be seen. However, the steel industry is particularly ripe for consolidation given its pervasive govern-ment interventions. As the government relaxes regulations, competition will further intensify in the future. Inefficient firms will therefore lose shares to and eventually be acquired by more efficient firms, leading to further consolidation.

Emerging new clusters　Intensified competition, the exit of poor per-forming firms and entry of more productive firms, and the consequential consolidation all affect regional agglomeration. During such processes of entry and exit, some regions attract more firms than others, creating new regional clusters by industry.

In the consumer products industry, there are two clear regional clus-ters: Guangdong and the Greater Shanghai area (including Shanghai, Jiangsu, and Zhejiang). In 1998, Guangdong controlled 33% of the mar-ket while the Greater Shanghai area controlled 26% of the market. As of 2009, the former represents over 55% and the latter 21%, together taking control of 76% of the manufacture of consumer products, as illustrated by Table 6.1. In particular, Guangdong acted like a magnet, attracting more consumer products firms, especially private firms. Guangdong also hosts a well-developed market of supporting industries like packaging, raw materials, sales, and distribution. This well-established supply chain also attracted local Chinese brands, e.g., Liby, Lonkey, Bluemoon, and global brands alike. P&G's operation is concentrated in Guangdong. Currently, there are more than 100 OEM consumer products firms in the region.[9]

The Greater Shanghai Area, also known as the Yangtze River Delta, also attracted many firms in consumer products thanks to its affluent customer base. Many foreign cosmetics brands, including Unilever, Shiseido, and L'Oréal, maintain their Chinese headquarters here. Compared to Guangdong, firms in the Greater Shanghai area take advantage of the strong R&D capabilities and local talents of the region's cities, including Shanghai, Hangzhou, Nanjing, and Suzhou. Several strong local firms like Shanghai Jahwa, White Cat, and Nice hail from this area. Like Guangdong, the Greater Shanghai area boasts a complete supply chain for the cosmetics industry, including upstream sectors such as packaging materials and raw materials and downstream sectors such as distribution and sales. For example, Hangzhou is strong in high-end skin care products, while Yiwu is well known for its makeup products market. This area also attracts global OEM customers for contract manufacturing. For instance, Suzhou Pach Fine Chemicals serves companies and brands alike, e.g., Hazeline, Lux, Dove, OMO, L'Oréal, Garnier, Revlon, Kose, Shanghai Jahwa.

Guangdong and Greater Shanghai traditionally served as hubs in the telecom industry, including transmission, exchange, and terminals. This changed drastically between 1998 and 2009 (see Table 6.1). While Guangdong's share increased from 33 to 48%, that of the Greater Shanghai area dropped from 41 to 13%. This change reflects the decline of the joint venture firms that previously dominated voice communication, e.g., Shanghai Bell, Siemens Shanghai Mobile Communications. On the other hand, Shenzhen-based firms like

Table 6.1. *Market share by region in five select industries*

REGION	AUTOMOBILES		CONSUMER PRODUCTS		TELECOM		BEER		STEEL	
	1998	2009	1998	2009	1998	2009	1998	2009	1998	2009
Beijing	4%	6%	2%	1%	9%	**17%**	5%	4%	5%	2%
Tianjin	**13%**	7%	5%	0%	2%	8%	0%	0%	4%	7%
Hebei	0%	0%	1%	2%	0%	1%	5%	2%	9%	**17%**
Shanxi	0%	0%	1%	1%	0%	1%	1%	0%	4%	3%
Inner Mongolia	1%	0%	0%	0%	0%	0%	2%	2%	2%	2%
Liaoning	0%	2%	1%	1%	1%	1%	5%	4%	**11%**	8%
Jilin	**12%**	**10%**	1%	0%	0%	0%	3%	2%	1%	1%
Heilongjiang	0%	1%	1%	0%	0%	0%	5%	3%	1%	0%
Shanghai	**37%**	**19%**	**15%**	5%	**22%**	7%	2%	1%	**14%**	4%
Jiangsu	1%	3%	4%	4%	8%	4%	4%	6%	8%	**14%**
Zhejiang	0%	1%	8%	**12%**	**11%**	3%	7%	4%	2%	4%
Anhui	2%	3%	4%	1%	0%	0%	4%	2%	2%	3%
Fujian	1%	0%	0%	1%	1%	1%	6%	4%	1%	2%
Jiangxi	4%	3%	0%	0%	0%	1%	2%	2%	1%	1%
Shandong	0%	7%	4%	4%	2%	6%	**14%**	**18%**	5%	8%
Henan	0%	1%	3%	2%	2%	0%	3%	8%	3%	4%
Hubei	**17%**	3%	3%	2%	4%	2%	5%	5%	6%	5%
Hunan	1%	0%	1%	2%	0%	0%	1%	2%	2%	2%
Guangdong	2%	**19%**	**33%**	**55%**	**33%**	**48%**	**13%**	9%	3%	3%
Guangxi	4%	4%	4%	1%	1%	0%	1%	3%	1%	2%
Hainan	0%	1%	0%	0%	0%	0%	1%	1%	0%	0%
Chongqing	0%	2%	3%	1%	0%	1%	2%	2%	1%	1%
Sichuan	0%	0%	3%	2%	1%	1%	5%	7%	6%	3%
Guizhou	0%	0%	1%	0%	1%	0%	0%	0%	1%	1%
Yunnan	0%	0%	1%	0%	0%	0%	1%	1%	1%	1%
Tibet	0%	0%	0%	0%	0%	0%	0%	0%	0%	0%
Shaanxi	1%	5%	1%	1%	2%	0%	1%	3%	1%	1%
Gansu	0%	0%	0%	0%	0%	0%	2%	2%	1%	1%
Qinghai	0%	0%	0%	1%	0%	0%	0%	0%	0%	1%
Ningxia	0%	0%	0%	0%	0%	0%	0%	0%	0%	0%
Xinjiang	0%	0%	0%	0%	0%	0%	1%	1%	1%	1%

Note: Market shares higher than 10% are in bold.

Huawei and ZTE quickly leveraged data communication to astronomical growth. As a result, Shenzhen is now the Silicon Valley of China. In addition to Huawei and ZTE, Shenzhen has also attracted electronics firms like Skyworth, Konka, TCL, and Lenovo. Shenzhen promotes an industrial policy geared toward the high-tech industries in the region. Specifically, Shenzhen set up the Technology Innovation Committee, the first in China, specially tailored to attract entrepreneurs to this region. The committee also allocates RMB 4 million to protect internet property rights and RMB 500 million to the internet industry development fund.[10]

Returning to the telecom industry, Beijing-Tianjin has likewise emerged as another key regional cluster, with its market share increasing from 11% in 1998 to 25% in 2009. Beijing's Tsinghua and Beijing Universities attract top scientists and engineering students while Tianjin, a three hour drive from Beijing, provides strong manufacturing infrastructure driven by the presence of such multinational firms as Motorola and Samsung. During the "eleventh five-year master plan" (2006–2011), the Tianjin government invested in mobile communication products, LCDs (liquid-crystal displays), set-top boxes, basic electronic components, and software products, while also opening several industrial parks to attract both foreign and local firms.

Regional clusters in the automobile industry also changed significantly over the last decade, as depicted in Table 6.1. Traditional regional clusters in the automobile industry centered on the Greater Shanghai area, where Shanghai Volkswagen and Shanghai GM are located; Jilin Province, where FAW and its joint ventures, including FAW Volkswagen, are located; and Hubei Province, where Dongfeng and its joint ventures are located. While the share of these three regions declined in the last decade, Guangdong emerged as a new hub. In 1998, Guangdong manufactured just 9800 vehicles. With FDI through joint ventures with Honda in 1997, Nissan in 2003, and Toyota in 2004, Guangdong emerged as a mecca of Japanese automobile manufacturing. Parts suppliers and other foreign firms like Volkswagen soon flocked to Guangdong.[11]

On the other hand, the steel and beer industries remain fragmented with small players in many regions. The government particularly encouraged steel firms to relocate to coastal areas to save on the transportation costs of raw materials, as China imports both iron ore and coal. The 2005 industrial policy proposed that 40% of total production should be located in coastal areas. For example, Wuhan Steel proposed new investments in Fangcheng Port in Guangxi Province. In response, Baosteel proposed a project in Guangdong's Zhanjiang Port, while Hebei Steel, Shougang, and Anben Steel all planned for investments in coastal areas with large ports. Like the steel industry, the beer industry is very fragmented and geographically dispersed. This is likely because the production of beer does not require scale economies in production (scale economies can, however, be helpful in advertising and distributing beer). The transport of beer is also expensive so decentralized production can actually save money.

As discussed in Chapter 2, regional concentration creates agglomeration economies by improving accessibility to specialized workers and resources, improving cross-learning among firms, and creating a common infrastructure, though it may nonetheless cause intensified competition among firms (Marshall 1920; Porter 1998). Although the Chinese government provides strong incentives to foreign firms to invest in western regions, established regional clusters in coastal areas like Guangdong and Greater Shanghai continue to offer appealing agglomeration economies. Thus, multinational firms should balance these positive agglomeration economies with negative agglomeration economies like wage hikes, congestion, and tough competition in their location decisions.

Wage Increase and Further Upgrading
As the Chinese economy experienced double-digit growth, workers' wages also increased sharply. Figure 6.3 shows the average wages of firms from 1995 to 2010. The average wage increased from RMB 5348 in 1995 to RMB 36,539 in 2010, almost seven times higher. The average wage in

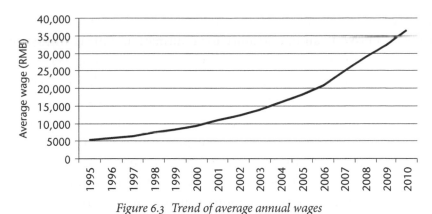

Figure 6.3 Trend of average annual wages

Note: Wages are based on urban workers from the National Bureau of Statistics.

Shanghai and Beijing in 2010 was even higher: over RMB 65,000. China is no longer a low-cost location for labor-intensive manufacturing. Several popular books address this topic with such titles as *The End of Cheap China.*[12] Facing rapid wage hikes, many multinational firms have moved their manufacturing operations to western or inland regions where wages are low compared to the coasts. As discussed earlier, in 2002, Unilever decided to close all factories in Shanghai and relocate to Hefei's industrial park located in Anhui Province to benefit from lower wages and provincial government subsidies. In 2010, Unilever reached an agreement with Hefei to expand their investment with construction of a second industrial park.[13] In addition to exploiting inland workers, relocation to inland areas might relieve social problems coming from migrant workers as the workforce of coastal regions is dominated by migrant workers from inland regions. Other firms hedge against the wage hike in China by opening manufacturing operations in lower wage countries like Indonesia and Vietnam. As mentioned earlier, multinational firms also have to balance the lower wages of relocating into inland areas with agglomeration benefits of remaining in coastal areas.

Further, higher wages are not necessarily bad news. Higher wages also mean higher disposable income, which in turn increases demand for high quality products. Higher wages and higher disposable income thus also provide an opportunity for multinational firms with strong technology or brands to expand their business throughout China. For example, demand for automobiles in China has skyrocketed. The sales of passenger cars jumped 33% to 13.8 million units between 2009 and 2010. Chinese consumers can now afford cars thanks to higher incomes. For example, the number of cars registered in Beijing more than quadrupled from 1 million in 1997 to 4.8 million in 2010. In 2010 alone, 800,000 new cars were added to the already overcrowded streets of Beijing, leading the Beijing municipal government to initiate a lottery system in 2011 to cap the number of cars on the streets. More than 1 million people entered the lottery for a chance of gaining one of the 20,000 available spots.[14]

P&G, Unilever, and other consumer product firms also seek to develop products tailored to more affluent local customers. While P&G spends more than $2 billion annually on R&D, its R&D centers used to be located only in developed countries. P&G added Beijing to its R&D docket so researchers could observe consumers in their daily activities and change prototypes of new products accordingly. For example, P&G developed Crest Pro Health toothpaste, a premium brand with a strong dose of fluoride, to appeal to health conscious Chinese customers. The Beijing R&D center also plays a critical role in developing low-end products targeted to the "$2 a day" customer. In response, P&G developed Tide Naturals, a skin-sensitive detergent for people who wash clothing by hand.[15] Similarly, Tsingtao and Yanjing now sell premium draft beer to woo affluent Chinese customers. Tsingtao's sales of its premium draft beer increased 11% in 2011, besting the flat sales of regular beer in terms of growth rate.[16] Tsingtao and Yanjing's expansion in the premium segment pose greater competitive challenges to multinational firms that have relied on premium markets.

Given these trends, multinational firms should, and did, upgrade their Chinese operations. Like P&G, several multinational firms set up R&D facilities in China. In 2010, GM sold 2.35 million vehicles in

China, more than in the US. GM set up the Advance Technical Center in Shanghai in 2011 to conduct serious technological innovation in China. In particular, GM takes advantage of the Chinese government's initiative to promote electric and hybrid cars. While wages of Chinese engineers are on the rise, they are still far below comparable engineers available in the West. The abundance of well-trained engineers available for a fraction of cost is a great advantage of operating in China. Multinational firms like GM and P&G recruit the best scientists and engineers from the top Chinese universities. According to Kevin Wale, CEO of GM China,

> What China does better than any place else in the world is to innovate by commercialization, as opposed to constant research and perfecting the theory, like the West. When the Chinese get an idea, they test it in the marketplace. They are happy to do three to four rounds of commercialization to get an idea right, whereas in the West, companies spend the same amount of time on research, testing, and validation before trying to take products to market. The Chinese have an innovative way of doing innovation, something that the rest of the world is struggling to understand.[17]

China is no longer just a market but a source of innovation for the rest of the world.

Chinese Firms' Outward FDI and Further Globalization of Competition

Local firms that emerged successfully from the cut-throat competition with multinational firms are now expanding overseas. Figure 6.4 shows the trend of overseas FDI by Chinese firms. China's outward FDI remained relatively miniscule until 2003, when it sharply increased. Outward FDI totaled $280 billion from 1990 to 2010. Outward FDI has already reached $243 billion during the shorter time period of 2004 to 2012. Among outward FDI between 2004 and 2010, 58% was destined for Hong Kong and Macao, while Asia, excluding Hong Kong and Macao, represents 8%. Investments to Latin American and African countries represent 18 and 5% of their outward FDI, respectively, suggesting that Chinese firms focus on these emerging markets for the locations of outward FDI. On the other hand, North America and Europe represent 2% and 6% of outward FDI, indicating that Chinese firms are cautious about entering developed country markets. This is consistent with the conventional theory of FDI, which emphasizes that firms incurring FDI should possess competitive advantages large enough to compensate for liabilities of foreignness. Chinese firms might not have strong enough advantages in technology or brand to overcome the liabilities of foreignness in developed countries. Developing country markets are thus more appealing. Figure 6.5 shows the destinations of outward FDI.

This push to globalization is consistent across the five industries used as case studies in this book. Private local firms Huawei and ZTE in the telecom industry exemplify this trend. Huawei operates 23 R&D centers worldwide. Its sales reached RMB 204 billion in 2011, 68% of which came from the overseas market. ZTE's sales reached RMB 86 billion in 2011, 54% of which came from overseas. Similarly, state-owned Chery and private local firms like Geely and BYD in the automobile industry tried to globalize by exporting and acquiring foreign firms. Chery has been the most aggressive in exporting and overseas expansion since 2003. Between 2003 and 2011, Chery

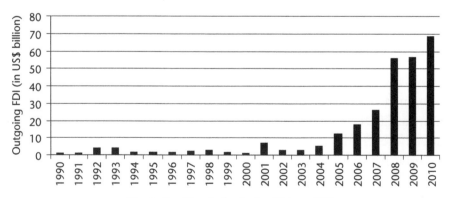

Figure 6.4 Trend of outgoing Chinese FDI

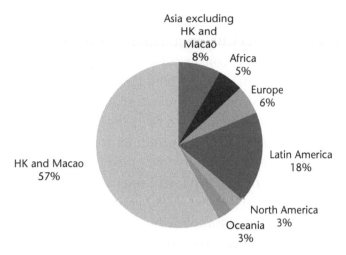

Figure 6.5 Destinations of outgoing Chinese FDI

Note: Destinations of outgoing Chinese FDI, totalling US$243 billion during 2004–10,
National Bureau of Statistics.

exported about 25% of its total production, making it the top Chinese vehicle exporter for nine consecutive years. Additionally, Chery set up 16 production bases, mostly using knock-down kits, in foreign countries like Egypt, Indonesia, Iran, Malaysia, Ukraine, and Venezuela, i.e., places neglected by established multinational firms. Geely set up Geely International, a subsidiary dedicated to the export business in 2002, similarly focusing on emerging markets in Eastern Europe, the Middle East, and Africa. In 2010, Geely surprised the world by acquiring Swedish car maker Volvo from Ford. With a $1.8 billion price tag, Geely gained access to Volvo's brand and technology, allowing it to compete with much bigger competitors in China and abroad. Geely is building plants in Chengdu in Sichuan Province and Daqing in Heilongjiang Province to produce Volvo cars for both domestic and export sales.[18] BYD likewise aggressively expanded overseas. In 2008, BYD began selling its mass-produced hybrid car, F3DM, not only in China, but also in Africa, South America, and the Middle East. BYD also exports its full electric car, e6, in developed countries like the

US. Compared to Chery, Geely, and BYD, incumbent local players in China that entered joint ventures with multinational firms like SAIC, FAW, and Dongfeng were rather conservative in globalizing. This might be due to the fact that joint ventures tend to focus on domestic markets with little interest in venturing aboard. Furthermore, these local joint venture firms faced difficulties in their initial expansions. China's largest automaker, SAIC, paid $500 million for a 49% stake in South Korea's SsangYong Motor in 2004. Doomed by its inability to manage the militant labor union, SAIC left Korea after a complete write-off of its investment.

Compared to the telecom and automobile industries, globalization of local Chinese firms in other industries is just beginning. In 2011, Baosteel, one of the most efficient steel producers in China, exported about 10% of their output to overseas markets, mostly in Asia. Baosteel and other Chinese steel firms did not actively seek foreign direct investments. During President Hu's visit to Brazil in 2009, Wuhan Steel signed an agreement to build a steel plant with LLX in Brazil, only to drop the plan in 2012. Baosteel had a similar withdrawal of an announced plan to set up a steel plant in Brazil in 2007.[19] Moving to the beer industry, Tsingtao beer is the largest and most well-known local beer brand. While it is available in 62 countries, overseas sales accounted for just 2.6% of its total sales in 2010. International expansion of consumer product companies like Shanghai Jahwa or Longliqi is likewise in its infancy, as these companies have not yet developed strong enough global competencies. The overall globalization of Chinese firms is still nascent.

While local Chinese firms actively seek globalization, they face tough challenges. First, these firms pursue rapid FDI expansion with limited international experience. Despite some export experience, they often lack knowledge regarding the management of international operations following FDI. Overseas expansion without sufficient experience leads to high liabilities of foreignness, which can negatively affect overseas performance. Quite often, these firms seek M&As in developed countries like the US and Europe, where their liabilities of foreign-ness could be greater than those in developing countries. For example, TCL-Thomson and Lenovo-IBM's PC business sought technology and brand via acquisition. However, these resource-seeking acquisitions in developed countries often create problems in post-acquisition integration if acquiring firms lack acquisition integration skills and deep understanding of local customs. When TCL acquired Alcatel's mobile phone business in 2005, it maintained a high welfare system for French employees, which proved to be a heavy burden for the company. After unifying the compensation system and cutting human capital costs, employees of Alcatel complained and many left the company. TCL experienced a huge loss after acquiring France's Thomson's TV business in 2004 and filed for bankruptcy in 2007. It is not uncommon for firms to face tough challenges in the early stages of internationalization due to their lack of experience. Japanese and Korean firms faced similar difficulties when they started to globalize in the 1980s and 1990s, respectively.

Second, these globalizing Chinese firms can be overambitious, which can lead to undue risk-taking. As mentioned above, SAIC's $500 million acquisition of Korea's SsangYong Motor in 2004 turned out to be a complete failure. SAIC also tried to acquire the British automaker MG Rover in 2005 but was outbid by another local Chinese firm, Nanjing Automobile. Competition between these two local firms led to a higher price tag for Rover. After this incident, SAIC acquired Nanjing Automobile in 2009. And, as mentioned above, Geely acquired Volvo for $1.8 billion. High profile overseas acquisitions with such hefty price tags often end up as failures, as in the case of TCL-Thomson. TCL chairman, Li Dongsheng admitted that he had underestimated the challenges involved in rescuing Thomson's business.[20]

Third, globalization may not necessarily improve firm performance when politically motivated. The Chinese government explicitly encouraged Chinese firms to globalize. The National Development and Reform Commission proposed several measures to encourage overseas investment by private firms in August 2012, including simplified approval procedures for overseas projects and strengthened risk management. For example, approval rights of projects related to resources under $300 million and non-resource projects under $100 million shifted from the national to the provincial level. Active globalization of local companies in the automobile industry, as in Geely, BYD, and Chery, is motivated by a desire to gain legitimacy, as the Chinese government has favored export to accumulate a trade surplus. By engaging in international operations, these firms may be able to secure various supports from the government. For these firms, active globalization is a political investment to gain legitimacy and to secure such government support. As globalization is politically, but not necessarily economically, motivated, these firms may experience severe losses from overseas operations. In particular, overly ambitious global expansion can be further damaging when urged by the Chinese government. That is, the Chinese government selected a few "national champions" in each industry and pushed them to become global companies. While globalization may foster national pride, it may not necessarily lead to profitability.

Fourth, globalizing Chinese firms face challenges concerning intellectual property rights. While Huawei and ZTE's international revenues represent more than half of their total revenues, they are mainly concentrated in emerging markets. Further, and relatedly, they face criticisms by governments and media in developed countries as an unfair competitor and a national security threat. Huawei and ZTE have faced criticism from the US government for allegedly stealing trade secrets from US companies like Cisco and Motorola.[21] The US opposed Huawei's acquisition of 3Com, an American network equipment company, in 2008 and 3Leaf, a bankrupt server technology firm, in 2011 on the basis of unspecified security reasons. Huawei was also blocked by the Australian government from participating in the construction of a new broadcasting system. While Huawei claims that it does not have any links to the Chinese military, its murky corporate governance system does not help alleviate such concerns. ZTE faces similar difficulties in the markets of developed countries. Local automobile firms like Geely, Chery, and BYD cannot sell their cars in developed markets because their products are largely criticized as copycats. As local governments and multinational competitors maintain a firm grip on intellectual property rights, globalizing Chinese firms need to tread gently.

This book has examined how winners came out on top of the fierce marketplace of China's economic reform. Specifically, it traced how successful multinational firms grew their operations in China and how successful local firms emerged from the restructuring process, as well as the competition between them. As a consequence of cut-throat competition, Chinese industries are increasingly consolidated. While the extent to which emerging local firms can challenge well-established multinational firms varies by industry, there are common characteristics of the winners within each firm type. A handful of multinational and local firms emerged victorious by acquiring small, weak, and regional players to become truly national players. During this process, weaker multinational firms were crowded out of the market by stronger multinationals as well as by emerging local powerhouses. The successful local firms that survive competition in China have global ambitions and venture into international markets, challenging foreign multinational firms in the global marketplace.

These successful multinational and local firms are clearly survivors of competition. Yet, as discussed in this chapter, they will likely face several future challenges. As the Chinese government relaxes regulations and pushes for further privatization, competition will be intensified and the consolidation trend will continue. Wage hikes, increasing demand from affluent customers, as well as continuing demand from less affluent customers, and strong state intervention pose great challenges to foreign multinationals and local firms alike. Both foreign multinationals and local firms should keep upgrading their technology and management systems to meet these challenges.

While one cannot predict the future, one thing is certain: whoever survives the competition to thrive in China will eventually be a winner in the global market.

Appendices

Appendix 1

Annual Industrial Survey and Definition of Firm Ownership Types

The annual industrial survey database from the Chinese National Bureau of Statistics (NBS) contains financial information for industrial firms with annual sales of at least RMB 5 million (roughly $732,000 using the 2009 year-end exchange). The data are available from 1998 to 2009. Prior to 1998, the NBS only collected information from firms above the township administrative level, so this database did not initially include information from private firms. In 1998, however, NBS expanded its coverage to encompass all SOEs and non-SOEs, including foreign firms. By law, all firms operating in China are required to participate in the NBS survey. Chow (1993) confirmed the accuracy and internal consistency of the NBS statistics, finding it suitable for empirical analysis. More recent works using the annual industrial firms database include Pan, Li, and Tse (1999), Buckley, Clegg, and Wang (2002), Park, Li, and Tse (2006), Chang and Xu (2008), Hsieh and Klenow (2009), and Brandt, Van Biesebroeck, and Zhang (2012). The period from 1998 to 2009 was critical because multinational firms expanded their operations in China while strong local firms emerged from the restructuring process. Longitudinal data over 12 years at an almost population level are really unique. Further, the database provides not only financial statements but also information on ownership and demographic information, including firm name, street address, names of managers, and government reporting relationship.

Foreign firms are legally defined by various relevant laws. In cases for which there are equity joint ventures or foreign-invested shareholding enterprises (including those from Hong Kong, Macao, and Taiwan, a.k.a. HMT foreign firms), the laws normally require the foreign partner to hold at least a 25% share of registered capital. The annual industrial survey provides the legal definition of foreign firms (HMT foreign firms or non-HMT foreign firms according to their registration information) as well as ownership stakes of foreign shareholders, also broken into HMT and non-HMT foreign owners.

The annual industrial survey classifies local firms into four types according to their registration status. It also divides ownership shares into private owners, legal person owners, state, and collectives. SOEs and collectives are two conventional firm types originating from the Communist regime. SOEs are firms directly owned by either the central or regional government. Collectives are owned by all the people in a given community. Yet, the people do not directly share the profits, nor do they have control rights over operations. Rather, the community's administration exercises ownership control by appointing executives and influencing production decisions (Tian 2000). Collectives differ from township and village enterprises (TVEs). According to Huang (2008: 74), TVE is a location-based designation, i.e., those firms located in townships and villages. While some TVEs are collectives owned by people in townships and villages, other TVEs have purely private ownership. Administratively, all non-private Chinese firms correspond to a level in governmental hierarchy. Some large SOEs function at the level of central ministries (their managers are ministry-level officials), while other firms correspond to regional or sub-regional hierarchies.

The 1993 adoption of the Company Law provides a legal framework for incorporated type firms, which includes limited liability firms and joint stock companies. Once an SOE or collective incorporates, its shares can be sold to a private party or come under SASAC ownership. The SASAC maintains an option to keep those shares in its portfolio, sell them to another party, or list them on the stock exchange. If a SASAC or holding company owns another firm, it shows up as a legal-person share. Although it may appear to be a non-state share, i.e., legal person share, these are affiliates or subsidiaries of the SOE. For example, the Shanghai government owns 100% of SAIC. If SAIC owns a firm, it shows up as a legal person share. But this is the same as state ownership. A 1998 constitutional amendment explicitly legalized private ownership. Yet, private firms existed prior to legalization. Some of these private firms were disguised as collectives, known as "red hat" firms, to avoid state expropriation.

Appendix Table 1.1 presents the general trend of ownership type by year. The proportion of SOEs and collectives declines over time, while that of private, incorporated, and foreign firms increases. Although the annual industrial survey covers all major firms, small firms under RMB 5 million sales are not covered in this data set. We compare industrial firms in the 2004 annual industrial survey with those in the 2004 economy-wide census, which includes all industrial firms, regardless of size. While about 81% of SOEs in the 2004 economy-wide census also appeared in the 2004 version of the annual industrial survey, the coverage of incorporated and foreign firms in the annual industrial survey database is 41 and 56%, respectively, while that of private and collective firms is 14 and 15%, respectively. This confirms that the annual industrial survey database is biased against small-sized private and collective firms due to its RMB 5 million threshold. Yet, in terms of economic activity, the sales and assets of firms that are included in the industrial survey represent more than 91% of total sales and 88% of total assets in the 2004 economy-wide survey.

Appendix Figure 1.1 displays the number of firms by year of establishment. While some firms trace their establishment year as far back as 1817, a clear trend emerges such that many more firms came into existence *after* China put its economic reform into motion in 1978. In fact, more than 92% of firms in the annual industrial survey were founded after 1979, and more than 81% of firms were established after the Company Law took effect in 1993. Yet this number may be even larger than reported. As newly entered firms would need some time to grow to meet the RMB 5 million threshold, more recent entries in Figure 1.1 might be under-represented in the annual industrial survey.

Appendix Table 1.1. *Number of firms in annual industrial survey by ownership type, 1998–2009*

YEAR	SOEs	COLLECTIVES	PRIVATE	INCORPO-RATED	HMT FOREIGN FIRMS	NON-HMT FOREIGN
1998	47,958	54,384	10,593	10,656	15,507	10,586
1999	42,878	50,068	14,458	13,273	15,529	10,901
2000	35,128	46,126	21,899	17,063	16,232	11,755
2001	27,318	39,186	35,402	22,608	17,953	12,931
2002	22,994	35,255	48,213	26,429	19,261	14,706
2003	17,510	29,406	65,754	30,338	20,826	17,184
2004	19,602	23,312	115,185	44,418	28,011	28,395
2005	11,606	20,374	118,826	44,740	27,128	28,368
2006	9,597	17,444	142,627	49,163	28,739	31,156
2007	6,539	16,039	168,332	55,093	31,450	34,909
2008	5,574	14,286	227,677	62,302	34,193	40,423
2009	5,118	12,917	219,277	61,218	31,199	37,024

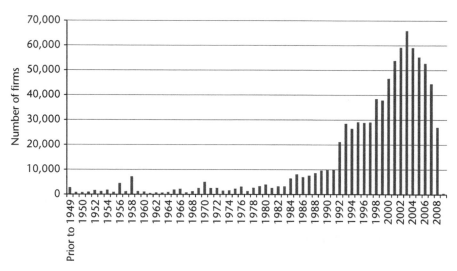

Appendix Figure 1.1 Number of firms in annual industrial survey by establishment year

Appendix 2

Entry Mode Decision

This appendix reports the results of statistical analyses on both dimensions of the entry mode decision: joint venture versus wholly owned subsidiary and greenfield investment versus acquisition. While there are a total of 150,910 foreign subsidiaries that appear in the annual industrial survey database, which include entries prior to 1998, this analysis focuses on the 83,657 foreign firms that entered between 1998 and 2009, as the most explanatory variables are available during this time period. Thus, this analysis focuses on the mode choices among more recent entries when joint venture requirements were not enforced except for in a few strategic industries like automobiles and steel. Among these 83,657 new entries, 51,310 cases came as wholly owned subsidiaries and 32,347 as joint ventures. Similarly, 76,219 cases entered via greenfield investments and 7438 via acquisition.

The analysis includes several sets of explanatory variables. Among subsidiary characteristics, *investment size* is captured by the equity value in thousands RMB (log transformed) of a foreign subsidiary. *Establishment year* is the calendar year when a foreign subsidiary was established. The *HMT foreign firms* variable is coded as one if the foreign parents are from Hong Kong, Macao, or Taiwan and zero if they are from other countries. For industry characteristics, industry-level *R&D* and *advertising intensities* are defined as the proportion of R&D or advertising expenditures to total sales, capturing the importance of intangible assets such as technology or brands, weighted by individual firm sales, defined at the 3-digit SIC level. Since R&D and advertising expenditures are available only for 2001–7, these variables are measured at the industry level. *Industry growth* captures the growth of industry shipment at the 3-digit SIC level compared to the previous year. *Industry export ratio* captures the total export by the industry divided by total industry shipment. *Herfindahl index* indicates industry concentration, defined as the sum of squares of individual firm market share.

Industry agglomeration effects are captured with three variables. First, *horizontal foreign firm presence* is defined as foreign equity participation. This is operationalized as the weighted average over all the firms in sector j, the weight for any given firm being its share of the output of sector j:

$$\text{Horizontal}_{jt} = [\sum_{i \text{ for all } i \in j} \text{FS}_{it} * Y_{it}] / \sum_{i \text{ for all } i \in j} Y_{it}, \tag{1}$$

where FS_{it} measures the share of foreign capital in firm i's total equity capital at time t and Y_{it} stands for firm i's real output at time t.[1] We draw on Javorcik (2004) for the proxies of the presence of foreign firms in downstream and upstream sectors. First, *upstream foreign firm presence* is defined as the weighted share of outputs produced by firms with foreign capital participation in sector j's upstream (or supplying) sectors. Following Javorcik (2004), we exclude from the calculation those goods that are produced by foreign affiliates for export (X_{it}), since only intermediate goods that are sold in the domestic market are relevant enough to capture spillover and competition effects:

$$\text{Upstream}_{jt} = \sum_{m:m \neq j} \sigma_{jm} \left[[\sum_{i \in j} \text{FS}_{it} * (Y_{it} - X_{it})] / [\sum_{i \in j} (Y_{it} - X_{it})] \right], \tag{2}$$

where σ_{jm} is the share of inputs purchased by sector j from sector m of the total inputs that are sourced by sector j. Similarly, the variable *downstream foreign firm presence* is a proxy for foreign presence in sectors supplied by sector j and is intended to capture the extent of potential contacts between domestic suppliers and multinational customers:

$$\text{Downstream}_{jt} = \sum_{k:k \neq j} \rho_{jk} \text{Horizontal}_{kt}, \tag{3}$$

where ρ_{jk} is the proportion of sector j's output supplied to sector k, taken from the 2002 input-output matrix. In addition, 2-digit region dummy variables are added to control for any region-specific factors that may affect entry mode decision.

The logit model estimates the impact of the explanatory variables on the probability that each entry mode will be selected. In this logit model, one entry mode must be designated as the base of reference, with its coefficients restricted to zero. The joint venture option and the greenfield investment option are chosen to be the reference point. Thus, all parameters should be interpreted as the marginal effect of an explanatory variable leading to the choice of a particular entry mode, i.e., wholly owned (as opposed to joint venture) and acquisition (as opposed to greenfield investment).

Models (1) and (2) of Appendix Table 2.1 compare the wholly owned versus joint venture decision. Model (2) adds industry characteristics to model (1), as the original includes only subsidiary characteristics. Results indicate that *investment size* and *establishment year* are positively signed and significant, suggesting that larger equity investment and more recent entries favor wholly owned subsidiaries over joint ventures. Multinational parents from Hong Kong, Macao, or Taiwan prefer wholly owned subsidiaries. These HMT foreign firms may possess local knowledge and thus obviate the need to have a local partner. Among industry characteristics, the industry-level *R&D intensities* variable is positively significant, suggesting that multinational parents favor wholly owned subsidiaries when they want to protect technology. *Industry growth* and *Herfindahl index* are negatively signed and significant, while *industry export ratio* is positively signed and significant, suggesting that wholly owned subsidiaries are preferred to joint ventures in mature and less concentrated but export-oriented industries, where multinational firms may prefer strong control over their subsidiaries.

Appendix Table 2.1. *Logit models of entry mode decision*

	WHOLLY OWNED VS. JOINT VENTURES		ACQUISITION VS. GREENFIELD	
	(1)	(2)	(3)	(4)
Investment size	0.068***	0.071***	-0.255***	-0.165***
	(0.005)	(0.005)	(0.008)	(0.009)
Establishment year	0.078***	0.075***	0.042***	-0.063***
	(0.003)	(0.003)	(0.005)	(0.005)
HMT foreign firms	0.079***	0.089***	0.075***	0.105***
	(0.016)	(0.016)	(0.027)	(0.030)
R&D intensity		47.728***		32.208
		(17.116)		(29.413)
Advertising intensity		-21.565		34.481
		(17.326)		(26.583)
Industry growth		-0.145***		-2.561***
		(0.024)		(0.029)
Industry export ratio		0.305***		-0.739***
		(0.068)		(0.128)
Herfindahl index		-2.921***		-0.799
		(0.694)		(1.131)
Horizontal foreign firm presence		0.787***		-0.156
		(0.090)		(0.164)
Upstream foreign firm presence		1.178***		-0.398
		(0.161)		(0.289)
Downstream foreign firm presence		0.385***		-0.203**
		(0.045)		(0.085)
Region fixed effects	Yes	Yes	Yes	Yes
Pseudo R-squared	0.073	0.084	0.046	0.218
Chi-squared (d.f.)	8161.6	9240.3	2296.1	10758.7
	(33)***	(41)***	(32)***	(40)***
Observations	83,657	82,661	83,654	82,658

*Note: Standard errors in parentheses. *** $p < 0.01$, ** $p < 0.05$, * $p < 0.1$. Joint ventures and greenfield are defined as reference groups, respectively. One region with three observations is dropped in models (3) and (4) due to collinearity.*

All three variables that capture *foreign firm presence* in horizontal as well as upstream and downstream markets turn positively signed and significant. The results suggest that wholly owned subsidiaries are preferred to joint ventures when there are many multinational firms already in the market, as wholly owned subsidiaries may help foreign firms respond to other foreign competitors' actions more swiftly. When there are foreign buyers and sellers in both upstream and downstream markets, multinational firms may not need the local knowledge that joint venture partners can provide and so prefer wholly owned subsidiaries.

Models (3) and (4) examine the decision between acquisition and greenfield investment. We identify an entry by a multinational firm as an acquisition if a local firm at time t switches to foreign firm status at a later date. The results show that *investment size* and *establishment year* are negatively significant, suggesting that large-scale investment and more recent entries favor greenfield investment. The *HMT foreign firms* variable is positively signed and significant, suggesting that firms from Hong Kong, Macao, and Taiwan prefer acquisition to greenfield investment. As above, they might possess local knowledge that could smooth the post-acquisition integration process. *Industry growth* is negatively signed and significant, suggesting that acquisition is preferred in low-growth, mature industries, likely because building new plants via greenfield investments will result in additional production capacity. *Industry export ratio* is negatively signed and significant, suggesting that foreign multinationals prefer greenfield investment in export-oriented industries, as the export-oriented industry does not require local knowledge given the overseas orientation. Among the agglomeration variables, only *downstream foreign firm presence* is negatively significant, suggesting that when there are more multinational customers in downstream sectors, firms prefer greenfield investment.

Appendix 3

Location Decision

This appendix explains the location choice decisions made by multinational firms between 1998 and 2009. As explained in Appendix 2, while there are a total of 150,910 foreign subsidiaries that appear in the annual industrial survey database, this analysis also considers the 83,657 foreign firms that entered between 1998 and 2009, as the most explanatory variables are available during this time period. Our sample firms face a set of location choices, each of which has different attributes. In this model, multinational firms choose which city or region to enter among 22 provinces, four major cities, and five autonomous regions. Thus, each firm has 31 options when choosing a specific location through which to enter China.

The location choice decision can be analyzed with a conditional logit model (McFadden 1974), widely used to understand how individuals or firms choose from a large set of alternatives. Because this model allows us to estimate how each attribute of each region increases or decreases the chance that a location will be chosen over other potential locations, it is applicable to the location choice analysis (Head, Ries, and Swenson 1995; Shaver and Flyer 2000). Since there were 31 regions from which firms could enter during our time study period, each of our 83,657 sample firms has 31 rows of data, with each row corresponding to a specific region. The maximum likelihood method is used to estimate coefficients to test whether various explanatory variables significantly affect the probability that one region will be chosen among all the regions in the choice set.

There are nine regional attribute variables. *Population*, measured in millions of people, and *per capita income*, defined as the regional level GDP divided by population in the region, capture the attractiveness of regional markets. The larger and the richer the market, the more attractive it is. The *marketiziation index*, constructed by the National Economic Research Institute (NERI) (http://www.neri.org.cn) annually, including the years between 1998 and 2009, captures the progress of marketization along different dimensions in each of the 31 provinces in each year. Its major categories include: 1) relation between government and market; 2) development of the non-state sector; 3) development of the product market; 4) development of the factor market; and 5) development of market intermediaries and the legal environment. Three other variables capture institutional barriers: *SOE sales share*, defined as the proportion of sales of SOEs to total industry shipment in each region, *government size*, defined as the proportion of state employees to total population in each region, and *government subsidy*, defined as the proportion of regional government subsidy to total fiscal expenditure in each regional government. We obtain these variables from the Chinese Annual Statistics Yearbook. *Horizontal agglomeration, downstream agglomeration* and *upstream agglomeration* are measured by the ratio of firm sales in the same region and in the same 3-digit SIC industry, analogous to Equations (1)–(3) in Appendix 2. Unlike in Appendix 2, however, here we measure foreign firm presence in the 3-digit SIC industry and in the same region. In this Appendix, we also define these variables with both local and foreign firms in model (2) and with foreign firms only in model (3). This allows us to observe whether agglomeration effects differ between foreign and local firms.

Appendix Table 3.1 displays the conditional logit models. In model (1), *population* and *per capita income* turn positive and significant, suggesting that foreign firms prefer regions with large populations and high per capita income, both of which reflect market attractiveness. *Marketization* is also positive and significant, suggesting that foreign firms prefer regions with higher levels of market development, which reflects less government intervention and greater reliance on market

Appendix Table 3.1. *Conditional logit models of location choice*

	(1)	(2)	(3)
Population	0.174***	0.099***	0.127***
	(0.002)	(0.002)	(0.002)
Per capital income	0.120***	0.119***	0.129***
	(0.006)	(0.007)	(0.006)
Marketization	0.525***	0.377***	0.405***
	(0.005)	(0.005)	(0.005)
Government subsidy	-0.002***	-0.001	-0.001
	(0.001)	(0.001)	(0.001)
Government size	-70.564***	-85.717***	-103.825***
	(2.112)	(2.176)	(2.245)
SOE sales share	-3.838***	-2.750***	-3.512***
	(0.065)	(0.063)	(0.064)
Horizontal agglomeration		0.434	
		(0.502)	
Downstream agglomeration		0.662***	
		(0.058)	
Upstream agglomeration		5.300***	
		(0.672)	
Horizontal foreign agglomeration			-0.402
			(0.680)
Downstream foreign agglomeration			1.209***
			(0.101)
Upstream foreign agglomeration			5.946***
			(0.902)
Pseudo R-squared	0.260	0.288	0.273
Chi-squared (d.f.)	169473.6	185141.3	175402.5
	(6)***	(9)***	(9)***
Observations	2,759,517	2,726,621	2,713,587

Note: Standard errors in parentheses. *** p < 0.01, ** p < 0.05, * p < 0.1.

price mechanisms. On the other hand, *government subsidy*, *government size*, and *SOE sales share* are negatively signed and significant, suggesting that foreign firms do not favor a location with large government subsidies, large governments, or larger shares of SOEs.

In model (2), we entered three agglomeration variables, capturing agglomeration of both foreign and local firms. In model (3), we entered the same set of variables, capturing agglomeration of foreign firms only. The agglomeration of firms in the same horizontal industry, whether we consider both foreign and local firms as in model (2) or just foreign firms as in model (3), does not have a significant impact on location choice. This result suggests that competition effects may offset any spill-over effects. Although there may be some positive benefits from agglomeration, competing directly with competitors in the same local markets may offset any such benefit. On the other hand, agglomeration in downstream and upstream sectors in a given region shows a strong positive impact on location choice. In other words, multinational firms tend to choose regions with well-established suppliers and buyers who will not compete with them but will simply share their knowledge.

Appendix 4

Performance Implications of Conversion of Joint Ventures to Wholly Owned Subsidiaries

Two research colleagues and I studied the impact of foreign subsidiary on performance when a firm switches from joint venture to wholly owned subsidiary (Chang, Chung, and Moon 2013). In order to single out the performance improvement associated with the changes from joint venture to wholly owned subsidiary, we compare the performance differentials between joint ventures that convert with comparable joint ventures that do not convert. In order to find the most comparable firms in each group, we use a technique called propensity score matching. The propensity score matching technique calculates the *ex ante* likelihood of a joint venture converting to a wholly owned subsidiary. If two firms have similar propensity scores, their *ex ante* likelihoods of conversion are the same, even though one converted while its match did not.

In order to maximize the contrast between pre-conversion and post-conversion, we focus on minority joint ventures in which the foreign partner owns between 25 and 50% of the equity.[2] We identify 31,435 minority joint ventures that appear between 1998 and 2006. Of these, 2991 converted to wholly owned subsidiaries and 28,444 remained joint ventures, either until they disappeared from the database or until 2006, the end of our period of analysis. Because we measure changes in performance from year t through year t+3 and because we include lagged explanatory variables when we calculate propensity scores, we restrict our sample to firms for which we have at least five consecutive years of observations, i.e., from year t-1 through year t+3, with firm conversion occurring in year t. Thus, we consider only the cases in which conversion occurred by 2003. Among the 19,557 minority joint ventures lasting for at least five consecutive years, 840 firms converted to wholly owned subsidiaries. We match each of these 840 firms with the most similar minority joint venture that did not convert during the sample period within the same 3-digit SIC industry and year.

We include other variables in the conversion model. We use return on assets (ROA), defined as net income divided by total assets, as our measure of financial performance. In order to address the concern that ROA may be sensitive to financial leverage or non-operating income, e.g., asset sales and tax payments, we also use operating return on assets (operating ROA), which is defined as operating income divided by total assets. The results are consistent. It is important to note that financial performance indicators based on subsidiary-level accounting data are susceptible to potential biases from transfer pricing, scope economies, and cross-selling. As far as transfer pricing is concerned, our research design poses a conservative test against any downward bias, as we expect higher profitability improvement in joint ventures-turned-wholly-owned subsidiaries compared to continuing joint ventures. It is usually harder to repatriate profits via transfer pricing schemes in joint ventures compared to wholly owned subsidiaries, as joint venture partners can monitor multinational partners' transfer pricing schemes.[3] We discuss potential income shifting activities of multinational firms in China in Chapter 6 and in Appendix 10.

We include several firm indicators to predict ownership conversion. To control for any size-related factors leading to conversion, we measure *firm size* as the logarithm of assets. We operationalize *firm age* as the calendar years passed since a firm's establishment. This controls for local knowledge and/or resources gained from a firm's joint venture experiences (Hennart 1991). *Leverage* is defined as total debt divided by total assets. We measure *export ratio* as export sales divided by total sales, which reflects a firm's export orientation. In calculating propensity score, we include ROA, leverage, and export ratio of a joint venture at one year prior to conversion to control for any real option values (Kogut 1991; Kogut and Chang 1996). For instance, a multinational parent is more likely to acquire a joint venture with higher profitability, a sound balance sheet, and export platform, as if it exercises a call option (option to acquire).

Intangible assets ratio measures the relative importance of a firm's intangible assets, defined as intangible assets divided by total assets. We believe that the intangible assets item on a foreign subsidiary's balance sheet is a key indicator of the transfer of intangible assets from multinational parents to foreign subsidiaries. R&D or advertising-related activities carried out in individual foreign subsidiaries would be regarded as current expenditures on subsidiaries' income statements, but technology, brands, and trademarks developed by multinational parents elsewhere and then transferred to their foreign subsidiaries are usually treated as investments in intangible assets that can be amortized over several years (Kieso, Weygandt, and Warfield 2010; Chapter 12). *Fixed assets ratio*, defined as fixed assets divided by total assets, indicates the firm's capital intensity. This variable also reflects technology transfer in the form of more sophisticated machinery or equipment, which shows up on the balance sheet as an increase in fixed assets. These intangible and fixed assets are important considerations in the joint venture conversion decisions. They also serve as key strategic indicators in observing changes after conversion.

In order to capture the characteristics of foreign parents and local joint venture partners, we look at joint venture ownership structure. *Conventional local parent* refers to joint ventures in which local parent firms are conventional local firms like state-owned enterprises or collectives, as opposed to modernized local firms like private enterprises or incorporated firms. *HMT foreign parent* captures the types of foreign parent: ethnic Chinese investors from Hong Kong, Macao, and Taiwan (HMT) or non-ethnic Chinese foreign multinational parents. Finally, we control for the level of foreign ownership by including *foreign share*, which is the percentage share held by foreign parents, and its squared term. We expect that the likelihood of conversion to wholly owned subsidiary will have an inverted-U relationship with the level of foreign ownership, as higher levels of foreign ownership obviate the need for conversion, while lower levels of foreign ownership render conversion more challenging.

Appendix Table 4.1 displays the probit regression results of the conversion decision, describing which joint ventures switch to wholly owned subsidiaries. The first column reports the coefficients from the regression using the full sample; the remaining four columns report coefficients from subsamples of high/low R&D and advertising-intensive industries. We conduct matching separately for each subsample of industries with high/low R&D or advertising intensity. Firm size is negatively significant, suggesting that joint ventures with more assets are less likely to convert, as the foreign partner requires more capital to buy out the local partner. Firm age is negatively significant, suggesting that older joint ventures are less likely to be converted. Conversely, smaller joint ventures and younger joint ventures are more likely to be converted to wholly owned subsidiaries. Joint ventures that are more profitable are less likely to be converted, as it would be expensive to buy out local partners from these profitable joint ventures. Financial leverage influences the conversion decision positively only in the case of low advertising industries. Export ratio is positively associated with the likelihood of conversion in the whole sample, as well as in the high R&D and low advertising-intensive industry samples, reflecting the real option value of an export platform (Kogut and Chang 1996). Ratios of intangible assets to total assets are positively associated with the likelihood of conversion in the high R&D-intensive industry, in line with transaction cost theory (Hennart 1982). This suggests that the higher the proportion of intangible assets, the more likely a venture in a high R&D-intensive industry will convert. The ratio of fixed assets to total assets also demonstrates a significantly positive association with the likelihood of conversion in all samples except for the low advertising-intensive industry subsample, thereby suggesting that firms that require a high fixed asset investment are more likely to be converted to wholly owned subsidiaries.

Appendix Table 4.1. *Conversion decision from joint venture to wholly owned subsidiary*

JV TO WOS CONVERSION	(1) ALL FIRMS	(2) HIGH R&D	(3) LOW R&D	(4) HIGH ADV.	(5) LOW ADV.
Firm size (t-1)	-0.07***	-0.09***	-0.06**	-0.07***	-0.07***
	(0.02)	(0.02)	(0.02)	(0.03)	(0.02)
Firm age (t-1)	-0.02***	-0.01***	-0.02***	-0.02***	-0.01**
	(4.0×10^{-3})	(5.0×10^{-3})	(6.0×10^{-3})	(6.0×10^{-3})	(5.0×10^{-3})
ROA (t-1)	-4.5×10^{-3}**	-5.1×10^{-3}*	-4.3×10^{-3}	-9.8×10^{-3}***	0.3×10^{-3}
	(2.0×10^{-3})	(3.0×10^{-3})	(3.0×10^{-3})	(3.0×10^{-3})	(3.0×10^{-3})
Leverage (t-1)	0.5×10^{-3}	1.1×10^{-3}	-0.4×10^{-3}	-1.9×10^{-3}	2.6×10^{-3}**
	(1.0×10^{-3})	(1.0×10^{-3})	(1.0×10^{-3})	(1.0×10^{-3})	(1.0×10^{-3})
Export ratio (t-1)	0.08*	0.13*	0.06	0.01	0.17**
	(0.05)	(0.07)	(0.07)	(0.07)	(0.07)
Intangible assets ratio (t-1)	6.0×10^{-3}	1.2×10^{-2}**	-1.3×10^{-3}	3.0×10^{-3}	7.2×10^{-3}
	(4.0×10^{-3})	(6.0×10^{-3})	(6.0×10^{-3})	(6.0×10^{-3})	(5.0×10^{-3})
Fixed assets ratio (t-1)	2.7×10^{-3}**	3.2×10^{-3}***	2.5×10^{-3}*	2.8×10^{-3}*	2.5×10^{-3}
	(1.0×10^{-3})	(1.6×10^{-3})	(1.4×10^{-3})	(1.8×10^{-3})	(2.0×10^{-3})
Conventional local parent (t-1)	-0.20***	-0.23***	-0.18***	-0.21***	-0.19***
	(0.04)	(0.06)	(0.06)	(0.06)	(0.06)
HMT foreign parent (t-1)	0.04	0.02	0.04	0.09*	-0.02
	(0.04)	(0.06)	(0.05)	(0.06)	(0.05)
Foreign share (t-1)	13.28***	12.94***	14.26***	16.76***	10.70***
	(1.78)	(2.62)	(2.50)	(2.80)	(2.23)

Appendix Table 4.1.

IV TO WOS CONVERSION	(1) ALL FIRMS	(2) HIGH R&D	(3) LOW R&D	(4) HIGH ADV.	(5) LOW ADV.
Foreign share	-15.80***	-15.79***	-16.63***	-20.27***	-12.42***
squared (t-1)	(2.33)	(3.47)	(3.25)	(3.69)	(2.90)
Industry fixed effects	Yes	Yes	Yes	Yes	Yes
Year fixed effects	Yes	Yes	Yes	Yes	Yes
Region fixed effects	Yes	Yes	Yes	Yes	Yes
Pseudo R-squared	0.14	0.14	0.15	0.18	0.11
Chi-squared	953.37***	446.40***	538.85***	619.31***	376.14***
Observations	19,557	9,195	9,603	8,757	10,262

Note: Standard errors in parentheses. *** $p < 0.01$, ** $p < 0.05$, * $p < 0.1$.

This table is reprinted with permission from the Wiley (Strategic Management Journal).

Appendix Table 4.2. Financial performance (ROA%) of JV-turned wholly owned subsidiary vs. continuing JV

WHOLE SAMPLE

YEAR	t-1	t	t+1	t+2	t+3
JV-to-WOS	4.20	4.86	5.73	5.49	5.31
JV	4.24	4.92	4.67	4.34	3.82
ATT			1.12**	1.21**	1.55**
S.E.			0.51	0.61	0.68
# Matches	799	799	799	799	799

HIGH R&D INTENSITY INDUSTRIES

YEAR	t-1	t	t+1	t+2	t+3
JV-to-WOS	3.96	4.43	5.65	5.63	4.92
JV	4.44	4.68	4.40	4.27	3.41
ATT			1.49**	1.60**	1.76**
S.E.			0.75	0.77	0.89
# Matches	388	388	388	388	388

LOW R&D INTENSITY INDUSTRIES

YEAR	t-1	t	t+1	t+2	t+3
JV-to-WOS	4.43	5.21	5.68	5.28	5.55
JV	4.91	5.05	5.08	4.32	4.00
ATT			0.44	0.80	1.39
S.E.			0.75	0.96	0.97
# Matches	410	410	410	410	410

HIGH ADVERTISING INTENSITY INDUSTRIES

YEAR	t-1	t	t+1	t+2	t+3
JV-to-WOS	3.44	4.08	5.63	5.37	5.11
JV	3.41	4.60	3.79	4.05	3.54
ATT			2.36***	1.84**	2.08**
S.E.			0.71	0.85	0.93
# Matches	414	414	414	414	414

LOW ADVERTISING INTENSITY INDUSTRIES

YEAR	t-1	t	t+1	t+2	t+3
JV-to-WOS	5.16	5.54	5.78	5.45	5.54
JV	5.39	5.77	5.15	4.56	4.94
ATT			0.86	1.12	0.83
S.E.			0.66	0.78	0.88
# Matches	386	386	386	386	386

Note: Standard errors in parentheses. *** $p < 0.01$, ** $p < 0.05$, * $p < 0.1$. ATT stands for average treatment effects for the treated. SE stands for standard error.

This table is reprinted with permission from the Wiley (Strategic Management Journal).

Among the parent type variables, joint ventures with conventional local firms are less likely to convert, as the foreign partner finds it harder to sever its relationship with state-owned enterprises or collectives because of their government backing. It may therefore be easier to convert joint ventures with private firms. On the other hand, foreign parent type—HMT foreign firm or non-HMT foreign firm—does not appear to influence the conversion decision. The foreign share variable is significant and positive, while its squared term is significant and negative, suggesting that, as predicted, the relationship between the level of foreign ownership and likelihood of conversion takes an inverted-U shape. Lastly, we include industry, region, and year fixed effects to control for their respective shocks. All unknown rational or irrational factors are commonly held by all firms and so treated as the error term in the probit model.[4]

With propensity scores calculated from this probit regression, we match these two groups of firms within the 3-digit SIC industry and within the same year to ensure a tight match. This matching procedure generates matches for 799 of the 840 converted wholly owned subsidiaries, with the same number of continuing joint ventures from the full sample of 19,557 minority joint ventures that remained in our database for at least five years. Appendix Table 4.2 shows the value of ROA for both converted and remaining joint ventures over time. This is based on the difference-in-differences estimation, which denotes the differences in the performance measure estimates for the 799 converted wholly owned subsidiaries relative to the performance of their counterparts in the control group. The average treatment effect on the treated (ATT) measures the difference in cumulative changes in ROA since the year of conversion (at time t) between the two groups. The results demonstrate that, for each of the first three years after conversion, converted wholly owned subsidiaries demonstrate 1.12, 1.21, and 1.55 average percentage point greater increase in ROA than firms that remained joint ventures with similar observed characteristics. Appendix Table 4.2 also displays the performance differences between the converted wholly owned subsidiaries and continuing joint ventures in subsamples of high/low R&D and advertising-intensive industries. This is analogous to De Loecker (2007), Girma and Görg (2007), and MacGarvie (2006), who present separate results between two subgroups. The difference in ROA increase of the converted wholly owned subsidiaries compared to continuing joint ventures seems to be present only in high R&D or advertising-intensive industries. In low R&D or advertising-intensive industries, the differences in ROA are insignificant. These results support transaction cost theory.

In order to identify potential sources for performance improvement, we trace the changes of key strategic indicators like sales, intangible assets, and fixed assets. Converted wholly owned subsidiaries show substantial increases in sales and intangible assets compared to continuing joint ventures. We expected that foreign parents would bring in more sophisticated technology or brands to their converted wholly owned subsidiaries. If a technology transfer or brand introduction is associated with conversion, there should be an increase in subsidiary-level intangible assets on the balance sheet. We find that fixed assets grow faster for converted wholly owned subsidiaries than joint ventures, which captures new investment in physical capital, e.g., the transfer of technology that is embedded in sophisticated machinery or equipment, especially in technology-intensive industries.[5] Please refer to Chang, Chung, and Moon (2013) for more details.

Appendix 5

Privatization and Firm Performance

This appendix addresses two key questions. First, it explores how the characteristics of firms that privatize versus firms that remain as SOEs and collectives differ. We define privatization as a change in a firm's legal status, as from an SOE or collective to a private or incorporated firm. As shown in Figure 3.3, and based on the annual industrial survey, there were 44,403 cases of privatization between 1998 and 2009. Second, this appendix asks if this transition improves performance by tracing the performance of privatized firms up to three years after privatization. In order to answer the second question, we must restrict our sample to firms with at least five consecutive years of data (from one year prior to privatization through three years after privatization). Of the privatization cases, 15,510 fit this requirement. We then match these 15,510 cases with most comparable firms from the pool of all other firms that continued as SOEs and collective firms using the propensity score matching technique.[6]

Appendix Table 5.1 displays the results of the statistical analysis used to determine which firms are more likely to privatize. First, we must create a data set containing all SOEs and collectives that privatized and all that remained SOEs and collectives during the same time period. To control for any firm-size related factors, *firm size* is measured as the log transformation of firm assets. *Firm age* is the calendar year since a firm's establishment, included to control for any age-related factors. We adopt two measures of firm performance: *return on assets* (ROA), defined as net income divided by total assets, and *productivity index*,

Appendix Table 5.1. *Probit model of the privatization decision*

	PRIVATIZATION (VS. REMAIN AS SOEs OR COLLECTIVES)
Firm size	0.106***
	(0.004)
Firm age	-0.010***
	(0.000)
Productivity	0.294***
	(0.019)
ROA	-0.042
	(0.053)
Leverage	-0.001***
	(0.000)
Export ratio	-0.001***
	(0.000)
Intangible asset ratio	0.018***
	(0.001)
Fixed asset ratio	0.003***
	(0.000)
Reporting to central/provincial government	-0.449***
	(0.023)
Reporting to city and township government	-0.099***
	(0.018)
Collectives (SOE is a reference group)	0.170***
	(0.015)
Industry fixed effects	Yes
Region fixed effects	Yes
Year fixed effects	Yes
Pseudo R-squared	0.146
Chi-squared (d.f.)	13257.4 (211)***
Observations	115,050

Note: Standard errors in parentheses. $***p < 0.01$, $**p < 0.05$, $*p < 0.1$.

defined as the productivity gap between a given firm and the average productivity in the same 3-digit industry. We measure firm productivity using a multilateral index developed by Caves, Christensen, and Diewert (1982) and later modified by Aw, Chung, and Roberts (2003) (see Equation 1 in Appendix 6). We expect that the higher the financial performance or productivity, the more likely firms will privatize, as this would make them more attractive to buyers. *Leverage* is defined as total debt divided by total assets. The more debt-ridden a firm, the less attractive it should be to potential buyers. We measure *export ratio* as export sales divided by total sales, a figure that reflects a firm's export orientation. Firms' domestic versus export market orientation may affect the chance that they will be privatized. *Intangible assets ratio* measures the relative importance of a firm's intangible assets, defined as intangible assets divided by total assets. *Fixed assets ratio*, defined as fixed assets divided by total assets, indicates a firm's capital intensity. The more fixed and intangible assets a firm possesses, the more likely it will privatize, as these assets would be attractive to potential buyers. These firm-level characteristics are quite comparable to those used in Appendix 4 to study the performance implications of the conversion from joint venture to wholly owned subsidiary.

In order to study privatization, the role of the different governments needs special attention, as they have the ultimate authority concerning privatization. As an administrative heritage of the Communist regime, SOEs and collectives reported to various levels of government, depending on their size and strategic importance. While some large firms and those in strategic sectors report to the central government, i.e., ministries in Beijing, others report to provincial, city, or township-level governments. Thus, this government reporting relationship is coded into three categories, resulting in two dummy variables, *reporting to central/provincial governments* and *reporting to city/township governments*. Reporting to governments lower than the township level serves as a reference group and so is indicated by a zero on both of these dummy variables. As SOEs and collectives may have different probabilities of privatization, a dummy variable denoting *collectives* (coded as one) is included with SOEs as the reference group. In addition, 3-digit industry, 2-digit region, and year fixed effects are added to control for these factors.

Appendix Table 5.1 displays the privatization decision. Positive and significant coefficients in this regression suggest a greater likelihood of privatization. *Firm size* is positively signed and significant and *firm age* is negatively signed and significant, suggesting that larger firms and younger firms are more likely to be privatized. On the flip side, perhaps small-sized SOEs and collectives find it difficult to attract attention from buyers. Older firms with greater inertia and, thus, resistance to change may similarly find it difficult to privatize. *Productivity* is positively significant, while *ROA* is insignificant for the privatization decision, suggesting that firms with higher productivity are more likely to be privatized. Financial performance does not seem to factor into the privatization decision. Usually, price tags for firms with high financial performance tend to be high, which can offset their attractiveness to potential buyers. *Leverage* and *export ratio* are negatively significant. Firms with higher debts are not attractive to buyers and are less likely to be privatized. Firms with lower export ratios that focus on domestic markets are more likely to be privatized than export-oriented firms. Both *fixed* and *intangible asset ratios* are positively significant, suggesting that firms with large fixed assets or intangible assets are more likely to find buyers. The dummy variables capturing relationship to the government are both negatively signed and significant, together suggesting that SOEs or collectives that report to central or provincial governments, which suggest that they may be of "strategic" importance, are least likely to be privatized, followed by those that report to city and township governments, and finally by those that report to governments below the township level. The results also show that collectives are more likely to be privatized than SOEs.

In order to examine the performance implications of privatization, we must find comparable firms that remain as SOEs and collectives and then compare their performance side by side with those that privatized. If firms are not appropriately matched, we would be comparing apples and oranges. For this purpose, we calculate the probability of privatization, calculated from the probit model in Appendix Table 5.1, and use it to match privatized firms and continuing SOEs and collectives within the 3-digit SIC industry, 2-digit region, and year to ensure a tight match. This propensity score matching technique generates matches of privatized firms with those that continue as SOEs and collectives, despite the fact the both firms have almost the same probability of being privatized. After matching these two sets of firms, we compare their performance side by side from the moment of privatization. The difference-in-difference technique compares two groups—the privatization group and the control group (those that were not privatized)—side by side by calculating changes since the privatization event. This matching procedure allows us to compare apples to apples and generates matches for 15,510 privatized firms with the same number of continuing SOEs and collectives that remained in our database for at least five years. Appendix Table 5.2 shows the value of ROA and productivity for both the privatized firms and continuing SOEs and collectives over time, based on the difference-in-differences estimation.

The average treatment effect on the treated (ATT) measures the difference in cumulative changes in ROA since the year of privatization (at time t) between the two groups. A t-test is then employed to determine whether the accumulated difference between these two groups is statistically significant. Results demonstrate that, for each of the first three years after privatization, privatized firms demonstrate an average of 0.47%, 0.58%, and 1.03% greater increase in ROA than firms that remained SOEs or collectives. In terms of productivity index, privatized firms, on average, similarly post 0.012, 0.014, and 0.019 points greater increase in productivity than firms that remained as SOEs and collectives. These results clearly demonstrate that the ownership restructuring of former SOEs and collectives into private or incorporated firms positively impacts firm performance.

Appendix Table 5.2 further explores which factors improve privatized firm performance. It compares such key indicators as sales, fixed assets, intangible assets, export ratio, and debt to equity ratio. We use the natural logarithm of sales, fixed assets, and intangible assets since the differences in the natural logarithm of these variables can be interpreted as percentage changes over time.[7] We find that, after three years since privatization, privatized firms have much greater sales growth (10.41 vs. 10.17%), fixed asset growth (8.82 vs. 8.63%), and intangible asset growth (2.60 vs.

Appendix Table 5.2. *Changes in key indicators between privatized firms and continuing SOEs and collectives*

a) ROA

	t-1	t	t+1	t+2	t+3
Privatized firms	5.53	6.31	6.77	7.41	8.04
Matched conventional firms	5.58	6.19	6.53	7.03	7.24
ATT			0.47***	0.58***	1.03***
SE			0.18	0.21	0.24

b) Productivity

	t-1	t	t+1	t+2	t+3
Privatized firms	0.102	0.118	0.140	0.153	0.167
Matched conventional firms	0.107	0.113	0.132	0.144	0.154
ATT			0.012***	0.014***	0.019***
SE			0.004	0.005	0.005

c) Log (sales)

	t-1	t	t+1	t+2	t+3
Privatized firms	9.90	10.04	10.18	10.31	10.41
Matched conventional firms	9.82	9.93	10.03	10.12	10.17
ATT			0.07***	0.11***	0.15***
SE			0.01***	0.01	0.02

d) Log (fixed assets)

	t-1	t	t+1	t+2	t+3
Privatized firms	8.49	8.57	8.66	8.75	8.82
Matched conventional firms	8.46	8.50	8.55	8.60	8.63
ATT			0.08***	0.13***	0.16***
SE			0.01	0.01	0.02

e) Log (intangible assets)

	t-1	t	t+1	t+2	t+3
Privatized firms	1.58	1.93	2.22	2.41	2.60
Matched conventional firms	1.29	1.40	1.58	1.68	1.85
ATT			0.36***	0.43***	0.46***
SE			0.05***	0.06	0.06

Appendix Table 5.2.

f) Debt to asset

	t-1	t	t+1	t+2	t+3
Privatized firms	64.16	63.65	62.72	62.05	61.73
Matched conventional firms	63.84	63.63	63.09	62.76	62.21
ATT			-0.67*	-1.03**	-0.79*
SE			0.36**	0.41	0.43

g) Export ratio

	t-1	t	t+1	t+2	t+3
Privatized firms	11.31	11.90	12.10	11.67	11.60
Matched conventional firms	11.41	11.75	11.52	11.43	10.95
ATT			0.68**	0.36	0.76**
SE			0.27	0.33	0.33

Note: Number of matches is 15,510. *** p < 0.01, ** p < 0.05, * p < 0.1. ATT stands for average treatment effects for the treated. SE stands for standard error.

1.85%) than their SOE and collective counterparts. Privatized firms also have lower debt to asset ratios (down by 2.43 vs. 1.63%) and higher export growth ratios (11.60 vs 10.95%). These results suggest that privatized firms could invest more in fixed assets, e.g., factories and machinery, as well as intangible assets, e.g., technology and brand, and thereby increase sales and lower their debt to equity ratio. This in turn creates higher profitability and productivity compared to matched SOEs and collectives, suggesting that privatization helps improve local firms and industries.

Appendix 6

Calculating Productivity

We measure firm productivity using the multilateral index developed by Caves, Christensen, and Diewert (1982) and later modified by Aw, Chung, and Roberts (2003). This productivity index offers several advantages over conventional parametric measures, e.g., the residuals from the Cobb–Douglas production function and its variants. First, the multilateral index is straightforward in computation and flexible enough to allow for heterogeneous production technology. Given that firms with varying degrees of technological sophistication compete with each other in China, this flexibility makes it particularly relevant to our setting. According to Van Biesebroeck, who examines the robustness of various productivity measures, "When measurement error is small (or outliers are properly controlled *ex post*), index numbers are among the best for estimating productivity growth and are among the best for estimating productivity levels" (2007: 529). Another advantage of the productivity index is that it allows for a consistent comparison of firm-level productivity across years. To compare any two firm-year observations that are transitive, this indicator expresses a firm's output and inputs as deviations from a single reference point. This reference point is a hypothetical firm that operates for each 3-digit SIC industry during the base time period, i.e., 1998, the first year of the annual database, using the industry average for input shares, inputs, and outputs. We perform robustness tests with alternative ways of measuring productivity. The productivity index is defined as follows:

$$Productivity_{it} = (lnY_{it} - \overline{lnY_t}) + \sum_{\tau=2}^{t}(\overline{lnY_\tau} - \overline{lnY_{\tau-1}}) - [\sum_{j=1}^{m}\frac{1}{2}(S_{ijt} + \overline{S_{jt}})$$

$$\left(lnX_{ijt} - \overline{lnX_{jt}}\right) + \sum_{\tau=2}^{t}\sum_{j=1}^{m}\frac{1}{2}(S_{j\tau} + \overline{S_{j\tau-1}})\left(\overline{lnX_{j\tau}} - \overline{lnX_{j\tau-1}}\right)] \tag{1}$$

where i denotes firm, t year, and j type of input ($j = 1,\ldots,m$). Y_{it} denotes output, and X_{ijt} denotes inputs including labor input, material input, and capital stock. S_{ijt} denotes input shares, defined as the ratio of labor costs to output for labor input, the ratio of material costs to output for material input, and one minus labor share and material share for capital input. The first term in Equation (1) captures the deviation of a firm's output in year t from the average industry output in that year. The second term reflects the change in industry average output across all years in the study. The third and fourth terms repeat the same for each input j, which are summed using the input share for each firm (S_{ijt}) and the average input share for each 3-digit industry in each year as weights. The productivity index measures the proportional difference between the productivity of firm i in year t relative to the hypothetical firm in the base year.

We make the following three adjustments to correctly capture inputs and outputs in calculating productivity index. First, following Brandt, Van Biesebroeck, and Zhang (2012), we adjust output and material input using input price deflators and industry-level output. The 1998 to 2003 annual industrial surveys contain information on the value of a firm's output in both nominal and real prices. We use the ratio of nominal output to real output to generate a firm-level price index, using 1998 as the base year. We then calculate the industry-level output price deflator by taking the weighted average of firm-level price indexes for each three-digit SIC industry using a firm's output as weights.[8] Because there is no information on firm-level nominal and real output information available for the years between 2004 and 2009, we use the ex-factory price index at the two-digit SIC industry level from the *China Statistics Yearbook* for these years. We calculate the input deflator by taking the weighted average of the output deflators using the input coefficients from the 2002 Input-Output table as a weighing factor for each industry.

Second, the NBS database provides accounting-based information on firms' nominal capital stock for each year, which allows us to trace capital stock increases from the time a firm appears in our annual data set. In order to estimate productivity, we also need to calculate the real capital stock for each year. For this purpose, we use the perpetual inventory method. For firms that appear in the 1994 NBS economy-wide census, we can observe their capital stocks as of 1994. For firms that are not in the 1994 economy-wide census, we can observe their capital stock when they first appear in the NBS annual industrial survey database. We can then estimate backward to determine firms' nominal capital stock at the time of their establishment. To do so, we need three additional pieces of information: average capital growth rate, capital depreciation rate, and the investment deflator (to control for price changes in capital goods). Because some firms appeared in both the 1994 economy-wide census and the 1998 annual industrial survey, we can calculate the capital stock increase between 1994 and 1998 for these firms and consider it to be the average rate of growth of nominal capital stock between 1994 and 1998. Given that the capital growth rate may vary by industry and region, we make this calculation for each 2-digit SIC industry for each region. Using this average capital stock growth rate, we calculate backwards to determine a firm's nominal capital stock at the time of establishment by discounting a firm's nominal capital stock in the first year the firm appears in the data set. The real capital stock at the time of establishment is obtained by deflating the nominal capital stock with the Brandt and Rawski investment deflator (Brandt, Van Biesebroeck, and Zhang 2012). Closely following Brandt, Van Biesebroeck, and Zhang (2012), we calculate the real capital stock at time *t* by applying a 9% depreciation rate and deflating the annual nominal investment using the Brandt and Rawski investment deflator. We can observe a firm's actual investment from 1998 forward with the annual industrial survey and, therefore, use the observed change in a firm's nominal capital stock for the nominal fixed investment for each year. We use the same depreciation and investment deflators to roll the real capital stock estimates forward. For firms that appear only in the 2004 economy-wide census, however, we cannot roll forward since we are unable to observe their actual investment history.

The third adjustment addresses labor costs. Because firms' official financial reports of wages, employee benefits, and unemployment benefits may underestimate labor costs, we follow the method employed by Hsieh and Klenow (2009), which inflates total labor compensation by a constant factor, such that the ratio of sector-level labor compensation to total inputs is equal to the same ratio in the 2002 Input-Output table in that sector. In other words, we assume that all firms in an industry pay their workers extra compensation in the same proportion paid to workers' official wages and benefits. Lastly, the 2008 and 2009 annual industrial survey lacks wage and material cost data. We extrapolate these factors by using previous years' information for the firms, if they existed prior to 2008. For firms that newly entered in 2008 or 2009, we use the industry average weighted by employment.

Appendix 7

Determinants of Foreign Firms' Market Share

In this appendix, I examine whether foreign firms command a large market share in industries characterized by a high level of intangible resources like technology and marketing knowhow. When an industry requires sophisticated technology or marketing knowhow, local competitors in emerging markets find it difficult to catch up with multinational firms by emulating their technology, design, or products. According to Kogut and Zander (1993), the more difficult it is to codify or teach technology and the more complex technology is, the more difficult it will be for competitors to imitate it. Similarly, marketing knowhow is difficult to emulate or copy, as it often resides in corporate culture or management systems. In other words, since it is not visible, it is difficult to copy. Thus, we expect that the higher the R&D and advertising intensity, the higher foreign firms' combined market share. Conversely, local firms are more likely to capture large market shares in industries low in technology or marketing knowhow.

In order to test this intuition, I ran simple regression models with foreign firms' combined market share as the dependent variable. Foreign firms' combined market share is measured at both the national and regional levels: 3-digit SIC industry in each region (provinces and special cities) and the overall 3-digit SIC industry (national level).

As for explanatory variables, *industry-level R&D* and *advertising intensities* are defined as the proportion of R&D or advertising expenditures to total sales, capturing the importance of intangible assets like technology or brands, weighted by individual firm sales, defined at the 3-digit

SIC level. These variables are measured at the industry level by aggregating individual firm expenditure. Foreign firms' share should be higher when industry level R&D and advertising intensities are high. *Industry growth* captures the growth of industry shipment at the 3-digit SIC level compared to the previous year. *Concentration ratio* is measured as the Herfindahl index of market concentration, reflecting whether an industry is controlled by a few large firms. Foreign firm market share should be lower in rapidly growing industries as they are likely slower than local firms in capturing business opportunities. Foreign firm share should also be lower in concentrated industries where a few large monopolies exist.

As for regional characteristics, to be included in models where foreign firms' market shares are measured at the regional level, i.e., 3-digit industry in a region, *per capita income* is defined as the regional level GDP divided by population in the region, capturing the attractiveness of regional markets. The larger and the richer the market, the more attractive it is and the higher the foreign firm market share. The *marketization index*, constructed by the National Economic Research Institute (NERI) annually from 1998 to 2009, captures the progress of marketization along different dimensions in each of the 31 provinces for each year. Its major categories include: 1) relationship between government and market; 2) development of the non state sector; 3) development of the product market; 4) development of the factor market; and 5) development of market intermediaries and legal environment. Two other variables capture institutional barriers: *SOEs sales share*, defined as the proportion of employment of SOEs to total industry employment in each region, and *government size*, defined as the proportion of state employees to total population in each region.

Models (1)–(3) of Appendix Table 7.1 use foreign firms' combined market share defined at the regional level. Model (1) is a baseline model with regional characteristic variables only. Model (2) adds industry characteristics variables. Model (3) adds industry fixed effects in addition to region and year fixed effects. Models (4)–(5) use foreign firms' combined market shares defined at the national level. Model (5) differs from model (4) in that it adds industry characteristic variables.

Table 7.1. *Determinants of foreign firms' combined market share*

VARIABLES	FOREIGN SHARE DEFINED AT THE REGIONAL LEVEL (3-DIGIT SIC IN A 2-DIGIT REGION)			FOREIGN SHARE DEFINED AT THE NATIONAL LEVEL (3-DIGIT SIC INDUSTRY)	
	(1)	(2)	(3)	(4)	(5)
Industry R&D		-0.502*	-1.619***		-6.506***
intensity (%)		(0.297)	(0.411)		(0.795)
Industry advertising		3.947***	4.728***		6.297***
intensity (%)		(0.140)	(0.198)		(0.544)
Industry growth		-0.000	-0.002*	0.000	0.001
		(0.001)	(0.001)	(0.001)	(0.001)
Concentration		-0.325***	-0.326***	-0.236***	-0.329***
ratio		(0.027)	(0.027)	(0.028)	(0.025)
Marketization	0.008***	0.006*	0.006*		
index	(0.003)	(0.003)	(0.003)		
Per capita income	0.011**	0.013**	0.013***		
	(0.005)	(0.005)	(0.005)		
Government size	4.232**	4.485**	4.523**		
	(1.847)	(1.849)	(1.773)		
SOE employment	-0.005	-0.007	-0.007		
share	(0.011)	(0.011)	(0.010)		
Industry fixed effects	No	No	Yes	Yes	Yes
Region fixed effects	Yes	Yes	Yes	-	-
Year fixed effects	Yes	Yes	Yes	Yes	Yes
Adjusted R-squared	0.267	0.284	0.342	0.549	0.570
Observations	42719	41904	41904	1700	1846

Note: Standard errors in parentheses. *** p < 0.01, ** p < 0.05, * p < 0.1.

Results indicate that industry R&D intensity is negatively signed and significant in all models, contrary to our expectation. This means that foreign firms' market share tends to be lower in technology-intensive industries in China. On the other hand, industry advertising intensity is positively signed and significant, suggesting that foreign firms' combined market share in advertising-intensive industries is high, consistent with expectations. This finding echoes the telecom industry case study presented in Chapter 4, as foreign firms' market share in the equipment market is declining with the rise of local competitors like Huawei and ZTE, while foreign firms' market share in mobile phones, where marketing and technology play an important role, remains high. The relatively low market share of foreign firms in technology-intensive industries might suggest that weak intellectual property protection might be a source of the problem.

As for other control variables, foreign firm market share tends to be lower in highly concentrated industries. Foreign firms tend to have high market share in regions characterized by high levels of marketization and per capita income. They also tend to be high in regions with large government presence. Industry growth and SOE employment share variables are not significant.

Appendix 8

Survival Analysis of Foreign and Local Firms

In my earlier work with a research colleague, we examined the survival rates of local and foreign firms as dependent on the relative size of spill-over and competition effects (Chang and Xu 2008). We define spillover effects as the positive influences caused by the presence of a group of firms on members of another group, which enhance the latter's chances of survival. Competition effects, on the other hand, are the negative influences caused by the presence of a group of firms on members of another group, which decrease the latter's chance of survival. Thus, spillover and competition effects are two sides of the same coin. A firm is simultaneously a source of knowledge spillovers and competition for other firms in the same industry. When competition is moderate, spillover effects are more likely to dominate; otherwise, competition effects will prevail. We rely on the competitive analysis framework of Chen (1996) and adopt two dimensions of competitive rivalry—market commonality and resource similarity—to gauge the level of competition among firms, and thus the relative size of spillover and competition effects. We argue that spillover effects are more evident in national markets, while competition effects are more apparent in regional markets. Similarly, spillover effects are more marked among groups of firms with dissimilar resource profiles, while competition effects are more often present among groups of firms with similar resource profiles.

We use firm survival as the criterion for assessing spillover and competition effects. We treat *survival* as a dichotomous variable that denotes survival/exit. Exit occurs when a firm disappears from the annual industrial survey. Firms that exited might have closed down or been sold off, or their sales could have dipped below RMB 5 million in the case of non-SOEs. In order to measure the sources of spillover and competition effects, we include three variables. *HMT foreign firm share* measures the combined market share of all firms from Hong Kong, Macao, and Taiwan. *Non-HMT foreign firm share* measures the combined market share of all firms not from Hong Kong, Macao, and Taiwan. *Reformed local firm share* measures the combined market share of private or incorporated firms in an industry. Because of their cultural origin, HMT firms enjoy some access to local knowledge and resources, and therefore may constitute a serious threat to local firms. The share of conventional local firms like SOEs and collectives serves as the reference group and is not included in the regression. We thus expect that HMT firms and reformed local firms may have greater resource similarity with each other, and in turn expect that competition effects may outweigh spillover effects between these two types of firms. On the other hand, non-HMT foreign firms and conventional local firms may not have a high degree of resource similarity, so spillover effects may outweigh competition effects between these firms. Following the convention of the FDI spillover literature, we measure both foreign and local firm presence by employment shares of various groups of firms. We measure this in terms of the *national market*, defined at the 3-digit SIC for the national level, and *regional market*, defined as the 2-digit region code in addition to the 3-digit SIC code.

As for controls, we measure *firm size* as the log-transformation of a firm's sales at time t and *firm age* as the number of years since establishment. We measure *profitability* as return on assets (ROA). We measure the degree of decentralized control for local firms with *decentralized control*. We also include a dichotomous variable, *reformed local firms,* to differentiate reformed local firms (coded 1) from conventional locals. For foreign firms, we use a dichotomous variable, *HMT firms*, to separate HMT firms (coded 1) from non-HMT foreign firms. We also measure ownership control by denoting whether foreign operations were created from scratch or formed by acquiring or creating joint ventures with local

Appendix Table 8.1. *Survival of local firms at time t+1 from 1998 to 2005*

	VARIABLE	ALL LOCAL FIRMS			REFORMED LOCAL FIRMS	CONVENTIONAL LOCAL FIRMS
		(1)	(2)	(3)	(4)	(5)
Employment share of firms in national markets	National non-HMT foreign firm share (t)	0.51 (0.17)***		0.54 (0.17)***	-0.55 (0.35)**	1.06 (0.24)***
	National HMT firm share (t)	-0.12 (0.15)		-0.05 (0.15)	-0.86 (0.22)***	0.27 (0.21)
	National reformed local firm share (t)	0.44 (0.07)***		0.50 (0.07)***	0.27 (0.11)**	0.50 (0.09)***
	National conventional local firm share (t)	0		0	0	0
Employment share of firms in regional markets	Regional non-HMT foreign firm share (t)		-0.03 (0.04)	-0.05 (0.04)	-0.19 (0.06)**	0.06 (0.06)
	Regional HMT firm share (t)		-0.11 (0.04)***	-0.13 (0.04)***	-0.37 (0.06)***	-0.43×10^{-2} (0.05)
	Regional reformed local firm share (t)		-0.05 (0.02)**	-0.08 (0.02)***	-0.12 (0.04)***	-0.06 (0.03)**
	Regional conventional local firm share (t)		0	0	0	0
Firm characteristics	Firm size (t)	0.34 (0.24×10^{-2})***	0.34 (0.24×10^{-2})***	0.34 (0.24×10^{-2})***	0.51 (0.52×10^{-2})***	0.31 (0.28×10^{-2})***
	Firm age (t)	0.01 (0.26×10^{-3})***	0.01 (0.26×10^{-3})***	0.01 (0.26×10^{-3})***	0.01 (0.46×10^{-3})***	0.01 (0.31×10^{-3})***

Appendix Table 8.1.

VARIABLE	ALL LOCAL FIRMS			REFORMED LOCAL FIRMS	CONVENTIONAL LOCAL FIRMS
	(1)	(2)	(3)	(4)	(5)
Firm profitability (t)	-0.13×10^{-2}	-0.13×10^{-2}	-0.13×10^{-2}	-0.16×10^{-2}	-0.85×10^{-3}
	$(0.15 \times 10^{-3})^{***}$	$(0.15 \times 10^{-3})^{***}$	$(0.15 \times 10^{-3})^{***}$	$(0.27 \times 10^{-3})^{***}$	$(0.18 \times 10^{-3})^{***}$
Level of control	0.47×10^{-3}	0.65×10^{-3}	0.59×10^{-3}	0.03	-0.05
	(0.19×10^{-2})	(0.19×10^{-2})	(0.19×10^{-2})	(0.27×10^{-2})	$(0.28 \times 10^{-2})^{***}$
Reformed local firms (vs. conventional locals)	0.30	0.30	0.30		
	$(0.01)^{***}$	$(0.01)^{***}$	$(0.01)^{***}$		
Intercept	-1.43	-1.35	-1.44	-3.41	-0.74
	$(0.04)^{***}$	$(0.04)^{***}$	$(0.04)^{***}$	$(0.08)^{***}$	$(0.05)^{***}$
Wald chi-sq (d.f.)	42327.7	42235.4	42353.6	19194.0	42358.6
	$(243)^{***}$	$(243)^{***}$	$(246)^{***}$	$(244)^{***}$	$(246)^{***}$
Observations	1,032,106	1,032,106	1,032,106	493,287	538,817

Note: *** $p < 0.01$, ** $p < 0.05$, * $p < 0.1$. 198 industry dummy variables, 30 region dummy variables, and six year dummy variables are not shown. Numbers in parentheses are robust standard errors adjusted for clustering on individual firms. In case all firms in our sample exit an industry in the same year, the industry dummy variable perfectly explains the exit likelihood and therefore those observations are dropped from the estimation. When we break up samples into conventional and reformed local firms, we tend to find more such cases. Thus, the number of observations in models (4) and (5) do not add up to that of the model using all local firms.

This table is reprinted with permission from the Wiley (Strategic Management Journal).

Appendix Table 8.2. Survival of foreign firms at time t+1 from 1998 to 2005

VARIABLE		ALL FOREIGN FIRMS			NON-HMT FOREIGN FIRMS	HMT FOREIGN FIRMS
		(1)	(2)	(3)	(4)	(5)
Employment share of firms in national markets	National non-HMT foreign firm share (t)	-1.66 (0.32)***		-1.61 (0.33)***	-1.30 (0.51)**	-1.59 (0.44)***
	National HMT firm share (t)	-1.19 (0.29)***		-0.74 (0.29)**	-1.04 (0.47)**	-0.72 (0.37)*
	National reformed local firm share (t)	-1.18 (0.16)***		-0.78 (0.17)***	-0.76 (0.27)**	-0.71 (0.22)**
	National conventional local firm share (t)	0		0	0	0
Employment share of firms in regional markets	Regional non-HMT foreign firm share (t)		-0.32 (0.08)***	-0.23 (0.08)***	-0.15 (0.11)	-0.26 (0.12)**
	Regional HMT firm share (t)		-0.68 (0.08)***	-0.61 (0.08)***	-0.48 (0.14)***	-0.68 (0.10)***
	Regional reformed local firm share (t)		-0.55 (0.07)***	-0.48 (0.07)***	-0.21 (0.11)*	-0.65 (0.10)***
	Regional conventional local firm share (t)		0	0	0	0
Firm characteristics	Firm size (t)	0.69 (0.01)***	0.70 (0.01)***	0.70 (0.01)***	0.71 (0.01)***	0.70 (0.01)***

Appendix Table 8.2.

VARIABLE	ALL FOREIGN FIRMS			NON-HMT FOREIGN FIRMS	HMT FOREIGN FIRMS
	(1)	(2)	(3)	(4)	(5)
Firm age (t)	-0.01	-0.01	-0.01	-0.01	-0.01
	(0.13×10^{-2})***	(0.13×10^{-2})***	(0.13×10^{-2})***	(0.20×10^{-2})***	(0.17×10^{-2})***
Firm profitability (t)	0.01	0.01	0.01	0.01	0.01
	(0.73×10^{-3})***	(0.73×10^{-3})***	(0.73×10^{-3})***	(0.11×10^{-2})***	(0.10×10^{-2})***
Foreign JV and acquisition (vs. green field investment)	-0.13	-0.13	-0.13	-0.17	-0.09
	(0.02)***	(0.02)***	(0.02)***	(0.03)***	(0.02)***
HK, Macao, Taiwanese firms (vs. other foreign firms)	-0.17	-0.15	-0.16		
	(0.02)***	(0.02)***	(0.02)***		
Intercept	11.76	11.53	11.91	-4.65	11.60
	(1.06)***	(1.08)***	(1.05)***	(1.03)***	(0.30)***
Wald chi-sq (d.f.)	9,038.7	9,046.8	9,097.0	5561.1	7129.3
	(229)***	(229)***	(232)***	(224)***	(224)***
Observations	241,069	241,069	241,069	106,961	134,024

Note: *** $p < 0.01$, ** $p < 0.05$, * $p < 0.1$. 182 industry dummies 30 region dummy variables, and six year dummy variables are not shown. Numbers in parentheses are robust standard errors adjusted for clustering on individual firms. In case all firms in our sample exit an industry in the same year, the industry dummy variable perfectly explains the exit likelihood and those observations are dropped from the estimation. When we break up samples into HMT and non-HMT foreign firms, we tend to find more such cases. Thus, the number of observations in models (4) and (5) do not add up to that of the model using all foreign firms.

This table is reprinted with permission from the Wiley (Strategic Management Journal).

firms. We measure *Foreign JV and acquisition* as a dichotomous variable, with foreign greenfield investment as the baseline.

We use the annual survey data from 1998 to 2005 for this study. Appendix Tables 8.1 and 8.2 show the results for local firm survival and foreign firm survival, respectively. As illustrated by Appendix Table 8.1, national non-HMT foreign firms' share and national reformed local firms' share are positively significant for local firm survival in model (1). This suggests spillover effects from non-HMT foreign firms and reformed local firms to other local firms in the national market. In model (2), regional employment shares of HMT firms and reformed local firms were significantly negative for the survival of local firms in their own regional markets. When we include employment shares for both national and regional markets, as in model (3), we find that competition effects are more likely to outweigh spillover effects in regional markets than in national markets. In models (4) and (5), we examine the survival of reformed local firms and conventional local firms in separate regressions. In general, conventional local firms enjoy more positive spillover effects than reformed local firms, due to the presence of both reformed local firms and foreign firms. Conventional local firms are crowded out only by the presence of reformed local firms in the same regional market. On the other hand, reformed local firms, whose resource profiles are similar to foreign firms, are crowded out by non-HMT foreign firms and HMT firms at the national and regional levels alike.

Appendix Table 8.2 displays the regression results for the survival of foreign entrants, including non-HMT foreign firms and HMT firms. The employment shares of non-HMT foreign firms, HMT firms, and reformed local firms in the national market were negatively significant for foreign firm survival in model (1). This suggests that competition was so intense that foreign firms were crowded out of the national market by both other foreign firms and reformed local firms. Model (2) shows that employment shares for these three groups in regional markets were negatively significant for foreign firm survival, indicating that foreign firms were also crowded out of Chinese regional markets. Counter to expectation, foreign firms face intense competition in both national and regional markets. This result suggests that foreign firms do not benefit from other firms' spillovers, at least not in China. Foreign entrants in China may instead rely on the proprietary assets of their own multinational operations. Whatever knowledge spillovers there are from other companies in China could be completely offset by competition from these same companies. The negative signs for national reformed local firm share and regional reformed local firm share indicate that, compared to conventional local firms, whose coefficients are set to zero, reformed local firms impose stronger competition effects on foreign entrants in both national and regional markets. The negative signs of the non-HMT foreign firm and HMT firm group variables at both the national and regional levels in model (3) are also consistent with our expectation of intense competition among foreign firms due to their similar resource profiles.

Overall, foreign firms appear more likely to be crowded out by HMT firms and reformed local firms that emulate their resource profiles than by conventional locals that rely on different resource endowments. We perform separate analyses for non-HMT and HMT foreign firms in models (4) and (5) of Appendix Table 8.2. Both show somewhat similar patterns, although the significance levels for the negative competition effects at the regional level appear to be stronger for HMT firms than for non-HMT firms.

Appendix 9

Profitability Analysis of Foreign and Local Firms

In this appendix, we compare foreign and local firm profitability. For this purpose, we run very simple regressions that include *firm size*, measured as the logarithm of assets, and *firm age*. We then add firm ownership type variables, denoting *private, incorporated, collective*, and *foreign firms*. SOEs serve as a reference group, coded as zero for all four binary variables. In model (1), we include the foreign firm dummy variable. In model (2), we break the foreign firm dummy variable into two categories: *HMT foreign firms* for those from Hong Kong, Macao, and Taiwan, and *non-HMT foreign firms* for those from other nations. In model (3), we break the foreign firm dummy variable into *joint ventures* and *wholly owned subsidiaries*. We include industry, region, and year fixed effects to control for any industry-, region-, and year-specific factors.

Appendix Table 9.1 displays these regression results. In model (1), the coefficients for firm ownership show that private and collective firms have the highest level of profitability, followed by incorporated and foreign firms, and finally the SOEs that serve as the reference group. Foreign firm profitability is about 2.2% lower than private and collective firms. This is surprising, as foreign firms tend to have stronger technology and brands than local firms. In model (2), we break the foreign firm dummy variable into HMT firms and non-HMT firms, but the sizes of the coefficients are about the same. In model (3), we break the foreign firm dummy variable into joint ventures and wholly owned subsidiaries. As wholly owned subsidiaries would allow foreign firms to bring

Appendix Table 9.1. *Profitability of firms by ownership type*

	(1)	(2)	(3)
Firm size	-0.016***	-0.016***	-0.017***
	(0.103 x 10^{-3})	(0.103 x 10^{-3})	(0.104 x 10^{-3})
Firm age	-0.456 x 10^{-3}***	-0.456 x 10^{-3}***	-0.471 x 10^{-3}***
	(0.134 x 10^{-4})	(0.134 x 10^{-4})	(0.134 x 10^{-4})
Private firms	0.058***	0.058***	0.055***
	(0.001)	(0.001)	(0.001)
Incorporated firms	0.040***	0.040***	0.037***
	(0.001)	(0.001)	(0.001)
Collectives	0.050***	0.050***	0.047***
	(0.001)	(0.001)	(0.001)
Foreign firms	0.036***		
	(0.001)		
HMT foreign firms		0.036***	
		(0.001)	
Non-HMT foreign firms		0.036***	
		(0.001)	
Joint ventures			0.035***
			(0.001)
Wholly owned subsidiaries			0.029***
			(0.001)
Industry fixed effects	Yes	Yes	Yes
Region fixed effects	Yes	Yes	Yes
Year fixed effects	Yes	Yes	Yes
Adjusted R-squared	0.148	0.148	0.148
Observations	2,733,839	2,733,839	2,716,397
Number of firms	841,589	841,589	839,276

Note: Standard errors in parentheses. *** $p < 0.01$, ** $p < 0.05$, * $p < 0.1$.

in more sophisticated technology and/or brands than joint ventures, we expect wholly owned subsidiaries to outperform joint ventures. The results, however, suggest that the profitability of joint ventures is actually higher than that of wholly owned subsidiaries. Further, the profitability of both joint ventures and wholly owned subsidiaries is still far below that of private firms.

This statistical analysis simply checks the average level of profitability of foreign firms vis-à-vis local firms. Yet it actually raises more questions than it answers. The relatively low profitability of foreign firms, whether from Hong Kong, Macao, and Taiwan or from other foreign countries, and whether in the form of joint ventures or wholly owned subsidiaries, compared to local firms counters to our expectation. Explanation for this anomaly can be found in Chapter 5.

Appendix 10

Income Shifting Practices in China

This appendix summarizes the major findings of my ongoing work with research colleagues that examines the degree of income shifting among multinational firms (Chang, Chung, and Moon 2012). If income shifting is occurring among multinational firms operating in China, foreign subsidiaries with parents from countries where corporate income tax rates are lower than that of China will have motivation to shift income to their parent firms in order to minimize global corporate tax liability (e.g., Grubert and Mutti 1991; Hines and Rice 1994).

In order to test this income shifting hypothesis, we first need to determine the nationality of multinational parents. The *Survey of Foreign-Invested Enterprises* conducted by the Chinese National Bureau of Statistics (NBS) in 2001 allows us to identify the nationality of multinational parents who together owned 150,435 foreign subsidiaries in 2001. We then match this information with the *Annual Industrial Survey Database* (2001–7) from NBS in order to acquire each firm's financial information. Matching the 2001 *Survey of Foreign-Invested Enterprises* and *Annual Industrial Survey Database* generates a list of 51,118 foreign subsidiaries. We further restricted our sample to firms whose parents are from OECD countries as of 2001 or from Hong Kong, Macao, Taiwan, or Singapore (HMTS), as well as to wholly owned subsidiaries. We focus on OECD countries since we can obtain reliable data on corporate tax rates. We also include subsidiaries from HMTS because they represent the lion's share of FDI inflows to China, though they are not members of the

OECD. Of the 42,388 firms from OECD or HMTS countries, 47.4% are from Hong Kong, 17.9% from Taiwan, 10.9% from Japan, 7.3% from the US, 6.9% from Korea, 2.2% from the UK, 1.6% from Germany, 1.5% from Macao, 0.8% from Australia, and 0.6% from France, the Netherlands, and Canada, respectively. These top 12 countries represent 98.08% of our sample firms. We also focus on wholly owned subsidiaries because here, parent firms command full control over wholly owned subsidiaries in deciding whether or not to income shift and adjust transfer prices. Of the 42,388 foreign subsidiaries of multinational parents from OECD and HMTS countries, 25,177 firms are wholly owned subsidiaries. We then build panel data for these 25,177 (104,105 firm-year observations). Our panel data for 2001–7 coincides with the aftermath of China's initiation into the World Trade Organization in 2001, when China officially removed various trade and investment barriers like joint venture requirements and restrictions on official repatriation of profits. Thus, we observe income shifting practices of foreign multinationals in China when there are no official barriers to profit repatriation.

We use *operating profit* as our measure of firm performance, defined as profit before deducting tax and financial expenses (in thousand RMB). We focus on operating profit as multinational firms' various uses of transfer prices, for the purpose of income shifting, will directly affect profits from their operations (e.g., Jacob 1996; Newberry and Dhaliwal 2001; Clausing 2003; Desai, Foley, and Hines 2004, 2006; Eden, Juarez Valdez, and Li 2005; Bernard, Jensen, and Schott, 2006). *Home tax rate* is the corporate income tax rate of the foreign parent's home country, measured by summing the national and average local corporate income tax rates, following the OECD's reporting standard as collected by the OECD Tax Database.[9]

Corporate tax information for HMTS countries is provided by KPMG (2007). We include the tax rates of our sample firms' countries of origin in Appendix Table 10.1. During our sample period, 2001–7, China's corporate income tax rate remained stable at 33%. During our sample period, there remained some tax benefits in various Special Economic Zones (SEZs). For instance, manufacturers in designated SEZs could

Appendix Table 10.1. *Combined corporate income tax rates by foreign firms' home countries*

OECD MEMBERSHIP	COUNTRY	2001	2002	2003	2004	2005	2006	2007
Yes	Australia	30	30	30	30	30	30	30
Yes	Austria	34	34	34	34	25	25	25
Yes	Belgium	40.2	40.2	33.99	33.99	33.99	33.99	33.99
Yes	Canada	40.51	38.05	35.95	34.42	34.36	34.07	34.09
Yes	Czech Rep.	31	31	31	28	26	24	24
Yes	Denmark	30	30	30	30	28	28	25
Yes	Finland	29	29	29	29	26	26	26
Yes	France	36.43	35.43	35.43	35.43	34.95	34.43	34.43
Yes	Germany	38.9	38.9	40.2	38.9	38.9	38.9	38.9
Yes	Greece	37.5	35	35	35	32	29	25
Yes	Hungary	18	18	18	16	16	17.33	20
Yes	Iceland	30	18	18	18	18	18	18
Yes	Ireland	20	16	12.5	12.5	12.5	12.5	12.5
Yes	Italy	36	36	34	33	33	33	33
Yes	Japan	40.9	40.9	40.9	39.54	39.54	39.54	39.54
Yes	Luxembourg	37.5	30.38	30.38	30.38	30.38	29.63	29.63
Yes	Mexico	35	35	34	33	30	29	28
Yes	Netherlands	35	34.5	34.5	34.5	31.5	29.6	25.5
Yes	New Zealand	33	33	33	33	33	33	33
Yes	Norway	28	28	28	28	28	28	28
Yes	Poland	28	28	27	19	19	19	19
Yes	Portugal	35.2	33	33	27.5	27.5	27.5	26.5
Yes	S. Korea	30.8	29.7	29.7	29.7	27.5	27.5	27.5
Yes	Slovakia	29	25	25	19	19	19	19
Yes	Spain	35	35	35	35	35	35	32.5
Yes	Sweden	28	28	28	28	28	28	28
Yes	Switzerland	24.7	24.4	24.1	24.1	21.3	21.32	21.32
Yes	Turkey	33	33	30	33	30	20	20
Yes	UK	30	30	30	30	30	30	30
Yes	US	39.26	39.3	39.33	39.31	39.28	39.3	39.26
No	Hong Kong	16	16	16	17.5	17.5	17.5	17.5
No	Macao	15	15	15	15	12	12	12
No	Singapore	25.5	24.5	22	22	20	20	20
No	Taiwan	25	25	25	25	25	25	25
No	China	33	33	33	33	33	33	33

Note: OECD data is from the OECD Tax Database (Section C, Table II. 1, accessible at www.oecd. org/ctp/taxdatabase), and non-OECD data is from KPMG (2007) Hong Kong Tax Competitiveness Series: Corporate Tax Rates.

enjoy 15% tax rates. Foreign firms located in various development zones and cities could also enjoy 24% tax rates, depending upon the location of the project. We thus need to control for these various economic zones with preferential tax rates. The dichotomous variable *Economic zones with preferential tax* denotes such locations.

In order to find evidence of income shifting at the subsidiary level, we follow the methodology developed by Bertrand, Mehta, and Mullainathan (2002) to trace the propagation of profit shock through a multinational firm. Consider, for example, a multinational firm with headquarters in a home country and a subsidiary in a host country. Suppose that the corporate income tax rate is lower in the home country than in the host country. Further, suppose that the subsidiary experiences a profit shock such as a sudden and unexpected increase in demand that would cause its profits to rise by RMB 1 in the absence of income shifting. Because the multinational firm has incentive to minimize corporate taxes, some increased profits in the foreign subsidiary may be shifted out of the country. As a result, the actual profits of the subsidiary will rise by less than RMB 1. If the home country has a higher corporate income tax rate than the host country, the situation would be reversed.

In order to calculate the predicted value of the operating profit of a subsidiary after experiencing a profit shock from an industry and a region where the subsidiary belongs, we first calculate the asset-weighted average profitability by dividing the aggregate operating profit of all local firms and foreign subsidiaries in the same industry and province by the aggregate assets of these firms in a given year. For each subsidiary i at time t, *predicted profit* is calculated by multiplying the asset-weighted industry-region-level average profitability for each industry-region pair JR with the total assets of each subsidiary using the following equation:

$$predicted\ profit_{it} = \frac{\sum\limits_{i \in JR} operating\ profit_{it}}{\sum\limits_{i \in JR} asset_{it}} \times asset_{it}, \quad (1)$$

Next, we use a subsidiary fixed-effect model to estimate a subsidiary's operating profit as a function of predicted profit using the following specification:

$$profit_{it} = \alpha + \beta \, (predicted \, profit)_{it}$$
$$+ \delta Size_{it} + Subsidiary_i + Year_t + \varepsilon_{it}, \qquad (2)$$

Since a fixed-effect model is used, both performance and predicted performance are measured as deviation from subsidiary-level averages, allowing us to interpret the deviation in predicted operating profit as a response to *profit shock*. Thus, the coefficient β captures the response of subsidiary performance with respect to market-level shocks in profitability.

$$profit_{it} = \alpha + \beta \, (predicted \, profit)_{it}$$
$$+ \gamma \, (predicted \, profit_{it} * subsidiary \, characteristic_{it})$$
$$+ \delta Size_{it} + Subsidiary_i + Year_t + \varepsilon_{it}, \qquad (3)$$

In equation (3), we add the interaction between predicted profit and home country tax rates. We also add the coefficient γ to capture the differential response of the performance variable with respect to market-level shocks in profitability according to those subsidiary-level characteristics. Additionally, we add the interaction between predicted profit and economic zones with special tax rates to control for any tax benefits for firms in those locations.

Appendix Table 10.2 reports the main results. Model (1) is the baseline model. The coefficient for predicted profit is 1.310, which means foreign firms increase their operating profit by RMB 1.310 for each RMB 1 profit shock in the market. Multinational firms may receive more benefit from unexpected profit shocks than local firms because foreign multinationals possess stronger technology or brands. In models (2) and (3), we enter the interaction term between predicted profitability and home country tax as a continuous variable and as a dummy variable. Model (2) shows

Appendix Table 10.2. The extent of income shifting according to tax rates among wholly-owned subsidiaries

SAMPLE	(1)	(2)	(3)	(4)	(5)
	ALL	ALL	ALL	ECONOMIC ZONES WITH SPECIAL TAX RATES	NON-ECONOMIC ZONES
Predicted profit	1.310***	0.668***	0.861***	0.143	0.843***
	(0.038)	(0.195)	(0.187)	(0.382)	(0.196)
Predicted profit * home tax rate		0.017***	0.011**	0.041***	0.012**
		(0.005)	(0.005)	(0.016)	(0.005)
Predicted profit * economic zones with preferential tax			-0.745*		
			(0.416)		
Predicted profit * home tax rate* economic zones with preferential tax			0.031*		
			(0.016)		
Log (assets)	-1,673.290***	-272.370	-936.175	-1,137.832	-512.492
	(391.825)	(494.241)	(646.907)	(938.245)	(603.454)
Year fixed effects	Yes	Yes	Yes	Yes	Yes
Firm fixed effects	Yes	Yes	Yes	Yes	Yes
Adjusted R-squared	0.941	0.942	0.945	0.868	0.983
Observations	104,105	104,105	104,105	69,578	34,527

Note: Standard errors in parentheses. *** p < 0.01, ** p < 0.05, * p < 0.1.

that wholly owned subsidiaries whose parents are headquartered in a country with higher tax rates report higher profits than expected from these market-level shocks. Other variables being equal, a firm whose parent company comes from a country with a 15% corporate income tax rate will report a RMB 0.923 (= 0.668+0.017*15) increase in operating profit when faced with a RMB 1 profit shock, whereas a firm whose parent comes from a country with 40% corporate income tax rate will report a RMB 1.348 (= 0.668+0.017*40) increase in operating profit in response to the same RMB 1 profit shock.

Model (3) uses the dichotomous variable *economic zones with special tax rates* and creates a two-way interaction term with predicted profit and a three-way interaction term with predicted profit and economic zones with preferential tax. The three-way interaction term is positively signed and significant, suggesting that firms in various economic zones with special tax rates respond positively to an external shock. Since the tax rates in these various economic zones are lower than other locations, foreign firms located in these economic zones report higher profits than those located elsewhere.

In models (4) and (5), we split the sample into firms located in economic zones with special tax rates and firms located elsewhere. Results show that the coefficient for predicted profit is insignificant for firms located in economic zones, suggesting that foreign firms in economic zones do not respond to industry-wide profitability. Rather, their reported profits depend entirely on the home tax rates. In other words, foreign firms whose home tax rates are high will report higher profits, while those whose home tax rates are low will report lower profits, even though both enjoy the same special tax rates in the same economic zones. Profits of foreign firms located in places other than economic zones also respond positively to their home country tax rate.

These results support our conjecture that the profits of foreign subsidiaries depend on home country corporate tax rate, regardless of location in China. Even foreign firms in economic zones with lower tax rates demonstrate similar patterns. This finding confirms extensive income shifting among foreign subsidiaries in China. Thus, the reported low profitability of foreign firms in China does not necessarily mean that they are unprofitable, rather, they just report less profit to the tax authorities in China.

Notes

Chapter 1

1. *China Economic Daily*, June 21, 2011. Foreign firms' shares in the Chinese economy are remarkably higher than those of any sizable economy. For example, in 2009, the US had a stock of incoming FDI of $3.1 trillion, while in 2008 foreign firms' share was 4.3% in employment and 18% in export. See Jackson (2012).

2. See Naughton (2007), Chapter 4 for more detailed information regarding specific reforms.

3. Collective firms, especially those in rural areas, towns, and villages (TVEs), may have represented an effective institutional response to the pre liberalization phase in order to avoid expropriation by the state (Walder 1995; Boisot and Child 1996; Tian 2000). However, due to vague property rights, I categorize both collectives and SOEs as conventional ownership firms and argue that neither fit post-liberalization competitive market conditions.

4. Initially, 195 non-financial firms were under the supervision of the SASAC. See Chapter 13 of Naughton (2007) for more information regarding how SASAC operates.

5. There are two types of joint ventures in China. The first type, equity joint venture, also common in other countries, occurs when a Chinese firm and a foreign firm invest capital and share financial profits and losses. The second type is the contract-based joint venture. First adopted in Guangdong Province, this occurs when the Chinese party contributes only the land while the foreign firm contributes the capital. The share of each party in the profits is determined by the contract, instead of by their share of capital (the land is not converted into shares of equity). Financial loss is borne by the foreign party up to the amount of their initial capital investment. When the contract expires or the venture is terminated, the remaining assets go to the Chinese party, unless otherwise contracted. This kind of venture solves the problem of capital constraints faced by the Chinese firms, while the foreign company usually takes a larger share of the profit. The legal procedure for government approval is usually faster in the contract-based joint venture. According to the annual industrial survey, about 12% of joint ventures in China are contract based.

6. For more detailed information on this law, please refer to National Development and Reform Commission (http://www.ndrc.gov).

7. Article 2 of the Foreign Invested Company Law specifies that, "Foreign invested corporations in this law refer to corporations wholly invested by foreign investors in China according to related laws, exclude branches set up by foreign companies and other organizations." This law was amended in 2000.

8. See full text in the laws and regulations section on the central government's website (http://www.gov.cn/flfg).

9. See Whalley (2011) for more information on taxes in China.

10. See KPMG (2007) for more information on tax reform.

11. The British Virgin Islands and the Cayman Islands are known tax havens where multinational companies set up paper companies to minimize tax exposure.

Chapter 2

1. "Interview with Wong Junrong, the former General Manager of Shanghai Volkswagen," www.sina.com (online media site), April 3, 2008.

2. Shanghai Volkswagen's 1996 Annual Report. Its production volume and local content are listed in annual reports, 1988–2011, available on its website (www.csvw.com).

3. We define wholly owned subsidiaries as firms in which multinational firms own and control more than 95%. Most empirical research, including Gatignon and Anderson (1988), adopts this definition.

4. Although joint ventures may also attenuate these hazards by holding partners in a mutual hostage situation (Kogut 1988), bilateral dependence between joint venture partners may further increase the degree of asset specificity.

5. "Comments: progress or threat? The acquisition of Chinese steel firms by foreign capital" (in Chinese), *China Industry & Commerce News*, November 2009.

6. "Analysis on the acquisitions by foreign capital in China's steel industry" (in Chinese), *China Market Research Network*, October 31, 2007.

7. The choice of entry mode has also been explained by cultural and national factors. Kogut and Singh (1988) hypothesized that differences in culture between home and host countries increased the level of risk in post-acquisition integration, leading firms to choose less risky entry modes. Their findings show that greater cultural distance was indeed associated with entry by greenfield investment rather than by acquisition. In addition, the investing firm's country of origin may be associated with preference for a particular entry mode, whether for cultural or institutional reasons (Franko 1976; Stopford and Haberich 1978; Wilson 1980). For example, Hennart and Park (1993) find that Japanese firms tend to prefer

entry through greenfield investment rather than acquisition, perhaps due to the strong ethnocentric orientation of the Japanese culture.

8. "P&G Greater China president: Choosing Guangzhou is the most wise decision" (in Chinese), *Guangzhou Daily*, July 30, 2007, which can be retrieved from P&G's website.

9. A recorded interview, *The Parlour of Netease Finance Channel*, 2010 Aug. The video clip is available on http://money.163.com/special/CTOBruceBrown/.

10. "Reform and open up for 30 year: The first wholly owned enterprise, Tianjin Motorola" (in Chinese), *China Daily*, October 30, 2008.

11. Henderson (1986) empirically demonstrates that agglomeration increases factor productivity. Saxenian (1994) documents how microelectronics firms clustered in Silicon Valley. Krugman (1991) develops a formal model in which agglomeration results from manufacturing firms' desire to locate in a place of larger demand in order to exploit scale economies and minimize transportation costs, while the location of demand depends on the location of manufacturers.

12. Early work in economic geography studied the impact of income, tax incentives, wage, and unionization on attracting greater FDI (Coughlin, Terza, and Arromdee 1991; Friedman, Gerlowski, and Silberman 1992; Wheeler and Mody 1992).

13. On the other hand, negative network externalities, such as groupthink and competition in product and factor markets, may be industry specific. It is not clear whether the marginal benefits and marginal cost schedules would intersect at a higher level of agglomeration for firms in the same industry or firms in different industries. Porter (1998) and Porter and Stern (2001) argue that intensified rivalry among firms in the same region actually promotes innovation, citing regional clusters like Silicon Valley for semiconductors as an example. The innovation promoting effects of intensified rivalry among firms in the same industry within a regional cluster tend to be greater than the negative consequences of intensified competition in the factor and product markets.

14. "A long-distance running of Unilever," *Information for Entrepreneurs*, 2008, Issue 1, pp. 104–6.

15. "Birth of a giant in telecom sector: Shanghai Bell was restructured into a foreign invested company" (in Chinese), *Liberty News*, October 24, 2001. Stocks owned by the Chinese parties were transferred to the SASAC of the State Council. This is viewed as an important action to tighten the ownership structure of Shanghai Bell.

16. "P&G promises 'full court press' in China," *China Daily*, August 9, 2010.

17. "GE makes $2b Chinese investment," *China Daily*, November 10, 2010.

Chapter 3

1. P&G Press release, February 18, 1994.
2. "White Cat stumbles," *Marketing Communication Network*, March 23, 2005.
3. "China's sleepy old cat awakes," *Sphere* 30, pp. 18–21.
4. In order to qualify as a "Group," a parent firm should have registered capital of more than RMB 50 million and at least five subsidiaries, while the combined capital of parent and subsidiaries should exceed RMB 100 million.
5. Nice Group website.
6. "Forerunners in China's SOE reform efforts: Shanghai Jahwa," *CCTV News*, May 8, 2012.
7. "Multinationals gaining ground, local groups fighting back" (in Chinese), *China Business News*, January 17, 2012.
8. "One-man show for foreign companies in skin care product: Local firms pressing on," *Information Times*, December 14, 2010,
9. "Multinationals besiege local brands by playing with Chinese traditional medicine concepts" (in Chinese), *Nanfang Daily*, September 8, 2010.
10. Government Document, "The National Economic & Trade Committee and the Notice on SOE Reform & Development in 1997."
11. Please refer to SASAC's homepage: http://www.sasac.gov.cn, which describes its main functions and responsibilities.
12. "Zhongxing Telecom: Developing stably with a bright future," *Economic Observation*, 2009.
13. To be precise, the State Economic and Trade Commission submitted a report to the Vice Premier in 1994, which was adopted by the Central Committee of the Communist Party in September 1995. See Garnaut et al. (2005) for more details.
14. There were several cases of "asset stripping" during the privatization process, by lowering the valuation and by selling assets at a low price to an interested party (Garnaut et al. 2005: 176–7). Haier's management buyout (MBO) plan in 2003 sparked a backlash and the government explicitly forbids the MBO of large state-owned enterprises.
15. "TCL mode preferred in Guangdong's SOE transition," *Chinese Business News*, April 29, 2005.
16. We ensured that firms that disappeared from the annual survey between 1998 and 2003 really did exit the market by comparing the list to firms in the 2004 full economic survey. Roughly 1.3% of firms that disappear from the annual industrial survey still exist in the 2004 economy-wide census, suggesting that their sales simply dipped below the RMB 5 million threshold. The other 98.7% firms that disappeared from the annual survey are therefore cases of real exit.
17. "Details of Jilin Tonghua Steel murder case," *China News Week*, August 5, 2009.

18. Several studies support the existence of such selection and learning effects, with most focusing on developed countries like the United States (Baily et al. 1992; Balasubramanian and Lieberman 2010), Canada (Baldwin 1995; Baldwin and Rafiquzzaman 1995; Baldwin and Gu 2006), Spain (Farinas and Ruano, 2005), and Germany (Wagner 2010). However, Baily et al. (1992) and Jensen, McGuckin, and Stiroh (2001) do not find a statistically significant relationship between firm age and productivity. Findings are also mixed for studies on transitional economies (Tybout 2000). For instance, Aw, Chung, and Roberts (2003) find that new entrants demonstrate lower productivity than incumbents in Taiwan, but find no difference in Korea.

19. Higher productivity of new entrants can be attributable to institutional barriers, defined as hindrance in the institutional environment that prevents market selection forces from functioning (Tybout 2000). My work with a research colleague argues that these institutional barriers create persistent survival advantages for incumbent firms, independent of their productivity. This in turn increases the fixed costs of doing business for new entrants (Chang and Wu 2013). As a consequence, only new entrants with higher productivity are able to enter and operate in the industry. Thus, institutional barriers truncate the productivity distribution of potential entrants, raising the average productivity of actual entrants. We further demonstrate that new entrants' superior productivity requirement to compensate for the institutional buffering effect is reduced when institutional barriers are lowered. When the institutional buffering effect is reduced by the removal of institutional barriers, the fixed cost of doing business is reduced, allowing more new firms to enter.

20. However, such labor turnover may also cause an adverse effect through, e.g., the occupational choices of skilled workers and domestic entrepreneurs (De Backer and Sleuwaegen 2003; Tian 2007).

21. "Valin Tube & Wire: The great benefits from the cooperation with Arcelor Mittal" (in Chinese), *China Securities Journal*, April 25, 2007.

Chapter 4

1. "ZTE telecom: Develop steadily with a bright future," *Economic Observation*, November 2, 2009.

2. "Cisco drops patent infringement suit," *New York Times*, July 29, 2004.

3. "Motorola sues Huawei for trade secret theft," *Reuters*, July 22, 2010.

4. "Ericsson, ZTE settle patent lawsuits," *PC World*, January 20, 2012.

5. "Sale of 3Com to Huawei is derailed by US security concerns" *New York Times*, February 21, 2008.

6. "Huawei's open letter to US," *Wall Street Journal*, February 25, 2011.

7. *Multinational Companies Research Group, Grow with China: P&G's 20 Years in China* (in Chinese), Peking University Press, April 2009. The entire book is available on P&G's website.
8. "The successful 'heart transplant' of Unilever" (in Chinese), *Anhui News*, March 9, 2010.
9. "Road rage in the West as copycat cars from China start to make their marque overseas," *The Independent,* September 9, 2007.
10. "GM charges Chery for alleged mini car piracy," *China Daily*, December 18, 2004.
11. "Did Spark spark a copycat?" *Business Week*, February 6, 2005.
12. "GM charges Chery for alleged mini car piracy," *China Daily*, December 18, 2004. GM executives demonstrated the extent of the design duplication, noting for example that the doors of the QQ and those of the Spark are interchangeable without modification. MotorAuthority.com and *Car and Driver* called the QQ a "carbon copy," while the *International Herald Tribune* referred to it as a clone in a 2005 article.
13. "P&G's epic campaign: War on fakes," *China Daily*, June 29, 2009.
14. "Software piracy costs US$63.4 billion in 2011: Study," *China Post*, May 16, 2012.
15. "Pro logo: Chinese consumers are falling out of love with fakes," *Economist*, January 14, 2012.
16. "In China, knockoff cell phones are a hit," *New York Times*, April 28, 2009.
17. "China tops US, Japan to become top patent filer," *Reuters*, December 21, 2011.
18. "Forerunners in China's SOE reform efforts: Shanghai Jahwa," *CCTV News*, May 8, 2012.
19. "The surge of Chinese herbal medicine group puts challenge on multinational daily products brands" (in Chinese), *Chinese Cosmetics* (www.zghzp.com is its website), May 3, 2012.
20. "Proper price increase helps the development of local Chinese brands" (in Chinese), *Xinhua News Agency*, December 19, 2011.

Chapter 5

1. "China beer market: Dragon ready to swallow US," www.just-drinks.com (online resource of the beverage industry), July 3, 2000.
2. "Analysis: Premium Chinese beer a bitter brew for foreign brands," *Reuters*, November 3, 2011.
3. After the repeal of the alcohol prohibition law in 1933, many brewers entered the US industry. In 1940, there were more than 611 beer companies, with the top five and top ten firms' market shares equal to just 16% and 23.6%, respectively (McGahan 1991: Tables 1 and 2). By 1958, the American brewing industry was

an oligopoly, with the top five and top ten firms' shares equal to 30.6% and 48.4%. As of 2007, the eight-firm concentration of the US beer industry is as high as 91.5%. Miller and Anheuser-Busch emerged as the dominant firms. Investment in production facilities, efficient distribution channels, and nationwide advertising played a critical role in this consolidation process (Greer 1971; McGahan 1991).

4. According to Elzinga (1982), 25 leading brewers made approximately 100 acquisitions, most of which were mid-size firms acquiring small firms.

5. "Heineken retreat from joint ventures in China due to internal and external difficulties," *Beijing Business,* November 8, 2011.

6. "The current situation of small and middle sized breweries" (in Chinese), *Dajing News,* November 11, 2011.

7. "Local firms are losing out the battle," *China Business,* July 21, 2012.

8. One might argue that spillover effects could also be greater among groups of firms with similar resource profiles, as similar resource profiles could suggest higher absorptive capacity among these groups. Nonetheless, the absorptive capacity argument—and its counterargument, the technological gap hypothesis—tend to be associated with level, not type, of resource (Cantwell 1989; Meyer 2004). Because our concept of resource similarity is based on resource type, we therefore cannot make inferences from the absorptive capacity argument.

9. "How foreign firms dodge taxes in China," *Asia Times,* April 11, 2007.

10. For instance, in a tax dispute case in the US, G.D. Searle had an average return on employed assets of -42% in the US compared to 119% in Puerto Rico, a zero effective tax rate jurisdiction (Wheeler 1988). In another case, the US Internal Revenue Service (IRS) charged that Japan's Toyota had systematically overcharged its US subsidiary on most of the cars, trucks, and parts sold in the US over several years, effectively shifting profits from the US back to Japan (Martz and Thomas 1991).

11. Using anecdotal evidence, Lall (1973) documents the extensive overpricing practices of imports by foreign firms in the Colombian pharmaceutical industry after the Colombian government passed Decree 444, which imposed various exchange controls and restrictions on the flow of funds by foreign investors. Harris (1993) identifies a mechanism of income shifting through transfer pricing by accounting for the different income shifting behaviors according to the "flexibility" possessed by multinational firms, which is proxied by interest payments, rent, R&D, and advertising expenses. Clausing (2003) provides comprehensive evidence regarding how the prices of intrafirm transactions differ from those of non-intrafirm transactions. Using monthly data from the Bureau of Labor and Statistics (BLS) on international prices from 1997 to 1999, he finds that US intrafirm export prices charged by parents are lower than (i.e., underpriced), and US intrafirm import

prices are higher than (i.e., overpriced), non-intrafirm transactions, as foreign country tax rates are lower.

12. Newberry and Dhaliwal (2001) find that US multinationals are more likely to issue bonds through a foreign subsidiary located in a country with high corporate statutory tax rates compared to the US. Desai, Foley, and Hines (2004) examine the capital structure of foreign affiliates and internal capital markets of US multinational firms, finding 10% higher local tax rates to be associated with 2.8% higher debt/asset ratios and that the internal, as opposed to external, debt from parent firms is particularly sensitive to taxes.

13. "Auto industry shall watch out FDI on 'income shifting'," *China Auto News*, June 17, 2005.

14. "How foreign firms dodge taxes in China," *Asia Times*, April 11, 2007.

15. "China to stop tax evasions for multinationals," *People's Daily Online*, July 29, 2009.

Chapter 6

1. "How did Du Shuanghua come here?" *Business Review*, November 2008.

2. "For global steel industry, China poses guessing game," *Wall Street Journal*, May 24, 2011.

3. "A farewell to Tieben," *Business Review*, 2010, Issue 2

4. "Ningbo Jianlong restructured amid qualms," *Ciajing*, January 10, 2005.

5. This acquisition grew complicated, when Rizhao struck a deal to sell his shares to Hong Kong-based investment company Kaiyuan, owned by Rizhao's founder, Du Shuanghua. This move avoided state expropriation. As of December 2012, Shandong Steel and Rizhao Steel are still negotiating on the equity structure of the merged unit.

6. "Why is the trend of 'the state advances, the private retreats' getting stronger in the steel industry?" *China Business Times*, June 19, 2009.

7. "The rise of state capitalism," *The Economist*, January 21, 2012.

8. "China fortifies state business to fuel growth," *New York Times*, August 29, 2010.

9. "The consumer products industry in Yangtze River Delta & Pearl River Delta," *China Washing & Cosmetics Weekly*, June 22, 2009.

10. "Why high-tech industry is booming in Shenzhen," *Guangming Daily*, May 14, 2011.

11. "Shishan, a town of Foshan, ambitions to build into an auto city," www.sina.com, June 18, 2012.

12. There are several books on related topics. See, for example, Rein (2012).

13. "The successful 'heart transplant' of Unilever" (in Chinese), *Anhui News*, March 9, 2010.

14. "Car plates applicants exceeded 1 million," *China Daily*, August 27, 2012.

15. "Can P&G make money in places where people earn $2 dollars a day?" *Fortune*, January 6, 2011.
16. "Premium Chinese beer a bitter brew for foreign brands," *Reuters*, November 3, 2011.
17. "Innovating in China's automotive market: An interview with GM China's president," *McKinsey Quarterly*, February 2012.
18. "Volvo cars prepares for Chinese production to start," BBC News, April 22, 2012.
19. "China's Wuhan Steel abandons plan to build Brazil mill-paper," *Reuters*, July 3, 2012.
20. "TCL to close most European operations," *Financial Times*, October 31, 2006.
21. "Huawei and ZTE face congressional grilling," *Financial Times*, September 13, 2012.

Appendices

1. We experimented with several alternative means of measuring the presence of foreign firms, such as employment and sales. The results are consistent.
2. Gatignon and Anderson (1988) use these criteria to distinguish among minority and majority joint ventures and wholly owned subsidiaries. We include 50:50 joint ventures in the category of minority joint venture.
3. While it is also possible to have upward bias in performances of wholly owned subsidiaries via transfer pricing (i.e., multinationals using transfer pricing to shift profits from their multinational headquarters to their Chinese subsidiaries), it is unlikely given the high corporate tax rates and regulations on profit repatriation in China.
4. The explanatory variables included in our probit model may not capture every factor affecting the conversion decision. For instance, profitability, leverage, and export ratios may not fully indicate the option value of a joint venture. Similarly, firm age may be an imperfect measure for differential learning among partners. Some multinational parents may simply favor wholly owned subsidiaries due to their organizational move toward more centralization or changes in their business portfolios (Franko 1971; Killing 1983). There are also some unknown rational reasons. For example, even though multinational parents with high R&D/advertising intensity seek to convert joint ventures to wholly owned subsidiaries, the negotiation may stalemate if they have difficulty finding local managers to oversee operations or if local partners demand an exorbitant price in return for the breakup. Sometimes, the conversion decision can be driven by irrational factors. For instance, some joint ventures, particularly those in industries with low intensity in R&D and advertising, may favor conversion out of imitative or herd behavior, despite no clear benefits (DiMaggio and Powell 1983; Yiu and Makino 2002).

Other joint ventures, on the other hand, may not convert despite being natural cases for conversion, like those in industries with high R&D and advertising.

5. We also trace export ratio and financial leverage for each time period in order to see whether the improved performance of converted wholly owned subsidiaries might be attributable to financial restructuring or an increase in multinational parents' export sales after conversion. We find no difference between these two groups. Results are available upon request.

6. 1688 observations were dropped due to no variation in the dependent variable in several industries and regions.

7. Let r_t be the rate of change in x_t over time, then: $\ln x_t - \ln x_{t-1} = \ln(x_t)/(x_{t-1}) = \ln(1+r_t) \approx r_t$, when r_t is small as in most of our cases.

8. Following Brandt, Van Biesebroeck, and Zhang (2012), we do not use the firm-level price deflator, as it tends to be very noisy due to extreme outliers. We only generate a 3-digit industry-level price deflator, which is less aggregated than the 2-digit industry-level deflator available in the *China Statistics Yearbook*.

9. This database is accessible at www.oecd.org/ctp/taxdatabase. See Section C, Table II.1.

References

Ahn, N., de la Rica, S., and Ugidos, A. (1999). "Willingness to move for work and unemployment duration in Spain," *Economica*, 66(263):335–357.

Aitken, B., and Harrison, A. (1999). "Do domestic firms benefit from direct foreign investment? Evidence from Venezuela," *American Economic Review*, 89(3):605–618.

Appold, S. (1995). "Agglomeration, interorganizational networks and competitive performance in the U.S. metalworking sector," *Economic Geography*, 71(1):27–54.

Arrow, K. (1974). *The Limits of Organization*. New York: W.W. Norton.

Arthur, B. (1990). "Positive feedback in the economy," *Scientific American*, 262 (February):92–99.

Aw, B., Chung, S., and Roberts, M. (2003). "Productivity, output, and failure: A comparison of Taiwanese and Korean manufacturers," *Economic Journal*, 113(November):F485–510.

Baily, M., Hulten, C., Campbell, D., Bresnahan, T., and Caves, R. (1992). "Productivity dynamics in manufacturing plants," *Brookings Papers on Economic Activity. Microeconomics*, 1992:187–267.

Balasubramanian, N., and Lieberman M. (2010). "Industry learning environments and the heterogeneity of firm performance," *Strategic Management Journal*, 31(4):390–412.

Baldwin, J. (1995). *The Dynamics of Industrial Competition: A North American Perspective*. New York: Cambridge University Press.

Baldwin, J., and Gu, W. (2006). "Plant turnover and productivity growth in Canadian manufacturing," *Industrial and Corporate Change*, 15(3):417–465.

Baldwin, J., and Rafiquzzaman, M. (1995). "Selection versus evolutionary adaptation: Learning and post-entry performance," *International Journal of Industrial Organization*, 13(4):501–522.

Barkema, H., Bell, J., and Pennings, J. (1996). "Foreign entry, cultural barriers, and learning," *Strategic Management Journal*, 17(2):151–166.

Barkema, H., and Vermeulen, F. (1998). "International expansion through start-up or acquisition: A learning perspective," *Academy of Management Journal*, 41(1):7–26.

Bernard, A., Jensen, J., and Schott, P. (2006). "Trade costs, firms and productivity," *Journal of Monetary Economics*, 53(5):917–937.

Bertrand, M., Mehta, P., and Mullainathan, S. (2002). "Ferreting out tunneling: An application to Indian business groups," *Quarterly Journal of Economics, 117*(1): 121–148.

Blalock, G., and Simon, D. (2009). "Do all firms benefit equally from downstream FDI? The moderating effect of local suppliers' capabilities on productivity gains," *Journal of International Business Studies*, 40(7):1095–1112.

Blodgett, L. (1992). "Factors in the instability of international joint ventures: an event history analysis," *Strategic Management Journal*, 13(6):475–481.

Blömstrom, M. (1986). "Foreign investment and productive efficiency: The case of Mexico," *Journal of Industrial Economics*, 35(1):97–110.

Blömstrom, M., and Kokko, A. (1998). "Multinational corporations and spillovers," *Journal of Economic Surveys*, 12(3):1–31.

Boisot, M., and Child, J. (1996). "From fiefs to clans and network capitalism: Explaining China's emerging economic order," *Administrative Science Quarterly*, 41(4):600–628.

Brandt, L., Van Biesebroeck, J., and Zhang, Y. (2012). "Creative accounting or creative destruction? Firm-level productivity growth in Chinese manufacturing," *Journal of Development Economics*, 97(2):339–351.

Buckley, P., and Casson, M. (1976). *The Future of the Multinational Enterprise*. London: Homes & Meier.

Buckley, P., Clegg, J., and Wang, C. (2002). "The impact of inward FDI on the performance of Chinese manufacturing firms," *Journal of International Business Studies*, 33(4):637–655.

Buckley, P., Clegg, S., and Wang, K. (2007). "Is the relationship between inward FDI and spillover effects linear? An empirical examination of the case of China," *Journal of International Business Studies*, 38(3):447–459.

Caballero, R., and Hammour, M. (1994). "The cleansing effect of recessions," *American Economic Review*, 84(5):1350–1368.

Cantwell, J. (1989). *Technical Innovation and Multinational Corporations*. Oxford: Basil Blackwell.

Caves, D., Christensen, L., and Diewert, W. (1982). "The economic theory of index numbers and the measurement of input, output, and productivity," *Econometrica*, 50(6):1393–1414.

Caves, R. (1971). "International corporations: The industrial economics of foreign investment," *Economica*, 38(149):1–27.

Caves, R. (1974). "Multinational firms, competition, and productivity in host-country markets," *Economica*, 41(162):176–193.

Chandler, A. (1962). *Strategy and Structure: Chapters in the History of the American Industrial Enterprise*. Cambridge, MA: MIT Press.

Chandler, A. (1977). *The Visible Hand: The Managerial Revolution in American Business.* Cambridge, MA: MIT Press.

Chandler, A. (1990). *Scale and Scope: The Dynamics of Industrial Capitalism.* Cambridge, MA: Harvard University Press.

Chang, S. (1995). "International expansion strategy of Japanese firms: Capability building through sequential entry," *Academy of Management Journal,* 38(2): 383–407.

Chang, S., Chung, J., and Moon, J. (2012). "Do multinational firms shift profit out of China?," Working Paper.

Chang, S., Chung, J., and Moon, J. (2013). "Do wholly-owned subsidiaries perform better than joint ventures?" *Strategic Management Journal,* 34(3):317–337.

Chang, S., and Park, S. (2005). "Types of firms generating network externalities and MNCs' co-location decisions," *Strategic Management Journal,* 26(7):595–615.

Chang, S., and Park, S. (2012). "Winning strategies in China," *Long Range Planning,* 45(1):1–15.

Chang, S., and Wu, B. (2013). "Industry dynamics and institutional frictions," in press, *Strategic Management Journal.*

Chang, S., and Wu, B. (2012). "Post-liberalization industry consolidation in China," Working Paper.

Chang, S., and Xu, D. (2008). "Spillovers and competition among foreign and local firms in China," *Strategic Management Journal,* 29(5):495–518.

Chen, M. (1996). "Competitor analysis and inter-firm rivalry: Towards a theoretical integration," *Academy of Management Review,* 21(1):100–134.

Chow, G. (1993). "Capital formation and economic growth in China," *Quarterly Journal of Economics,* 108(3):809–842.

Christensen, C. (1997). *The Innovator's Dilemma: When New Technologies Cause Great Firms to Fail.* Boston, MA: Harvard Business School Press.

Chung, W., and Alcacer, J. (2002). "Knowledge seeking and location choice of foreign direct investment in the United States," *Management Science,* 48(12):1534–1554.

Clausing, K. (2003). "Tax-motivated transfer pricing and US intrafirm trade prices," *Journal of Public Economics,* 87(9–10):2207–2223.

Cohen, W., and Levinthal, D. (1990). "Absorptive capacity: A new perspective on learning and innovation," *Administrative Science Quarterly,* 35(1):128–152.

Coughlin, C., Terza, J., and Arromdee, V. (1991). "State characteristics and the location of foreign direct investment within the United States," *Review of Economics and Statistics,* 73(4):675–683.

Davidson, W. (1980). "The location of foreign direct investment activity: Country characteristics and experience effect," *Journal of International Business Studies,* 11(2):9–22.

Dawar, N., and Frost, T. (1999). "Competing with giants: Survival strategies for local companies in emerging markets," *Harvard Business Review*, 77(2):119–129.

De Backer, K., and Sleuwaegen, L. (2003). "Does foreign direct investment crowd out domestic entrepreneurship?" *Review of Industrial Organization*, 22(1):67–84.

De Loecker, J. (2007). "Do exports generate higher productivity? Evidence from Slovenia," *Journal of International Economics*, 73(1):69–98.

Desai, M., Foley, C., and Hines, J. (2004). "A multinational perspective on capital structure choice and internal capital markets," *Journal of Finance*, 59(6):2451–2488.

Desai, M., Foley, C., and Hines, J. (2006). "The demand for tax haven operations," *Journal of Public Economics*, 90(3):513–531.

Dierickx, I., and Cool, K. (1989). "Asset stock accumulation and sustainability of competitive advantage," *Management Science*, 35(12):1504–1512.

DiMaggio, P., and Powell, W. (1983). "The iron cage revisited: Institutional isomorphism and collective rationality in organizational fields," *American Sociological Review*, 48(12):147–160.

Doz, Y. (1996). "The evolution of cooperation in strategic alliances: Initial conditions or learning processes?" *Strategic Management Journal*, 17(S1):55–84.

Du, J., Lu, Y., and Tao, Z. (2008). "Economic institutions and FDI location choice: Evidence from US multinationals in China," *Journal of Comparative Economics*, 36(3):412–429.

Dunning, J. (1988). "The eclectic paradigm of international production: A restatement and some possible extensions," *Journal of International Business Studies*, 19(1):1–31.

Eden, L., Juarez Valdez, L., and Li, D. (2005). "Talk softly but carry a big stick: Transfer pricing penalties and the market valuation of Japanese multinationals in the United States," *Journal of International Business Studies*, 36(4):398–414.

Elzinga, K. (1982). "The beer industry," in W. Adams (ed.), *The Structure of American Industry* (6th edn). New York: Macmillan, 128–154.

Farinas, J., and Ruano, S. (2005). "Firm productivity, heterogeneity, sunk costs and market selection," *International Journal of Industrial Organization*, 23(7–8):505–534.

Fosfuri, A., Motta, M., and Rønde, T. (2001). "Foreign direct investment and spillovers through worker's mobility," *Journal of International Economics*, 53(1):205–222.

Foster, L., Haltiwanger, J., and Syverson, C. (2008). "Reallocation, firm turnover, and efficiency: Selection on productivity or profitability?" *American Economic Review*, 98(1):394–425.

Franko, L. (1971). *Joint Venture Survival in Multinational Corporations*. New York: Praeger.

Franko, L. (1976). *The European Multinationals: A Renewed Challenge to American and British Big Business*. Stamford, CT: Greylock Publishers.

Friedman, J., Gerlowski, D., and Silberman, J. (1992). "What attracts foreign multinational corporations? Evidence from branch plant location in the United States," *Journal of Regional Science*, 32(4):403–418.

Garnaut, R., Song, L., Tenev, S., and Yao, Y. (2005). *China's Ownership Transformation: Process, Outcomes, Prospects.* Washington, DC: International Finance Corporation and International Bank for Reconstruction and Development.

Gatignon, H., and Anderson, E. (1988). "The multinational corporation's degree of control over foreign subsidiaries: an empirical test of transaction cost explanation," *Journal of Law, Economics, and Organization*, 4(2):305–336.

Gilley, B. (2001). "Breaking barriers," *Far Eastern Economic Review*, July 12:12–19.

Girma, S., and Görg, H. (2007). "Evaluating the foreign ownership wage premium using a difference-in-difference matching approach," *Journal of International Economics*, 72(1):97–112.

Greer D. (1971). "Product differentiation and concentration in the brewing industry," *Journal of Industrial Economics*, 19(3):201–219.

Gregory, A. (2003). "Chinese trademark law and the TRIPs Agreement—Confucius meets the WTO," in D. Cass, B. Williams, and G. Barker (eds), *China and the World Trading System.* Cambridge: Cambridge University Press, 321–344.

Gregory, N., Tenev, S., and Wagle, D. (2000). *China's Emerging Private Enterprises: Prospects for the New Century.* Washington, DC: International Finance Corporation.

Groves, T., Hong, Y., McMillan, J., and Naughton, B. (1994). "Automony and incentives in Chinese state enterprises," *Quarterly Journal of Economics*, 109(1):183–209.

Grubert, H., and Mutti, J. (1991). "Taxes, tariffs and transfer pricing in multinational corporate decision making," *Review of Economics and Statistics*, 73(2):285–293.

Guo, Y. (2012). *Global Big Business and the Chinese Brewing Industry.* London: Routledge.

Hannan, M., and Freeman, J. (1977). "The population ecology of organizations," *American Journal of Sociology*, 82(5):929–964.

Harris, D. (1993). "The impact of U.S. tax law revision on multinational corporations' capital location and income-shifting decisions," *Journal of Accounting Research*, 31(3):111–140.

Haskel, J., Pereira, S., and Slaughter, M. (2007). "Does inward foreign direct investment boost the productivity of domestic firms?" *Review of Economics and Statistics*, 89(3):482–496.

Head, K., Ries, J., and Swenson, D. (1995). "Agglomeration benefits and location choice: Evidence from Japanese manufacturing investments in the United States," *Journal of International Economics*, 38(3):223–247.

Hejazi, W., and Safarian, A. (1999). "Trade, foreign direct investment, and R&D spillovers," *Journal of International Business Studies*, 30(3):491–511.

Helfat, C. (1997). "Know-how and asset complementarity and dynamic capability accumulation: The case of R&D," *Strategic Management Journal, 18*(5):339–360.

Henderson, R., and Clark, K. (1990). "Architectural innovation: The reconfiguration of existing product technologies and the failure of established firms," *Administrative Science Quarterly, 35*(1):9–30.

Henderson, V. (1986). "Efficiency of resource usage and city size," *Journal of Urban Economics, 19*(1):47–70.

Hennart, J. (1982). *A Theory of Multinational Enterprise.* Ann Arbor: University of Michigan Press.

Hennart, J. (1991). "The transaction costs theory of joint ventures: An empirical study of Japanese subsidiaries in the United States," *Management Science, 37*(4):483–497.

Hennart, J., Kim, D., and Zeng, M. (1998). "The impact of joint venture status on the longevity of Japanese stakes in U.S. manufacturing affiliates," *Organization Science, 9*(3):382–395.

Hennart, J., and Park, Y. (1993). "Greenfield vs. acquisition: The strategy of Japanese investors in the United States," *Management Science, 39*(9):1054–1070.

Heracleous, L. (2001). "When local beat global: The Chinese beer industry," *Business Strategy Review, 12*(3):37–45.

Hines, J., and Rice, E. (1994). "Fiscal paradise: Foreign tax havens and American business," *Quarterly Journal of Economics, 109*(1):149–182.

Hitt, M., Dacin, M., Levitas, E., Arregle, J., and Borza, A. (2000). "Partner selection in emerging and developed market contexts: Resource-based and organizational learning perspectives," *Academy of Management Journal, 43*(3):449–467.

Hofstede, G. (1980). *Culture's Consequence: International Differences in Work-Related Values.* Beverly Hills, CA: Sage Publications.

Hopenhayn, H. (1992). "Entry, exit, and firm dynamics in long run equilibrium," *Econometrica, 60*(5):1127–1150.

Hsieh, C., and Klenow, P. (2009). "Misallocation and manufacturing TFP in China and India," *Quarterly Journal of Economics, 124*(4):1403–1448.

Huang, Y. (2003). *Selling China: Foreign Direct Investment during the Reform Era.* New York: Cambridge University Press.

Huang, Y. (2008). *Capitalism with Chinese Characteristics: Entrepreneurship and the State.* New York: Cambridge University Press.

Hymer, S. (1976). *The International Operations of National Firms.* Cambridge, MA: MIT Press.

Jackson, J. (2012). *Outsourcing and Insourcing Jobs in the US Economy.* Congressional Research Service, 7-5700.

Jacob, J. (1996). "Taxes and transfer pricing: Income shifting and the volume of intra-firm transfers," *Journal of Accounting Research, 34*(2):301–312.

Javorcik, B. (2004). "Does foreign direct investment increase the productivity of domestic firms? In search of spillovers through backward linkages," *American Economic Review*, 94(3):605–627.

Jensen, J., McGuckin, R., and Stiroh, K. (2001). "The impact of vintage and survival on productivity: Evidence from cohorts of U.S. manufacturing plants," *Review of Economics and Statistics*, 83(2):323–332.

Johanson, J., and Vahlne, J. (1977). "The internationalization process of the firm: A model of knowledge development and increasing foreign market commitment," *Journal of International Business Studies*, 8(1):23–32.

Jovanovic, B. (1982). "Selection and the evolution of industry," *Econometrica*, 50(3):649–670.

Katz, M., and Shapiro, C. (1985). "Network externalities, competition, and compatibility," *American Economic Review*, 75(3):424–440.

Keller, W. (2002). "Geographical localization and international technology diffusion," *American Economic Review*, 92(1):120–142.

Keller, W., and Yeaple, S. (2009). "Multinational enterprises, international trade, and productivity growth: Firm-level evidence from the United States," *Review of Economics and Statistics*, 91(4):821–831.

Khanna, T. (2008). *Billions of Entrepreneurs*. Boston, MA: Harvard Business School Press.

Khanna, T., and Palepu, K. (2010). *Winning In Emerging Markets: A Roadmap for Strategy and Execution*. Boston, MA: Harvard Business School Press.

Kieso, D., Weygandt, J., and Warfield, T. (2010). *Intermediate Accounting* (13th edn). Hoboken, NJ: John Wiley and Sons.

Killing, J. (1983). *Strategies for Joint Venture Success*. New York: Praeger.

Kim, L. (1996). *From Imitation to Innovation*. Boston, MA: Harvard Business School Press.

Kogut, B. (1983). "Foreign direct investment as a sequential process," in C. Kindleberger and D. Audretsch (eds), *The Multinational Corporation in the 1980s*. Cambridge, MA: MIT Press, 38–56.

Kogut, B. (1988). "Joint ventures: Theoretical and empirical perspectives," *Strategic Management Journal*, 9(4):319–332.

Kogut, B. (1991). "Joint ventures and the option to expand and acquire," *Management Science*, 37(1):19–33.

Kogut, B., and Chang, S. (1996). "Platform investments and volatile exchange rates: direct investment in the U.S. by Japanese electronic companies," *Review of Economics and Statistics*, 78(2):221–231.

Kogut, B., and Singh, H. (1988). "The effects of national culture on the choice of entry mode," *Journal of International Business Studies*, 19(3):411–432.

Kogut, B., and Zander, U. (1993) "Knowledge of the firm and the evolutionary theory of the multinational corporation," *Journal of International Business Studies*,
24(4):625–646.

KPMG (2007a). "China's new tax system and its implications," *TaxAdviser*, December,
21–22.

KPMG (2007b). *Hong Kong Tax Competitiveness Series: Corporate Tax Rates.* Hong
Kong: KPMG.

Krugman, P. (1991). "Increasing returns and economic geography," *Journal of Political
Economy*, 99(3):483–499.

Lall, S. (1973). "Transfer-pricing by multinational manufacturing firms," *Oxford Bulletin
of Economics and Statistics*, 35(3):173–195.

Lau, L., Qian, Y., and Roland, G. (2000). "Reform without losers: An interpreta-
tion of China's dual track approach to transition," *Journal of Political Economy*,
108(1):120–143.

Lee, G. (2009). "Understanding the timing of 'fast-second' entry and the relevance of
capabilities in invention vs. commercialization," *Research Policy*, 38(1):86–95.

Li, D. (1996). "Ambiguous property rights in transitional economies," *Journal of
Comparative Economics*, 23(1):1–19.

Li, H., and Zhou, L. (2005). "Political turnover and economic performance: The
incentive role of personnel control in China," *Journal of Public Economics*,
89(9–10):1743–1762.

Liebowitz, S., and Margolis, S. (1995). "Path dependence, lock-in, and history," *Journal
of Law, Economics, and Organization*, 22(1):1–2.

Lin, J. (2009). *Economic Development and Transition.* Cambridge: Cambridge
University Press.

Lin, J. (2012). *Demystifying the Chinese Economy.* New York: Cambridge University
Press.

Liu, X., Siler, P., Wang, C., and Wei, Y. (2000). "Productivity spillovers from foreign direct
investment: Evidence from UK industry level panel data," *Journal of International
Business Studies*, 31(3):407–425.

Liu, X., Wang, C., and Wei, Y. (2009). "Do local manufacturing firms benefit from trans-
actional linkages with multinational enterprises in China?" *Journal of International
Business Studies*, 40(7):1113–1130.

McFadden, D. (1974). "Conditional logit analysis of qualitative choice behavior," in P.
Zarembka (ed.), *Frontiers in Econometrics.* New York: Academic Press, 105–142.

McGahan, A. (1991). "The emergence of the national brewing oligopoly: Competition
in the American market, 1933–1958," *Business History Review*, 65(2):229–284.

MacGarvie, M. (2006). "Do firms learn from international trade?" *Review of Economics
and Statistics*, 88(1):46–60.

Madhok, A. (1997). "Cost, value and foreign market entry mode: The transaction and the firm," *Strategic Management Journal*, 18(1):39–61.

Marshall, A. (1920). *Principles of Economics* (8th edn). London: Macmillan.

Martz, L., and Thomas, R. (1991). "The corporate shell game," *Newsweek*, April 15, 32.

Marukawa, T. (2006). "The supplier network in China's automobile industry from a geographic perspective," *Modern Asian Studies Review*, 1(1):77–102.

Meyer, K. (2004). "Perspectives on multinational enterprises in emerging economies," *Journal of International Business Studies*, 35(3):259–276.

Ming, Z., and Williamson, P. (2007). *Dragon at Your Door: How Chinese Cost Innovation Is Disrupting Global Competition.* Boston, MA: Harvard Business School Press.

Mitchell, W. (1989). "Whether and when? Probability and timing of incumbents' entry into emerging industrial subfields," *Administrative Science Quarterly*, 34(2):208–230.

Naughton, B. (2007). *The Chinese Economy: Transitions and Growth.* Cambridge, MA: MIT Press.

Naughton, B. (2009). "Loans, firms, and steel: Is the state advancing at the expense of the private sector?" *China Leadership Monitor*, 30:1–10.

Nelson, R., and Winter, S. (1982). *An Evolutionary Theory of Economic Change.* Cambridge, MA: Belknap Press.

Newberry, K., and Dhaliwal, D. (2001). "Cross-jurisdictional income shifting by U.S. multinationals: Evidence from international bond offerings," *Journal of Accounting Research*, 39(3):643–662.

Pan, Y., Li, S., and Tse, D. (1999). "The impact of order and mode of market entry on profitability and market share," *Journal of International Business Studies*, 30(1):81–103.

Park, S., Li, S., and Tse, D. (2006). "Market liberalization and firm performance during China's economic transition," *Journal of International Business Studies*, 37(1):127–147.

Porter, M. (1998). "Clustering and the new economics of competition," *Harvard Business Review*, 76:77–90.

Porter, M., and Stern, S. (2001). "Innovation: Location matters," *Sloan Management Review*, 42(2):28–36.

Puck, J., Holtbrügge, D., and Mohr, A. (2009). "Beyond entry mode choice: Explaining the conversion of joint ventures into wholly owned subsidiaries in the People's Republic of China," *Journal of International Business Studies*, 40(3):388–404.

Qian, Y., Roland, G., and Xu, C. (1999). "Why is China different from Eastern Europe? Perspectives from organization theory," *European Economic Review*, 43(4–6):1085–1094.

Qian, Y., Roland, G., and Xu, C. (2006). "Coordination and experimentation in M-form and U-form organizations," *Journal of Political Economy*, 114(2):366–402.

Rawski, T. (1980). *China's Transition to Industrialism: Producer Goods and Economic Development in the Twentieth Century.* Ann Arbor: University of Michigan Press.

Redding, G., and Witt, M. (2007). *The Future of Chinese Capitalism*. New York: Oxford University Press.

Rein, S. (2012). *The End of Cheap China: Economic and Cultural Trends that Will Disrupt the World*. Hoboken, NJ: Wiley.

Reuer, J., Zollo, M., and Singh, H. (2002). "Post-formation dynamics in strategic alliances," *Strategic Management Journal*, 23(2):135–151.

Saxenian, A. (1994). *Regional Advantage*. Cambridge, MA: Harvard University Press.

Scherer, F., Beckenstein, A., Kaufer, E., and Murphy, D. (1975). *The Economics of Multi-Plant Operation*. Cambridge, MA: Harvard University Press.

Scherer, F., and Ross, D. (1990). *Industrial Market Structure and Economic Performance*. Boston, MA: Houghton Mifflin.

Schipani, C., and Liu, J. (2002). "Corporate governance in China: Then and now," *Columbia Business Law Review*, 1:1–69.

Schumpeter, J. (1934). *The Theory of Economic Development: An Inquiry into Profits, Capital, Credit, Interest, and the Business Cycle*. Cambridge, MA: Harvard University Press.

Shaver, J., and Flyer, F. (2000). "Agglomeration economics, firm heterogeneity, and foreign direct investment in the United States," *Strategic Management Journal*, 21(12):1175–1193.

Slocum, T., McMaster, R., Kessler, F., and Howard, H. (2005). *Thematic Cartography and Geographic Visualization*. Upper Saddle River, NJ: Pearson Education.

Smith, D., and Florida, R. (1994). "Agglomeration and industry location: An econometric analysis of Japanese-affiliated manufacturing establishments in automotive-related industries," *Journal of Urban Economics*, 36(1):23–41.

Sosa, M. (2009). "Application-specific R&D capabilities and the advantage of incumbents: Evidence from the anticancer drug market," *Management Science*, 55(8):1409–1422.

Stinchcombe, A. (1965). "Social structure and social organization," in J. March (ed.), *Handbook of Organizations*. Chicago, IL: Rand McNally, 142–193.

Stopford, J., and Haberich, K. (1978). "Ownership and control of foreign operation," in M. Ghertman and J. Leontiades (eds), *European Research in International Business*. Amsterdam: North Holland, 141–167.

Sutton, J. (1991). *Sunk Costs and Market Structure: Price Competition, Advertising, and the Evolution of Concentration*. Cambridge, MA: MIT Press.

Sutton, J. (1997). "Gibrat's legacy," *Journal of Economic Literature*, 35(1):40–59.

Tian, G. (2000). "Property rights and the nature of Chinese collective enterprises," *Journal of Comparative Economics*, 28(2):247–268.

Tian, X. (2007). "Accounting for sources of FDI technology spillovers: Evidence from China," *Journal of International Business Studies*, 38(1):147–159.

Tripsas, M. (1997). "Unraveling the process of creative destruction: Complementary assets and incumbent survival in the typesetter industry," *Strategic Management Journal*, 18(Summer Special Issue):119–142.

Tybout, J. (2000). "Manufacturing firms in developing countries: How well do they do, and why?" *Journal of Economic Literature*, 38(1):11–44.

United States International Trade Commission (2010). *China: Intellectual Property Infringement, Indigenous Innovation Policies, and Frameworks for Measuring the Effects on the U.S. Economy*, Investigation No. 332-514. USITC Publication 4199, November 2010.

Van Biesebroeck, J. (2007). "Robustness of productivity estimates," *Journal of Industrial Economics*, 55(3):529–569.

Vernon, R. (1971). *Sovereignty at Bay: The Multinational Spread of U.S. Enterprises*. New York: Basic Books.

Wagner, J. (2010). "Entry, exit and productivity: Empirical results for German manufacturing industries," *German Economic Review*, 11(1):78–85.

Walder, A. (1995). "Local governments as industrial firms: An organizational analysis of China's transitional economy," *American Journal of Sociology*, 101(2):263–301.

Whalley, J. (2011). *China's Integration into the World Economy*. Singapore: World Scientific Publishing.

Wheeler, D., and Mody, A. (1992). "International investment location decisions: The case of U.S. firms," *Journal of International Economics*, 33(1):57–76.

Wheeler, J. (1988). "An academic look at transfer pricing in a global economy," *Tax Notes*, 40(1):87–96.

Williamson, O. (1991). "Comparative economic organization: The analysis of discrete structural alternatives," *Administrative Science Quarterly*, 36(2):269–296.

Wilson, B. (1980). "The propensity of multinationals to expand through acquisitions," *Journal of International Business Studies*, 11(1):59–65.

Yang R. (2002). "China suffers 30 billion-yuan loss from tax evasion by multinationals," *China Daily Online*, July 31.

Yiu, D., and Makino, S. (2002). "The choice between joint venture and wholly owned subsidiary: An institutional perspective," *Organization Science*, 13(6):667–683.

Young, A. (2000). "The razor's edge: Distortions and incremental reform in the People's Republic of China," *Quarterly Journal of Economics*, 115(4):1091–1135.

Zeng, M., and Williamson, P. (2007). *Dragons at Your Door*. Boston, MA: Harvard Business School Press.

INDEX